Nicholas II, The Last Tsar

Nicholas II,
The Last Tsar

MICHAEL PATERSON

ROBINSON

ROBINSON

First published in Great Britain in 2017 by
Robinson

1 3 5 7 9 10 8 6 4 2

A CIP catalogue record for this book
is available from the British Library.

ISBN: 978-1-47213-683-1

Typeset in Scala by TW Type, Cornwall
Printed and bound in Great Britain by CPI
Group (UK), Croydon CR0 4YY

Papers used by Robinson are from well-
managed forests and other responsible sources.

Robinson
An imprint of
Little, Brown Book Group
Carmelite House
50 Victoria Embankment
London EC4Y 0DZ

An Hachette UK Company
www.hachette.co.uk

www.littlebrown.co.uk

Contents

NOTE

The titles used in this book are confusing, because they are entirely interchangeable. Tsar – the Russian rendering of Caesar and thus the word for Emperor – was spelled as Czar throughout the nineteenth and into the twentieth century. Tsar, Czar, Emperor, Tsarina, Czarina and Empress are all used to refer to the same people and the same positions.

Introduction

The sixth of May, 1868. St Petersburg. The River Neva, blue beneath an early summer sky. From across the water the loud, repeated banging of guns – a sound that seemed to go on forever. It rattled windows, brought a booming echo from the façades of the great houses along Palace Quay, and caused bystanders to block their ears. The saluting-battery on the rampart of the Peter-Paul Fortress, shrouded in white smoke. It was firing a 101-gun salute to announce the birth of the newest member of the Imperial Family: Nicholas Alexandrovich, grandson of the Tsar. The succession was safe for another generation.

The thirteenth of March, 1881, St Petersburg. The River Neva, solid-frozen under a leaden, late winter sky. This time there were only two explosions, and they heralded not an arrival but a departure. The same Tsar, Alexander Nikolaivich, was returning home in his carriage when he was the target of a terrorist bomb. He was uninjured. His escort, and a passing delivery boy, bore the brunt. He himself could have escaped – had he not ignored advice and got out of his vehicle to see to the wounded. Another terrorist threw a second bomb and this one landed in front of him. He lost his left foot, and his right leg was mangled. His wounds were fatal and he knew it, for his blood lay in great patches on the snow. 'To the Palace,' he whispered, 'to die there.' He was carried up the marble staircase, dripping more blood on the way, and was laid on a divan in his study. He lingered long enough to be visited by his family, to see them and to hear their farewells. Among them was his 36-year-old son, who would very shortly become the third Tsar Alexander, and the 12-year-old boy who would, much later, succeed him as Nicholas II. When the child was shown him, he looked through the one eye he could still use and managed the semblance of a smile, but he could not speak. Both Alexander and his son were to remember this scene vividly all their lives. The timing of this event had been extraordinary. No more than a few hours earlier, the Tsar had signed legislation that would have set his country on the path to representative government. That document would never now be ratified. An unkind fate had nipped in the bud the notion of even a nascent democracy in Russia. The sudden death of the reform-minded 'Tsar Liberator' would put an immediate end to the hopes of Russian liberals that their country would develop peacefully into a constitutional monarchy. This single act was to ensure that the reigns of the next – and last – two tsars would be a time of stern and repressive reaction.

CHAPTER ONE

Romanovs

The greatest present given by fate to Nicholas II was the Kodak camera, for it has put posterity on his side. Never, surely, can 'despotism' have looked so adorable. He and his family – he had, as everyone knows, a wife, four daughters and a son – lived, by accident of circumstance, in the era of the popular camera and the moving image. He and his children possessed Kodaks, a novelty – a craze – that they shared with millions of others. The albums filled with pictures – both by them and by the Empress's closest friend – of their holidays and their leisure pursuits were never intended for us to see. When tragedy overwhelmed them these were left behind, as were many hundreds of their other possessions, and became familiar to a wider public. It is through these images that we know them, and there can be few of us who look at the photographs in the forms that they have come down to us – in expensive coffee-table volumes or as illustrations in histories and biographies – and are not enchanted. We view them, their country and the regime they represented with indulgence because of how they look.

They seem so perfect – a handsome, athletic man, so benign in his expression, so dignified in his array of uniforms, so visibly indulgent of his children. His beautiful, distant wife – so gorgeously dressed, so stylish when seen amid the interiors she created and inhabited, but so obviously anxious over their son that she is seldom far from his side. Four daughters of electrifying beauty and grace whose progress from winsome childhood to adolescent loveliness is a journey on which we can accompany them. In their identical clothing, which so often involved white dresses and huge picture-hats, they seem the epitome of Edwardian young womanhood. Their brother, also strikingly attractive in his sailor suits and miniature uniforms, looks so impish as he larks about or, endearingly tries to look precociously grave while attending state occasions. They seem like characters from one of the magical children's novels of E. Nesbit – they could be *The Railway Children* or *The Treasure Seekers*.

Their private photographs are naturally the most evocative because they are the most informal, spontaneous, appealing. Though a few of these images were released at the time and found their way into books or journals at home and abroad, the majority were unknown during the lifetime of those they depicted. We see them swimming, playing tennis, having picnics, laughing, grimacing for the camera, careering along on roller skates, dancing the mazurka with naval officers on the deck of their yacht. We feel we know them because we have shared with them these private moments of light-heartedness and relaxation, as well as the milestones on their way to maturity. We have seen them so often that we can tell them apart. We are familiar with their traits, their tastes, their foibles, as if they were characters in a soap opera or a favourite novel.

They look like people we would like to know, and we do. Today they have serious admirers who have favourite family members, and have made it their business to devour all the details available about them. Even in this age of the computer they have a place. A glance at YouTube will show that each of the children has at least one website devoted to pictures of them, sentimentally captioned ('Olga, Warm-hearted Girl', 'Tatiana, the Beautiful One', 'Maria, the Blue-Eyed Angel', 'Anastasia, the Wild Child') and accompanied by a soundtrack of inappropriate modern balladry. When we think of the Romanov dynasty, we think at once of them. To the layman, Imperial Russian history begins with Peter the Great and ends with Rasputin. The other rulers – the first Tsar Michael, Elizabeth, Peter III – did not live in the age of the photograph. Nicholas did and so he is accessible while they are not.

And yet the life of this family was so abnormal. The Tsar, though seen affably smoking, hiking, shovelling snow, lived under a huge and growing strain that was to exhaust and age him, before it finally proved insupportable. Nothing, nothing in his life went well except for the happiness he gained from his family and the momentary pleasures of a few minor hobbies – walking, shooting game, reading, motoring, canoeing or playing billiards. The Empress was a martyr to a wide range of medical complaints, including the agonies of sciatica, and spent much of her time immobilised, in bed or in a wheelchair. She did not get on with her husband's relatives, especially her mother-in-law, with whom relations ranged from distant to hostile. She did not share the liking for outdoor exercise that made the lives of her husband and children seem so robust and enjoyable. She also knew she was disliked in her adopted country. Other than her family, her faith and the company of a tiny circle of friends, she had little pleasure in life.

The children had very few playmates. The girls, when adolescents, knew virtually no young women of their own age, and met few people from outside the Court. They had an almost pathetic fascination with the very ordinariness of those outsiders they did encounter, latching onto the domestic details given them, for instance, by crew members on the Imperial Yacht. They met almost no men apart from officers and had no chance to develop the relationships of normal young women. How bored they sometimes look, attending reviews, accompanying their parents on formal visits, meeting groups of officials, walking arm in arm in procession with aged, Grand-Ducal relatives. They were isolated from their contemporaries and hemmed in by stifling etiquette. Who among us would have wanted the life they had?

The images of them fascinate and enchant us largely for two reasons. Firstly, because they show what seems to be a world of almost impossible luxury and deference, surroundings and facilities – yachts and trains as well as palaces – that are beyond our reach. We can inhabit it vicariously through them. Secondly, because we know that this lifestyle, and those who had it, were about to vanish. As we look through the umpteen picture-books about them and read the dates in the captions, we cannot help making mental calculations and thinking that there were only five years, or three years, or one year left before the *Götterdämmerung* of 1914 that would ultimately end the Empire and their lives. Had the children all grown up to live out normal lifespans in peaceful obscurity as did their royal contemporaries in, say, Sweden, they would surely not have had this fascination for us. We speculate about what they would have been like, who they would have married, what they might have achieved, just as we wonder what would have become of Russia if it had had the opportunity to develop in peace instead of becoming a considerably worse form of totalitarian state.

Our fascination with them is not really morbid. We do not want to dwell on their deaths. Indeed these are so horrible to read about that many admirers avoid any description of them. The Romanovs seem, after all, like old friends, and we do not want to know about the suffering and annihilation of those of whom we are fond.

However criticised Nicholas may have been in his lifetime, his troubles and his faults are largely forgotten in the West. And it is in the West that the cult of the Romanovs has flourished. In their homeland the story of these people, and even their likenesses, were suppressed for generations. After the end of communism, many of their compatriots were astonished to learn about them through books and museum exhibitions ('No one told us this!' exclaimed one woman after discovering that the ladies had worked as wartime nurses). It was suddenly possible to search for records of them in archives, to see their letters and belongings and to study pictures of them. For many Russians, however, their era is too remote to seem relevant. It is simply another tragedy in a century littered with misfortune and with the violent deaths of their countrymen. The Romanov dynasty has nothing to do with their nation's present problems, conditions or aspirations.

Some of them certainly find it surprising that in the West, where there is no shortage of living, functioning monarchies, people should be so fixated with the memory of theirs. In 1998, when the Family were about to be returned from their distant graves for reburial in St Petersburg, a colleague of mine in Russia, answering a query I had sent him about the event, ended his faxed message with the words: 'But why are you interested in this?' He was unaware that in the West a virtual industry in books, films, articles and exhibitions has, for decades, driven an intense public fixation. Almost a generation later, he is probably no longer wondering. A visit to any bookshop in Moscow or Petersburg would reveal a multitude of publications in both Russian and English on the tsars – individually and collectively – on their palaces (a particular passion for foreigners), their jewellery, their art collections, their costume, letters and diaries, as well as their ubiquitous photograph albums. The descendants of Nicholas's subjects have long-since realised what a harvest of tourist income the dynasty brings in. Lenin, Stalin and the other unmentionables of more recent history could not possibly claim this level of interest.

For many years, fascination throughout the wider world was fuelled by speculation about what became of Nicholas and his family. With no definite proof that they had been killed in Siberia, and with claimants emerging for years after 1918 (Anna Anderson, who lived a long life insisting that she was Anastasia, was simply the best known among several) excitement was maintained in perpetuity. It was periodically brought to boiling-point by books or documentaries that – plausibly or otherwise – claimed to have new evidence, or simply to have applied better logic, to the commonly accepted narrative that all were dead. Like other great mysteries – the identity of Jack the Ripper, or the existence of the Loch Ness Monster – the fate of Russia's royal family was a question that both writers and readers could not leave alone. The question was, of course, answered with the revelation of their graves in 1991 – though not without a lingering whiff of intrigue because the remains of two of them, Alexis and one of his sisters, would not be found until some time later. This has not ended the fascination, rather it has refocused it. Their tombs in the Peter-Paul Fortress are now a place of pilgrimage, as is the church built on the site of their murder. The State Hermitage Museum, and several other institutions, have taken from storage their costumes and furniture, books and toys, and used them to recreate their surroundings. We now have greater access to their world than has ever previously been possible.

To the newspaper-reading, Western public of his own day, Nicholas II was a reactionary despot whose country – underdeveloped, semi-barbaric, expansionist but dangerously unstable – was a threat to world peace. He was seen as responsible for the mass killing of innocent demonstrators and the imprisonment of thousands. Our view of him is kinder because, through his letters and diaries and several accomplished biographies, we have access to his own thoughts and views. Though these often reveal maddening faults – dithering and indecisiveness, failure to stand up for himself, inflexibility, lack of vision, a refusal to learn from past mistakes, a regrettable inability to confront difficult people or issues – they also suggest a shy and gentle, humorous and well-meaning man, devoted to his country and his family and doing his best amid circumstances that would have overwhelmed many a more able ruler. These things are often enough to put us on his side, consciously or otherwise. We view the calamities of his time with sympathy because we understand the stress under which he was placed by his son's illness. We may even ignore what was perhaps the most terrible scar on his reign – the pogroms that he neither prevented nor condemned – because we know that his life too was to end in violence and horror. We admire the saintly, even Christ-like, detachment he was somehow able to maintain during his last months of life.

His story cannot be separated from those of his wife, son and daughters. And all of them were attractive personalities. Though vilified as meddlesome and blamed for introducing the spectre of Rasputin to the Court, Alexandra was under even greater strain than her husband, for she bore the burden of guilt at having brought into the family the disease that affected their son. Of German origin – a fact that increased her unpopularity after 1914 – she made sincere efforts to understand the culture and religion of her adopted country, but failed to win the affection of Russians and was always to be compared unfavourably with her predecessor and mother-in-law, the Empress Marie. As with Nicholas, her resignation in captivity and humiliation has given her a posthumous sanctity.

The four daughters, Olga, Tatiana, Marie and Anastasia, were beautiful by the standards of any age, and all were different in personality. They died just as they were emerging into adulthood, and it is enthralling to speculate about the lives they would have led. Any notion of them as spoiled brats is banished by the things we read in any memoir by those who knew them, and by the knowledge that they actively worked for charity. We also know that during the War the two eldest, like their mother, trained as nurses and assisted in operations on wounded soldiers. Had they been members of a modern royal family, subject not only to demands that they be informal and accessible but to more intrusive media attention, they would have been a triumph. Stylish, smiling, friendly and outgoing, they would have had much the same public appeal as some more recent British princesses, and for the same reasons. We can imagine how the fashion press and charity organisations would have loved them. Even within their own lifetimes, photographic postcards, showing them singly and collectively, sold in the hundreds of thousands all over the world.

The Tsarevich, Alexis, whose debilitating illness adds considerable poignancy to his memory, is perhaps the most tragic of the Romanovs. He would, even given a normal chance to grow up, probably not have lived into adulthood, and to us this death sentence is written on all the images we see. Photographed in uniform, or seen on film being carried by a burly Cossack or sailor, he more than all the others symbolises the sorrow that befell his family. The sight of his teddy bear or his scarlet Cossack coat, now on display, can move some to tears.

As for Russia itself, the atrocities and privations of the Stalin era make the rule of the tsars seem, from our perspective, comparatively mild. Theirs was despotism, but a benign and well-meaning one, after all. The overthrow of tsardom seems to us inevitable, given its failure to cope with the twentieth century, but the killing of the Romanovs was a crime that shocked the world. The centenary of these events – the abdication and murder – will see major commemorations in Russia and elsewhere, and doubtless there will be re-examination of their lives and of their role in history. After that, it is unlikely there will be 'closure'. The Romanovs and their story will continue to haunt the world's imagination for a very long time to come.

CHAPTER TWO

Nicholas

No misfortune has been spared to Nicholas II, and had he
only understood their importance, he would have been the
most unhappy man in the whole of his vast Empire.

Count Vassili

Though Nicholas has been befriended by later generations, he had few
friends in his lifetime. He was seen as a disappointment by virtually
everyone, and from the moment of his accession. To Russian monarchists and even to members of his own family he lacked the personality
and the presence to be an effective ruler. Liberals had hoped he would
institute change and political reform when he ascended the throne,
but were told more or less at once by the Tsar that such notions were
unthinkable. That he later oversaw the establishment of nascent representative government offended traditionalists. His choice of wife was
unpopular with his family for several reasons and, once she arrived
in Russia and married him, her behaviour alienated his relatives, the
Court, the aristocracy and the wider Russian community.

Abroad, it was his position rather than his personality that brought
criticism. Autocracy did not sit comfortably with public opinion
in any liberal Western country. In Britain and France, the Russian
Emperor had been a popular demon ever since Nicholas I (1825–55)
had suppressed the Decembrist revolt and triggered the Crimean War.
Foreigners had long made a point of describing, or reading about,
Russia's savage law enforcement, spies and secret police, brutal pris-
ons and convict-settlements, and the work of Russian writers helped
to spread this image (Tolstoy's *Resurrection* was a bestseller abroad). It
had long been assumed by Britain that Russia was the likely opponent
in a future European war. Whitehall saw Russian expansion in Central

Asia as a threat to Britain's Indian Empire, and was to feel some satisfaction at the Tsar's defeat in the Russo-Japanese War not only because it put a rival out of the way but because it revealed Russia's military weakness.

Across the Atlantic, the Russian system of government was so alien to American ideals that hostile opinion could be virtually taken for granted. Moreover, both Britain and the United States possessed influential Jewish communities which reacted with understandable outrage to the pogroms that followed the first revolution. Nicholas's considerable problems, both international and domestic, evoked little sympathy in other countries, though democracies would applaud his attempts to introduce representative government once circumstances had obliged him to do so.

Though it is not difficult to sympathise personally with the Tsar, anyone seeking to admire Nicholas II has found it uphill work. He is blamed for the collapse of a nation that covered one-sixth of the earth's land area, of a regime that had lasted three hundred years and a system of government that had endured for five hundred. He is the culprit for allowing a regime of horrific oppression to take over Russia – although he himself was one of its victims – and caused the collapse of an entire civilisation. In fact, nobody could effectively have stood in the way of these calamities and prevented Russia from changing drastically. It was simply his fate to stand on the fault line between the old and the new and, by actions that seemed to him reasonable, to help cause the earthquake.

Nicholas was in some ways a very positive symbol of Russia, and might have begun his reign on a wave of hope for the future. As a figurehead, he certainly looked the part. He was very handsome. He wore his uniforms with flair. He looked impressive taking the salute, inspecting troops or when mounted at parades. He was athletic, skilled in riding and shooting. He was a man of his time, with a very modern passion, for instance, for motoring. He suffered no noticeable forms of ill-health and he kept fit by walking and by doing gymnastics. He had charming manners – diplomats and officials frequently remarked on the courtesy with which they were received, and he could converse fluently in several languages. He appeared personally modest, even shy, yet he made the effort to talk – with apparent ease – among even the humblest of his subjects. He was deeply religious in a country where this was of the profoundest importance – indeed he was perhaps the most devout personality to occupy the throne since the Tsar Alexis (1645–76), the ancestor he most admired and after whom he named his son. His wife was beautiful and the children they produced were equally attractive. All of these things should have made him popular but, beyond a small circle of friends and courtiers, he developed a general *un*popularity that simply went on increasing with every year he was on the throne.

Part of his trouble was that he followed a predecessor who had been overwhelming. Alexander III was physically powerful, immensely strong-willed and blunt-spoken. With his bear-like build and huge beard, he could have been mistaken for a droshky driver. Dogmatic and brutal – he too carries the indirect but ultimate blame for terrible pogroms – he had the nickname 'Tsar-Moujik' which, according to how it was interpreted, could mean that he had the manners and bearing of a peasant or that he was a ruler who identified with his people and reflected their simple qualities. His strength was respected even where his repressive measures were feared. Where he had been solid, his son was slim and slight. Nicholas was considerably more refined and more regal-looking yet, with his natural modesty, he did not have the presence to dominate a room or a situation in the way that Russians had known his forebears to do. Where Alexander had been forceful and ruthless, Nicholas was sensitive, hesitant, nuanced, indecisive and anxious not to give offence. Russians admired the strength of Alexander and despised the weakness of Nicholas, which they rightly recognised as a fatal flaw in a state in which a single man was the government. Had Nicholas been a constitutional monarch, his shy and diffident nature might have been an endearing attribute – as it was to be for the much-loved King George VI – but it was the wrong personality for one whose task was to rule the Russian Empire and to face down both internal and external enemies.

It can be argued with justice that he failed to understand his people or his time. It can also be said that he had no ideas and no ideals. His notion of ruling seemed simply a matter of grimly hanging on, keeping everything as near as possible to the way it had always been, regardless of changing circumstances. His years in power were an increasingly ineffectual rearguard action against the inevitable. If he did not understand his people, they had little opportunity to understand him. They saw him very seldom, unless they were members of some institution he was visiting. If he were travelling through their streets, they and their neighbours might be evicted until he had passed, for people looking from their windows posed a threat to security. Even his ministers did not know him well, for his conversation gave little clue to his thoughts, and his sincerity could not be relied upon. As one anonymous wag remarked: 'he doesn't lie, but he doesn't tell the truth either'. He did not lead his people, in the sense of making great public speeches – indeed his communications with his subjects were in the form of printed proclamations called *Ukase* which simply stated the intentions of his government.

Nicholas was not, of course, a candidate for elective office, whose practice it is to promise a bright future. It is not the function of a monarch – even in an autocracy – to be idealistic. Rather, they are there to ensure a sense of continuity and to represent the traditions of the nation and its people. While others win battles, build railways, write great literature or make fortunes through trade, a sovereign presides over rather than shapes an era. His function is to endure the formalities of government and ceremonial, reward achievement on behalf of the nation, act as a figurehead (it was his purpose, in other words, to keep the institutions together as best he could). These things – the essence of his job – Nicholas did with patience, commitment, determination and even enthusiasm.

The public persona that Nicholas and his family presented to their subjects was, in most ways, unfortunately a negative one. His wife, for all her attractiveness, was not an asset, because she was perceived as aloof and humourless. Brought swiftly to Russia as her husband was about to inherit the throne, she had no opportunity – as had Alexander's wife – to settle into her new country, meet its people or assimilate before she was married and assumed her official position. She was both painfully shy and somewhat shocked by the licentiousness of St Petersburg society, a disapproval she did not conceal. She was overshadowed by the still-very-much-in-evidence Dowager Empress Marie, by whom she was snubbed and bullied, and was aware that her mother-in-law's popularity was much greater than her own, as was that of her sister the Grand Duchess Elizabeth. She suffered from continuing ill-health and had five pregnancies. Small wonder that she spent years of her husband's reign in a kind of semi-purdah. Seen in photographs she smiles rarely, and commonly wears an expression that could be variously interpreted as nervous, timid, resigned, haughty or hostile.

Her four daughters, though they were beautiful, kind and dutiful, were not seen as an enhancement of the monarchy or the Imperial Family. Rather, they were living proof of the Empress's failure to produce a son. So much depended on this in an autocracy that one can only imagine the Tsarina's grief as each new arrival proved to be female. When in 1904 a boy was finally born, the event was met with appropriate national rejoicing, yet within a few years it was widely rumoured that the Heir suffered from an unspecified illness and was not strong or healthy enough to inherit (at one point, in 1912, it had to be made public that he seemed about to die). Some courtiers, who knew the history of Europe's royal families, guessed that his disease was haemophilia, carried by women and given to male children. The Empress certainly knew, and blamed herself for the rest of her life. There can surely have been few unhappier consorts in history. It is therefore significant that, amid all the troubles of Nicholas's reign, informed observers knew that the future was bleak. The Heir was unlikely to reach manhood, and would quite possibly predecease his father. There would thus be a succession crisis on top of everything else. There was little hope, in other words, that the country's difficulties would last less than several decades. Many went further, and saw tsarism itself as doomed because of these two problems – the complete ineptitude of the system presided over by their current ruler and the absence of anyone to succeed him. They felt they were living at the end of an age, and history was to prove them right.

While Nicholas thus had a 'bad press' during his lifetime, we are able to assess him more objectively. Setting cliché aside, we have the opportunity to study his character through the memoirs of some of those who knew him best. More importantly, we have access to his private thoughts through his diaries, meticulously kept from his young manhood until the end of his life. These were largely a prosaic record of events and did not include trains of thought or flights of fancy, but they nevertheless reflect and show us his pragmatic and meticulously dutiful nature. More revealingly, we can also read the letters he exchanged with his wife. We have the opportunity, as his contemporaries did not, to see him as a personality rather than a symbol. The Russian historian Edvard Radzinsky has written that: 'The Revolution punished him without trial, not allowing him a final say. The portrait of this puzzling man was created only after his death – by his opponents and supporters.'

What was Nicholas like? Almost everyone has seen pictures of him. They show a man of something below middle height (he was five-feet-six), full-bearded and of slim but powerful build. Much is made of his close resemblance to his cousin, King George V, who was the same height and colouring and who also had a beard. Some seem to have regarded them as identical. We must believe the accounts of those who saw them or knew them, but it is difficult when studying photographs to see how – at close quarters at least – confusion was possible, for there were fundamental differences in their appearance. Nicholas had a thinner face and a sharp nose that was almost retroussé, as well as deep-set, close-together eyes, while George had inherited the prominent, bulging eyes that can be seen in portraits of Victoria and George III. Nicholas had blue-grey eyes, George's were the shade called 'china-blue,' which he had, once again, inherited from his grandmother.

George's beard was always short and close-cropped. That of Nicholas was pointed, and his moustaches were longer, wilder and more curling.

Contemporary descriptions of Nicholas constantly refer to his smallness of stature. Though he was eye to eye with George V and was slightly taller than another cousin – the German Kaiser – historians seldom mention *their* height. With Nicholas this only seemed significant because his subjects were accustomed to rulers who were built on a larger scale. Peter the Great had been a huge man – he was six-feet-four – but height had really come into Nicholas's family only with the nineteenth century, from Alexander I (1800–25) onward. He was followed by another giant, his brother Nicholas I, and then the two further Alexanders. It is true that all of them had a striking physical presence which, when enhanced by uniform or ceremonial robes, could dazzle and overawe observers, but Nicholas's slighter build was not, as we have seen, untypical among monarchs of his day. And did this actually matter? One later commentator, the Englishman Sacheverell Sitwell, thought so. He wrote of Alexander III as Heir that: 'This prince, six foot five inches tall and strong in proportion, was the last of the huge Romanovs. It is probably true to say that it was the physical height and strength of these giant men that supported the Russian monarchy through the nineteenth century until the accession of the puny Nicholas II.' If he is correct, then Nicholas will certainly have been a disappointment from the beginning.

Radzinsky has described him in the following terms: 'He is of ordinary height. His body is not perfectly proportioned: his muscular torso rather massive, and his strong legs relatively short. His neck is unusually powerful for his small, neat head. A pleasant face and a small nose, reddish moustache, tobacco-yellow beard. His eyes are changeable – first bluish-grey, then sky-blue . . . and sometimes steely-green . . . '

A contemporary, and unambiguously critical, observer, the journalist Carl Joubert, said of him: 'He is spare and short in stature, with narrow shoulders, and he has none of the outward characteristics of his father or grandfather. Like most little men he is highly endowed with self-importance. He is not remarkable for physical or for moral courage, and he lives in a perpetual state of nervous anxiety.'

Perhaps so, but those who knew him remarked on his kindness and charm. His essential decency is perhaps best captured in an anecdote told by Sydney Gibbes, an Englishman who was engaged as tutor to the children. One day he was at the Emperor's wartime headquarters, giving a lesson to the Tsarevich while Nicholas worked in the room. Alexis had admired a cut-glass ball that hung from the chandelier above them, and told Gibbes he would take it home with him when he returned. The Tsar was shocked. 'Alexis!' he cried out, 'that's not *ours!*'

A friend, Princess Bariatinsky, wrote in her memoirs that: 'I am happy and grateful to Providence that I was allowed to see the Emperor so closely and to have the opportunity of appreciating his simplicity, his kindness and affability. What an irresistible charm of manner he had! To begin with, his voice had such a deep, clear, sympathetic ring; his eyes had a peculiarly sweet expression, and when he smiled they lighted up and smiled too. They were the mirror of his soul, which was pure and noble. All who came into contact with the Emperor fell under his charm and adored him.'

Another contemporary author, George Shavelsky concurred: 'His free and easy manner and simplicity could charm absolutely anyone. One could talk to him about anything at all, talk simply, not choosing one's words, not reckoning with etiquette. He was well-versed in history, archaeology and church matters.'

Sydney Gibbes, the Englishman, agreed that he was personable but felt, as others did, that though his shy manner was a pleasant characteristic in an individual it was unsuitable for a ruler: 'He knew well how to guard his dignity; one never dreamed of taking liberties, his presence was so quietly, naturally self-possessed. But it evoked awe, not fear. His wonderful eyes (of a most delicate blue) looked you straight in the face with the kindest, tenderest expression. It was his great charm and politically his great weakness, for the inculcation of fear is more than halfway to victory.'

His cousin, King George V, described him succinctly after his death as: 'the kindest of men and a thorough gentleman; He loved his country and his people.'

However likeable on a personal level, his glaring faults were summarised by Aleksander Blok, who considered him: 'Stubborn and weak-willed, nervy yet lackadaisical, harassed and cautious in speech.' Joubert wrote of him in 1905 that: 'His disqualifications for rule are many, but chief among them is that by nature he is a weak man, with a mind incapable of grasping the principles of government or of forming a consistent policy. It is generally admitted that in his private life he is a good husband and father, and a dutiful son, but unfortunately it is not by qualities such as these that a great nation can be governed single-handed. He is, furthermore, unfitted for his position by the fickleness of his nature and by his ridiculous love of adulation.'

Count Benkendorff, who had served at the court of the last two Alexanders, assessed the final Romanov ruler rather more charitably thus: 'He was very young when he ascended the throne, with no experience of life or of affairs, and his character never had a chance of being formed. To the end of his life he lacked balance, nor could he grasp the principles that are necessary for the conduct of so great an Empire. Hence his indecision, his limitations and the fluctuations which lasted throughout his reign. He was very intelligent, understood things at once, and was very quick [and] well-meaning, his character did not allow him to respond to the gigantic events of the closing years of his reign.'

There is no question that he was conscientious in his work. He sat for long hours each day at his desk, making notes in his concise, neat hand in the margins of documents. He read things slowly and tried, whether he could or not, to understand them.

Lacking from all accounts of his reign are any descriptions of the Tsar sitting with a group of advisors and discussing with them the problems of the day, in the way that any president or prime minister would do. There was no practice of hearing arguments batted back and forth and coming to a balanced conclusion. What happened instead was that the Tsar saw individual ministers, listened to them, made judgements by himself and then changed his mind as soon as he was visited by someone else. His decision would then be issued to his subjects as a *Ukase*, or proclamation, and he could in theory send these out as often as he wanted, even issuing a new one within hours to contradict the last. Because he was answerable to no one and did not even employ a secretary (in the sense that that functionary exists among statesmen), he reigned in a vacuum – a solitude of responsibility that must have given him a sense of dangerous helplessness. Small wonder that he made a confidante of his wife and listened so intently to her advice. It was said that he was like a pillow – marked with the impression of the last person to lie on it. He based decisions partly on such advice and partly on whatever he thought – or was told – his father might have done in the circumstances. In 1905, when faced with the national crisis that war and revolution brought about, Sergei Witte was asked what could be done. He pointed at a portrait of Alexander III and said: 'Resurrect him!'

With hours of paperwork to deal with each day, Nicholas spent much of his time as a bureaucrat. There were always scores of documents to look over, to sign and to stamp with the big gold-and-crystal Imperial seal, including the regular reports he received from every provincial Governor throughout his territories. He took this duty seriously and worked conscientiously.

He stated, at the outset of his reign, that: 'I try not to ponder over anything and I find that is the best way to rule Russia.' To a large extent he believed that it was counter-productive to look too much into detail, that bureaucracy could run itself, and that while he might make occasional pronouncements and periodically come to a major decision, he need not interfere too much in most matters. Professional administrators, with their training and experience and their trusted routines, would ensure that the country muddled along. This is, to an extent, true. A similar attitude was held by at least one other monarch, Napoleon III, and even by Adolf Hitler.

Critics spread the notion that he was impulsive and scatter-brained, that he might fix on a few minor details of an issue while ignoring the main points, and there is some evidence of this. He did have a fear of decision, and sometimes he would put off any definitive action for as long as possible, tinkering at the edges rather than addressing what really mattered. Because it was what he most enjoyed, he was extremely good at what might be called the 'public relations' side of his position, insofar as it involved answering letters, responding to requests, acknowledging gifts or municipal greetings. He would often write at length and with genuine appreciation. These, however, are precisely the things that even in a constitutional monarchy, let alone an autocracy, are delegated to Private Secretaries, ladies-in-waiting or other Court officials. They did not merit the full attention of a busy head of state. It seemed as if the more trivial a matter the more trouble he would take over it. Because of this personal interest in some of his subjects, the Tsar was able to impress deeply a small percentage of them and encourage a limited but deep devotion, though the number of those affected in this way would never be significant.

We can identify, in fact, a pattern of self-deception: his detailed attention to unimportant matters gave him the delusion that he was working hard. If he had sat up all night to answer a letter, he could feel that he was doing his utmost for his people, pushing himself to his physical and mental limits. 'Let all know,' he said in a famous address to a delegation of Zemstva members, 'that I, devoting all my strength to the good of the nation, will preserve the principles of autocracy as firmly and steadfastly as my unforgettable parent did.' If he exhausted himself with work he was making good this promise, even if he achieved nothing of importance. Once again Carl Joubert was unimpressed:

He will sit in his library to all hours of the night ransacking books of every description to find an apt quotation in answer to some flattering letter, and this while the Ship of State is drifting on to the rocks. He will jump up from the breakfast table to change a word in the draft of his reply to some laudatory address which a deputation from Kazan or Novgorod has presented. His mind is never concentrated on one point for more than a few minutes at a time; but he jumps from one thing to another like a caged canary.

Another hostile contemporary, Count Paul Vassili, echoed this sentiment: 'Nicholas II is one of those timid, weak creatures who nevertheless like to assert themselves at certain moments in matters utterly without importance, but which, to their eyes, appear to be vital ones. His mind is as small as his person; he sees the biggest events go by without being touched, or being even aware of their great or tragic sides.' He added that he found the Tsar to be: 'personal in everything, shallow-minded, weak, well-intentioned, but only in so far as it did not interfere with his own comfort, indifferent to all the necessities of his country and governed entirely by his sympathies or antipathies without considering anything else. After he had reigned a few months everyone who came into contact with Nicholas II realised that he was the echo of everyone else's opinion except his own.' This was, to a large extent, true, but we must not assume it was the whole picture. For one thing, Nicholas was genuinely interested in a number of the issues with which he dealt, whether these related to the army, the peasantry or the national railway system. He would therefore have given them more attention, had more decided views on them or made decisions based on personal knowledge. Secondly, he did this type of work every day for almost twenty-three years and we can assume that, as he matured and gained experience, he got better at it.

As a ruler, Nicholas was a watered-down version of Alexander. Joubert in fact summed up his outlook by naming the two living people who most decidedly influenced him: 'For all practical purposes it is still Alexander III who rules, through his wife, Marie Dagmar (sic) and M. Pobodonostseff.' In other words his mother, and the reactionary tutor chosen by his father to educate him, continued to rule the country through him. Joubert, however, misses the point that the new Tsar wanted as much as these others did that the policies of Alexander should continue. What he offered was a continuation of his father's outlook, albeit without the experience, the ability or the native intelligence to carry it out effectively, or the vision to see that circumstances were changing so rapidly as to make old practices obsolete.

What did these critics expect from a young man of twenty-six who, with no adequate background, had in the space of a few weeks been taken from a regimental officers' club and put on the throne? Naturally he would rely upon, and imitate, the only example he knew, and naturally he would make mistakes, utter regrettable statements and disappoint or offend some. Nicholas gained a reputation for ineptitude that he never lost – as witness the fact that the views quoted here were written not at the beginning of his reign but in its middle years.

Weak men who know, or suspect, that others despise them will often be angry and resentful as a defensive measure. Nicholas could sense the frustration and contempt of some of those with whom he dealt, and was infuriated. He was also a reader of the foreign press, and thus was aware of the disrespect with which many foreign observers viewed him. For the disaster of the war with Japan and the revolution that followed it, who else could be blamed, in a country with no popular representation? Everything was his fault. The nation's loss of prestige and of great power status was laid at his door.

Though he spent many hours each day at the service of his country, he felt that he was entitled to escape when he could. Following the assassination of Stolypin, his replacement as Minister of the Interior, Kokovtsov, visited the Tsar at Livadia, his palace in the Crimea. In the midst of what was a grave and anxious time for the nation he found Nicholas unwilling to discuss issues with him, intent instead on hanging a series of prints on the wall. After avoiding serious conversation several times, Nicholas finally told him that he had come to the Crimea for a holiday and did not want to be bothered with work, which could be left until he returned to Tsarskoe Selo. Such moments of weakness and selfishness – even had they been rare or untypical – seriously undermined confidence in the Tsar among his servants.

Alexander III had had, perhaps, less education than his son, and yet had known by some God-given instinct how to be an effective ruler. This in fact owed less to intelligence than to physical presence and force of personality. Nevertheless, he was right in his belief that for a monarch it is of no benefit to be an intellectual. High intelligence and an over-curious mind are a drawback. A ruler must have a marked tolerance of boredom and routine, must either be comfortable with a life of stultifying ceremonial and administration or be able to pretend this, must have good judgement of the character and opinions of others and an ability to weigh advice and to act decisively. If at all possible, he should be devout and morally upright so as to lead his country by personal example. Between them, Alexander and Nicholas covered all of these virtues – the latter undoubtedly had the gift of tolerating boredom and routine – but to have found all of them in one person would have been asking too much of Fate.

How did Nicholas compare with his other recent predecessors? Could he have been Alexander I, making an alliance with Napoleon and then leading the nation against him in desperate times, with the loss of territory and lives? No, he did not have the qualities necessary for that task. Nicholas I, who personally crushed the Decembrist revolt in 1825, strengthened the autocracy and presided over almost thirty years of prosperity before he involved Russia in the unsuccessful Crimean War – he too had virtues of strength, decisiveness and self-belief that his namesake was to lack. Alexander II emancipated the serfs and planned further social reforms. Nicholas would have been too conservative by nature (he was, after all, taught by Russia's arch-conservative) for such a course of action, even without Alexander II's assassination to bolster his reactionary inclinations.

Nicholas was patriotic almost to the point of obsession. He had a passion for his country and people that was deeply impressive. He devoured Russian literature. He hated the use of non-Russian words or expressions in reports or official documents, and habitually crossed them out with a red pencil. He liked to dress, when in private, in the type of loose-fitting garments worn by millions of his peasant subjects. He loved the traditional Muscovite architecture and design that was having a conspicuous revival in his lifetime (the Church of the Holy Redeemer on the Spilled Blood, opened in 1907 on the site of his grandfather's murder, is an example of this). He admired Russian art, and music and costume (he toyed briefly with the notion of dressing his thousands of retainers in seventeenth-century Muscovite liveries instead of Western-inspired uniforms, but this proved too costly). He loved the armed forces – all his life he was proud to have served in the Army, and he was most at ease in the company of officers and soldiers. He loved the peasantry – or at least he loved the *idea* of them.

Above and beyond all, he loved the Orthodox Church, of which he was head. He had a deep personal Christian faith and was well informed in matters of theology.

All of this, together with the physical isolation in which he lived, gave him a view of Russia that was dangerously false. He loved meeting the simple folk of the rural areas – those not educated enough to stray beyond social orthodoxies – and would make statements like: 'It is my chief preoccupation to discover the needs of the peasants, who are so dear to me.' When he opened the Duma, he made a point of spending longer with the peasant delegates than with the others, as if folk-costume was somehow a guarantee of loyalty and political conservatism. Cheered by thousands of soldiers at a parade or by streets lined with peasants, receiving delegations from remote districts with their loyal addresses and deferential manner, he would assume that these expressed the total and touching devotion of their entire class. He saw his realm as an idealised place of trusty servants, brave soldiers and devout peasantry. The real Russia was to him a country of traditional values and institutions, focused upon God and upon himself as God's viceroy. He was slow to appreciate the danger that was growing as the country industrialised and created an urban proletariat unhappy with living and working conditions. We must not, however, assume that he remained incapable of grasping reality. He was informed of everything that went on in his Empire and knew of all the discontent, disturbance and violent protest that occurred. Rather, his sentimental vision reflected his country as it *ought* to be or should aspire to be – an idealised place. Much the same attitude would be expressed by another head of state, Charles de Gaulle, when he wrote: 'I have a certain idea of France...'

During the years that Nicholas was Heir and then Tsar, Russia was experiencing a massive cultural flowering that was truly breathtaking and which has, to a large extent, defined the nation's culture ever since. It was the time of Tolstoy, Tchaikovsky, Chekov, Chaliapin, Diaghilev, Repin and Serov. Russia's 'Silver Age', as it came to be known, forms a glorious and enduring monument to the spirit of the nation at this time. Never, before or since, has Russia known such soaring heights of international prestige in the arts. It seemed a gift of Fate that Nicholas – a man who loved literature and music – should have come to preside over such an era, yet it seems strange that he was so little identified with it.

As a young man unexpectedly thrust into prominence, Nicholas initially benefitted from a general goodwill. People both in Russia and abroad wished him well. Many who saw his picture in the press thought him an agreeable, capable-looking young man. There were considerable hopes that this new ruler, of whom little was known because there was little to know about his life or opinions, would be sympathetic to new attitudes, perhaps be a child of his era, infected with modern notions and blessed with the energy and enthusiasm to make them possible. The fact was, of course, that he had no such notions. One observer after another discovered instead his weakness, his lack of focus, his indecisiveness.

He was indeed that most dangerous of combinations, a weak man who was also obstinate. He had been brought up to believe in the Divine Right of Kings – to see himself as appointed by God and answerable to the Almighty for his stewardship of his Empire, but also to think that criticism of himself was criticism of an infallible God. As well as this, he had a responsibility to both past and future generations. He was aware that he would be measured against his predecessors and that he must preserve intact the heritage – the autocracy – he had inherited. He must pass it on intact to his son.

Nicholas was not well served by his family. His mother, who was a presence throughout his entire reign and who would outlive him by a decade, much influenced his decisions, supported her favourites for appointment to important positions, and was constantly at hand to compare him unfavourably with his father – though it must in fairness be said that he often welcomed her advice. His uncles – the four younger brothers of Alexander III (Grand Dukes Vladimir, Alexis, Sergei and Paul) – were also a continuing source of judgement, argument and largely self-interested advice. As regarded his siblings, there was genuine affection between them, but none were of much help. Of his two younger brothers one, George, was an invalid who had to live in the Caucasus because he suffered from tuberculosis, and died young. The second, Michael, was charming and dutiful but would lose his right to the succession by marrying against the Tsar's wishes and outside royal circles. He was, as a result of this, banished from the country and allowed to return only at the outbreak of the Great War (because he was second in line to the throne after the Tsarevich Alexis). He was to become Tsar, for less than twenty-four hours, when Nicholas abdicated and at a stage when it was much too late for anyone to stave off the end of the dynasty. He had even less aptitude than Nicholas, and he could not have made an adequate ruler even in peacetime let alone during war and revolution. The sisters, Xenia and Olga, were good women but the latter – who was Nicholas's favourite – married a man considered completely unsuitable. She made a love-match with a handsome and devoted cavalry officer, but paid the usual price of losing caste.

History has judged him harshly, but with so much at stake, and given the baleful consequences for the world of his failure (a stand-off between ideologies that lasted more than seventy years) this is not surprising. But he had had no hope of succeeding in any case. He came to the throne too early. He had insufficient, and inadequate, preparation or experience. Nature had not endowed him with any of the attributes necessary to be an effective ruler. Though he recognised his inadequacy he did nothing to rectify it, like a sick man who does not seek medical help. He struggled with a whole series of crippling handicaps – in his family circumstances, in the domestic affairs of the Empire, in the international arena. He was obliged to meet a whole series of upheavals and crises that neither he nor anyone else could have solved.

The most vital moment of his reign was when he granted a constitution following the 1905 Revolution. Even had he been entirely sincere in his desire to do this – if he had recognised the need for change, planned it intelligently and carried it through – there would not have been time for the country and its institutions to adapt before the cataclysm came in 1914. Indeed society might well have split into factions, with conservatives and reformers at loggerheads, and perhaps even civil war, the fault line more or less where it was to be when such a war did come in the 1920s. Russia would thus have been dangerously weak when the Great Powers went to war, and her western lands could quickly have been overrun by an enemy that was able to exploit her preoccupation.

Revolutionaries – the fanatics of Bolshevism and Menshevism – would not have been content with Nicholas's constitutional concessions, no matter how generous or wide-ranging these might have been. They would still have wanted to overthrow the dynasty, still have hated any state run by bourgeois parliamentarians, and would have carried on with their bombings and murders. Much of the violence that characterised the last years of autocracy might well have happened even under a more enlightened and populist form of monarchy. In giving ground to reformers, the Tsar could thus have satisfied neither conservatives nor revolutionaries, and earned the enmity of both in more or less equal measure. It is not at all fanciful to imagine him being stalked and killed by right-wing extremists, a fate that could have befallen him following any of the crises of his reign and which he might have been spared largely because there was no plausible or popular Romanov candidate to replace him.

Russia was in any case undergoing such immense change that fixed practices could not hold back the tide. Industrial revolution, which had come to Britain in the eighteenth century and to France,

Germany and America in the nineteenth, was sweeping Russia in the twentieth. Even had war and revolution and haemophilia not been decisive factors and had the succession therefore carried on, the country over which Alexis ruled would have been a very different place, perhaps unrecognisable to traditionalists. If Nicholas had not eventually made the major and fundamental adaptations in the way the country was run, his successor would have been the one who had to do so. But such speculation is pointless. This state as he knew it could not have survived.

CHAPTER THREE

Background

He was born at Tsarskoe Selo, the place where he was to spend much of his adult life. The date was, as we have seen, 6 May 1868. This was the Orthodox feast of 'Job the long-suffering' and all his life the Tsar would see himself as similarly afflicted with ill-fortune. Because he had a deep and sincere faith in God, he believed it was his lot to suffer. This would lend to his nature a noticeable fatalism and lack of initiative. He believed that events were played out according to God's will and that there was no resisting this. It was to mean, in several fateful moments, a lack of direction and leadership on his part that was to seal the fate of his regime and of many of those around him.

Though he was not yet the Tsarevich – the direct successor to the throne – he was accustomed from birth to both opulence and deference. Within three weeks of his arrival he had been invested with five of the highest awards of the Russian state, including the Orders of Alexander Nevsky, of St Anne, St Stanislas and – most illustrious of all – of 'St Andrew the First-Called'. Peter the Great had founded this but had not deemed himself worthy of membership, and was not among the original knights. As was customary, Nicholas was also appointed colonel-in-chief of several regiments. All the men, and even the boys, in his family wore uniform virtually every day.

Unlike many in his position, he had a very happy childhood – so far as the circumstances of an increasingly embattled dynasty allowed. His family was close and his parents genuinely affectionate. His father had not expected to become Tsarevich – he was a younger brother and only the sudden death, in 1865, of his older sibling, who would otherwise have succeeded as Nicholas II, placed him in that position. Alexander had not only inherited the direct succession but the fiancée of his brother, and had married Princess Dagmar of Denmark, who adopted the Russian name Marie Feodorovna. Though Nicholas was not the favourite among the five children they eventually had – that would be his youngest brother Michael – he was highly regarded by his mother and father. Alexander disliked formality and ceremonial. He also disliked the capital and elected not to live there. The Winter Palace, in which his own father had died, would never be the permanent home of a Tsar again after March 1881. For his visits to Petersburg he used the much smaller Anitchkov Palace, further up the Nevsky Prospect, whose windows looked out on the pavement with its hurrying pedestrians, or on the drifting barges along the Moika Canal.

Alexander's family home, however, was the palace of Gatchina, about thirty miles west of the city. He chose it for reasons both of security and privacy (though in fact its park and some of its rooms were open to the public). Here he disappeared so effectively from the life of the capital that he was nicknamed 'the Hermit of Gatchina'. Built by the Italian architect Rinaldi for Gregory Orlov, the favourite of Catherine the Great, the palace had been conceived as a rural idyll and surrounded by an extensive park that, in the English style, was meticulously designed to look as if it had been accidentally created by nature. It passed, after Orlov's death in 1784, to Catherine's son Paul, who remodelled the building and trimmed it of some of its opulence. Though grand, and not without charm (one modern guidebook describes the yellow stone used in its construction as being 'the colour of captured sunlight') it did not have the beauty of Tsarskoe Selo or Peterhof. While some of the interiors are designed to be breathtaking, there is a simplicity about much of the building that reflects the unpretentious personal preferences of generations of Tsars. From the outside, Gatchina has a barrack-like starkness. Its angular towers and severe, neo-classical façade look down on vast courtyards in which the ill-fated Paul spent long hours drilling his troops. After his death, Gatchina was used intermittently by his descendants, and his personal rooms were restored as a memorial to him. The Imperial Family did not live in the grand chambers but on the first floor, in small apartments that had formerly housed minor functionaries and even servants, so that although there were wonderful things around

Nicholas, there was no question that he grew up taking luxury for granted. Visitors were sometimes shocked by their meanness, the lack of space and by the sheer awfulness of the wallpaper, the pictures and the furniture. It was decidedly bourgeois in character.

Life here was as simple and unaffected as possible, and came close to the Russian idyll, familiar to us from Chekov and Turgenev, of a minor aristocratic family on a country estate. All of the children were to remember with great fondness the years they spent there. Nicholas's sister Olga, thirteen years his junior, was to be one of the few members of the Family to survive the Revolution. She left a beautiful picture of life in the Palace, playing hide-and-seek in the Chinese Gallery, concealed behind priceless oriental vases that were twice the size of her; being disappointed at not seeing the ghost of Tsar Paul, which was believed to walk the galleries; or tramping the park with their father and learning from him about the natural world. The Palace had nine hundred rooms and was staffed by some five thousand servants indoors and outdoors. These included – surely an Arabian-nights wonder for children – the Tsar's 'Ethiopians', a cohort of towering negroes, with turbans and voluminously baggy trousers, whose costumes can still be seen in the State Hermitage Museum. Originally, six of these men had been sent to the Tsar by their ruler, the Negus of Abyssinia, and replacements must have been recruited later. No doubt modern opinion would see these men as 'exploited', but they enjoyed considerable prestige and responsibility as the silent guardians who stood outside the monarch's study. In Alexander's reign at least one of them, Mario, was a genuine native of Ethiopia but another, called Jim Hercules, was actually an American citizen who went home periodically to see his family. He brought back jars of guava jelly as presents for the children.

It was fortunate that they had this sanctuary, for during the years of Nicholas's childhood the country was becoming increasingly dangerous. Seven years before his birth his grandfather, Alexander II, had carried out one of the most significant acts in Russian history. He had proclaimed the emancipation of the country's serf population, thus freeing an estimated twenty-three million of his subjects from slavery. This had earned him the title of 'Tsar Liberator' and worldwide admiration, but it had encouraged many of a radical inclination to see this as a crack in the façade of autocracy and to seek further and wider reforms. Russia was a highly regulated nation, with not only a vast police and secret police but with one of the world's largest armies to maintain public order. The Tsar, personification of the State and the only instrument of government, was well protected but by no means impossible to attack. During the years that followed there developed a political activism that became the first modern terrorism. This situation was new. Alexander had, in the earlier part of his reign, been able to walk the streets of his capital, recognised but with impunity. His father, Nicholas I, had been known to take a solitary walk from the Winter Palace every afternoon. The timing was more or less common knowledge and his route could easily be guessed. He was willing during these excursions to meet his subjects, whom he might stop and question about their circumstances or occupations. He could be handed petitions, and often listened to grievances. Though the same might have been true at that time of American Presidents and British Prime Ministers, this was nevertheless impressive 'democracy' in a country that was seen as inhumane and tyrannical. It epitomised the traditional notion of the Tsar as father of his people. Though surrounded by pomp, he was within reach of even the humblest of his subjects and would concern himself with the problems of shopkeepers and shoe-blacks.

In April 1866, however, an activist called Dmitri Karakozov shot at the Tsar and, though his attempt was unsuccessful, a rubicon had been crossed. It spawned further plotting, harsher preventive measures and a climate of permanent suspicion. By the 1870s freedom of movement for the Imperial Family was unaffordable. They became prisoners within their palaces. Even within their own living spaces they were not safe, however. One evening in February 1880 a stock of dynamite, concealed in the dining room of the Winter Palace, exploded at the moment they were due to enter it, causing considerable destruction. The device had been planted by a man who had – in the manner of terrorists ever since – gained access to the building as a low-level employee, attracted no attention and waited for an opportunity.

And then, on a March afternoon, a further attempt – the seventh altogether – succeeded. While the Tsar travelled by carriage beside the Catherine Canal in Petersburg, a bomb was thrown by a member of the People's Will, a revolutionary group already responsible for other plots. When Alexander left his carriage the police had a tight grip on the man responsible – it was a curious point of honour with these savage idealists that they remained at the scene and faced arrest. A bomb thrown by a second terrorist killed him. This was the reward for allowing political reform, and there would be no more.

Nicholas began his education at the age of eight. As was the usual custom among royal families, he and his siblings would not attend school or even learn in the company of other children, for there was no general conception that associating with the sons and daughters of subjects would be helpful for a future ruler (interestingly his cousin, later Kaiser William II, did have this type of upbringing, attending school and university, but that was highly unusual). The Tsar's children were to be taught in a palace schoolroom by tutors who had been recruited by word of mouth from other prominent families. The programme of study was drawn up not by a teacher but by a senior army officer – the Adjutant General, Danilovich. The boy was to undertake a course of general studies that would last for eight years. He would be instructed in history, geography and foreign languages. He did not learn mathematics, though he did learn some sciences – biology, chemistry and mineralogy – and he was directed to read comprehensively in Russian literature. Of these subjects, he developed a lifelong affection for two: he loved history, remarking that 'if I was a private individual I would devote myself to historical studies', and literature. He would devour Russian novels. His librarian would lay out for him each month a series of books. The Tsar would examine them and place them in the order in which he would read them, then he would go through them in precisely that sequence. His reading habits, in other words, were as methodical as everything else about him. For a man of such rigid mental discipline it is somewhat unusual that he should take such pleasure in the fancies of poets and novelists. Nevertheless he genuinely loved the work of the great Russian writers: Pushkin, Lermontov, Gogol, Dostoevsky, Chekov.

In terms of languages, he learned well. He spoke and wrote fluently in French and English, and his German was good enough to conduct correspondence. He also had some command of Danish, learned from his mother and developed through holidays in her country.

Though Nicholas might seem to us to have been a lonely man, he grew up with a very close friend – his brother George. The two were three years apart in age, and they shared a room, and many tastes, as well as an education. George was many things that his brother was not – he was more outgoing, more expressive, and he had a sense of humour that delighted Nicholas, who wrote down many of his witticisms and kept them.

For the education of the princes both his parents seem to have been responsible. Alexander, a simplistic man not given to imaginative outlook, appears to have thought that the boys would be adequately equipped with a few hints in the right direction and a good deal of military discipline. Marie, who had a great deal of influence in the matter, had had an extremely simple childhood and felt that this was the best background for her own children. The fact that she had been brought up in a small and relatively informal court and prepared for a life in which she would not govern but simply marry and produce children seems not to have mattered. 'We had no governesses when we were children,' she said when asked if her own elder daughter should have the guidance of a tutor.

Nicholas's teachers were by any yardstick a very able body of men, but then they had been chosen because they were at the top of their various fields. His tutor in economics, Nicholas Bunge, had been Minister of Finance in the 1880s. A former Foreign Minister, Nicholas Girs, taught him about international relations. He learned strategy and other martial subjects from General Genrikh Leyer, who was the editor of Russia's most comprehensive military encyclopedia. He studied fortification under a general of Engineers, and military history with several experts from the General Staff Academy, whose pupils were normally majors and colonels. Another teacher was Charles Heath, an Englishman who, a generation before, had taught two other Romanov princes. Heath was to be a formative influence on the Tsar, who would one day introduce him to Queen Victoria. Nicholas had, in other words, a good grounding in a range of more-or-less relevant subjects given by men of ability, but he was never tested in any way – his understanding was never assessed, nor was he ever required to develop ideas, let alone defend them in debate. Just as significantly, he never experienced criticism. He had no notion of being wrong, or being told that his thoughts or actions were mistaken. He had never had any need to change his mind, to listen to others, to see anyone else's point of view.

Most important by far among his teachers was the Russian Konstantin Pobedonostsev (1827–1907). A clergyman and mystic, he held the important post of Procurator of the Holy Synod. Pobedonostsev had been tutor to Alexander III and had exercised a vital influence upon his life and reign. An inflexible – indeed fanatical – advocate of autocracy and orthodoxy, he came to prominence the year before the killing of Alexander II and found that his reactionary conservatism fitted well with the times that followed. He convinced two generations of his country's rulers that any form of representative government was entirely alien to the Russian mentality and that no concessions to reform must be allowed. Alexander's personal inclinations followed much this course and he had no difficulty accepting such views. Nicholas, who had the same indoctrination and who saw his father as a model, also had no hesitation in agreeing. Pobedonostsev, who would resign his Synod post in 1906 after the establishment of the Duma and die the following year, is regarded by historians as a grey eminence who, more than any other figure, symbolised the reactionary spirit of tsarist Russia.

We can imagine Nicholas, sitting in the schoolroom in his dark sailor suit, the grey-blue eyes watchful and attentive but reflecting no passion or enthusiasm. He was always diligent, writing notes in a neat and careful hand, never asking for clarification or for further explanation. If he was not an inspiring pupil, at least he was not a troublesome one. If he showed no zeal for learning, at least he was not overtly lazy or disrespectful. In the midst of these schoolroom years he suddenly became an adult, in that on his sixteenth birthday he came of age according to his family's custom, and was required to swear an oath of allegiance to his father in front of the assembled Court. He therefore had no chance to forget his destiny or treat these years as carefree and unimportant.

He had no lack of loyalty to his father. Throughout history it has been common in royal families that a ruler and his heir do not like each other. The father imagines the son waiting impatiently for his demise. The son may collect around him a party of friends, men whose fortunes have not prospered under the present regime and who place their hopes in a future reign. They are opponents of those at present in power and are thus disliked by those around the throne. With Alexander and Nicholas there was none of this. The father was not resented, the son was anything but impatient to take over, and would indeed have liked to delay this for long years. There was no objection by Nicholas to his father's advisors, none of whom he wished to replace when he became Tsar. There was no clash of generations. Alexander was demonstratively affectionate with his children, and genuinely loved Nicholas.

The Tsarevich avoided becoming another stereotype – the pleasure-loving young man typified by Shakespeare's Prince Hal, the future Henry V. Though he enjoyed the comparatively irresponsible period – a tragically short phase lasting only four years – between leaving the schoolroom and ascending the throne, he did not throw himself into a life of idleness or vice. He did not have a phase of cocking a snook at authority. He similarly did not seem to wonder about other young people of his age, or show any desire to meet them. He appeared to live comfortably within the limits of his position, and this will have owed much to his incurious and passive nature.

His basic grounding was followed by a further five-year course of advanced study – the equivalent of the senior years at school and then a university education, or rather that of a military academy. He would now study those most serious of subjects – economics and law – but would concentrate particularly on military sciences. These, of course, were an entire field of their own, and while theory can be taught in a classroom the necessary practical skills need company. To obey on a drill field is difficult unless one is in formation with others, and learning to command is equally problematic if there is no one to carry out one's orders. Nicholas accepted as normal his individual instruction with the same passivity that he accepted everything else that life brought him.

He remained a diligent, if uninspiring, student. His position did not save him from any of the monotony of the classroom, the long hours of instruction or the need to study and prepare in his own time – his workload involved some thirty one-hour lessons a week – yet he never complained. In fact he did not usually react in any way to what was being told him. To make matters worse for his instructors, they were still forbidden to test him by any means, verbal or written – or even to ask him questions while teaching. He himself did not ask them anything, and so they left the room after each class without any idea how much he had understood.

Count Vassili described Nicholas's formative years in highly negative terms that we know to be exaggerated even if they contained some truth: 'The love of learning was never inculcated; reading serious books was never encouraged; the discoveries of science were only explained as things which existed, but not as things capable of further development. In a word, the Tsarevich received quite a middle-class training.'

He went on:

His education had been neglected, and he was brought up as befitted an officer in the Guards, not as the heir to a mighty

Empire. For a number of years after he had emerged from his teens he was treated as a little boy, and not allowed the least atom of independence. The instruction of the children had been conducted slowly, and instead of fostering the development of their minds, it had been kept back as much as possible by their teachers. The Tsarevich lived in two small rooms – those which he was later on to inhabit for the first months that followed upon his marriage – in the Anitchkov Palace, and he stood always in considerable awe of his parents, perhaps more of his mother than of his father. He had no companions, no friends; no artistic tastes, no interest in anything – not even in military matters.

The nearest he came to normality during his upbringing was the visits he made to Denmark. His maternal grandfather, King Christian IX, was known as 'the father-in-law of Europe' because of his children's extensive marriages throughout the continent. In particular, his daughter Alexandra had married the Prince of Wales and her sister Dagmar the Tsarevich, linking his small country with two of the most powerful empires on earth. The huge extended family that resulted from these various alliances gathered in the summer at his palace of Fredensborg. For his daughters it was a chance to revisit the scenes of a carefree youth. For the younger generation of Romanovs it provided an intriguing opportunity to live in a lilliputian kingdom, beautiful and historic, yet with an endearing informality and a welcome lack of terrorism. Here they were among cousins – British and Greeks as well as Danes – with whom they could romp as children and flirt as adolescents, for among those with whom they shared these summer days might well be their future spouses. United by a common status, they could be 'normal' – silly and juvenile – in a way that they could not in any company at home. Though their elders were always at hand to enforce good behaviour, and the old King who was their host might have been a stern patriarch, these were happy interludes of comparative freedom.

With the almost limitless resources they had at their disposal, it perhaps surprises us that the Romanovs should have shown such lack of imagination – such almost wanton incompetence – in the educating of their children. Today we are accustomed to the notion that the best way that heirs to thrones can possibly be brought up is to treat them like all other children. Because they will have a demanding official life in the future, it is the mantra in palace nurseries that they must be allowed to live years of normality and quietude before they begin. We see present-day European princes attending local schools, playing football or going on outings with others from their neighbourhood, experiencing the typical upbringing of those they will one day rule (the present King of the Netherlands was, as a teenager, bought a second-hand moped by his parents as a birthday present). It is therefore difficult for us to understand a world in which these things were unthinkable, or just not possible. Royal families did not look to the wider community for examples of how to educate, but to their own past. Royal children did not need to learn the same things as their subjects. They required an entirely different 'skill set' and with limited time there was no point wasting resources on what was irrelevant. They must know the ways of the Court and of officialdom, they must know the armed forces that they would one day head, since these men might be asked to die for them. They must have a grasp of the geography and characteristics of their land and they must have some knowledge, too, of other dynasties, since their marital partners would come from these and from no other source.

The next phase of his life began when he was gazetted to His Majesty's Imperial Rifles, and then transferred to the smart and aristocratic Preobrazhersky Regiment. Nicholas loved the army. It was the only happy period of his life. He had been steeped in its culture for as long as he could remember, and so many of his relations were involved in it that it did not seem like leaving home at all. His father and grandfather had both been in the Preobrazhensky Regiment. Two of his fellow-officers were his cousins, Alexander and Serge Maikhailovich, and his uncle, Grand Duke Serge Alexandrovich, was the Commanding Officer. The Guards regiments were in such close contact with the Imperial Family that, in any case, he was constantly seeing other Romanovs.

He adapted well. He liked precision and, once taught to march, he never lost the distinctive gait of the guards officer – a characteristic that others would remark upon for the rest of his life. He willingly obeyed orders and certainly did not stand on privilege with his seniors. He enjoyed the clear and usually uncomplicated tasks that regimental duty involved and he was intrigued to meet the men – his soldiers – and to work with them. With the infantry he had two drill sessions a day, together with shooting practice and the usual inspections of kit, quarters, the men's feet, their rations. He enjoyed the company of other officers and, although he did not share any of the vices associated with rich young men of that sort, they liked him. He may not have known that his father, who despised the morals of the army, had given detailed instructions to his son's regiments about how the officers were to behave while he was serving.

For anyone in his position, a love of military spectacle was, if not essential, at least preferable. The Tsar would wear some sort of uniform almost every day of his life (even when on holiday on his yacht he would dress as an Admiral) and attend regimental parades, military school graduations or other ceremonies at a rate of several times a week. It is fortunately not difficult for monarchs to enjoy these occasions, however. The spectacle of men, horses and shining steel, the colour, the discipline and precision and the blare of march music are enough in themselves, but the knowledge that all this is for your approval and protection adds even more to the occasion.

He would have absorbed since birth the notion that Russia's mighty army, victorious in many, if not all, wars, was at the service of his family, that it was among the biggest, best dressed and most courageous fighting forces in history, that it focused the loyalty of the aristocracy and the peasant class alike on useful service to the State, and that to be in any way associated with it was a privilege. Nicholas was not to spend all his service in the same regiment, where he could form lasting friendships and learn about the men he led. Rather he was to experience the three main branches of the army – infantry, cavalry and artillery. He was gazetted first to the Preobrazhensky, smartest of the foot guards regiments. After a spell here he was transferred to His Majesty's Hussar Guards, which was quartered at Tsarskoe Selo. Finally, he went to the Guards Horse Artillery as commander of a section in its First Battery. Since service in the artillery required technical knowledge as well as the ability to lead, it is probable that the Heir was 'shadowed' by a professional officer who actually did the necessary work. Nicholas was, naturally, outside the usual progression of ranks, because he must climb the ladder much faster, to reach the very top when he succeeded to the throne. While his fellow officers must wait years to become captains and majors, and many would not reach a colonelcy at all, the Tsarevich was therefore promoted to Colonel, in August 1892, only three years after his military career had begun.

In all cases his comrades, the regimental officers, had initially been awestruck and curious. To their great pleasure, they discovered that the heir to the throne could be congenial company and could take a joke. The statesman Sergei Witte, whose opinion was favourable (he considered Nicholas 'kind and extremely well brought-up'), was to say of him that he 'had the education of an average Guards colonel of good family'. If this is a criticism, it is perhaps a little harsh – after all he liked literature, which was not a common trait among officers. To a large extent, however, it is true that he felt at ease with this uncomplicated view of the world – patriotic, dutiful, disciplined but without imagination, let alone vision. There was not one among the kings or princes of his generation who did not spend his formative years in the armed forces of his country, involved in much the same round of drill, exercises, administration and socialising. Commanding a company of men, or captaining a naval vessel, was seen as running a kingdom, or an empire, in microcosm.

The life of a fashionable regiment in the Petersburg garrison can easily be imagined. There were not, as there would be today, refresher courses to attend or strenuous exercises to participate in. When not carrying out regimental duties – and these had normally ended by five o'clock in the afternoon – the young men's time could be taken up with pleasures. Lacking a public-school background of organised games, Russian officers did not have the same passion for sport that was seen in their British counterparts. They did not ride to hounds, take part in steeplechases, or play golf or tennis (though a polo club was established by one of them during these years) and their taste ran more to drinking and gambling and actresses. Nicholas was neither a heavy drinker nor given to games of chance (he liked playing only dominoes and billiards) but he met a woman with whom he quickly became infatuated. Mathilde Kschessinska was a ballerina. She was very beautiful, and talented above the average. Nicholas pursued her, and understandably she quickly surrendered. Their affair became an open secret, and Society understood. There has always been a sense of tolerance with regard to heirs to the throne sowing wild oats, and the relationship would have been good for Nicholas. It was certainly good for Kschessinska, whose career ascended to new heights (she was to become principal dancer at the Mariinsky Theatre). Two people who did not show sympathy for this flirtation were Nicholas's parents, however. They did not want their son mired in scandal and enmeshed in unsuitable, compromising relationships. Alexander decided to get the boy out of the way for a time. As so often happens in Victorian novels, a long trip abroad was seen as the most effective way to kill off a friendship that was unprofitable and damaging.

And what was he like on the verge of adulthood? We already know that he lacked many important qualities. Vassili describes him: 'As Tsarevich he was always timid, almost painfully so, and when by a strong effort of will he conquered that timidity, he came out with what he wanted to say in an almost brutal manner, which made him many enemies. Often quite unjustly. He never had any opinions of his own, except in purely personal matters.'

One opinion he expressed – though only in the privacy of his diary – was recorded on 6 May 1890, his twenty-second birthday. He wrote: 'Today I finished my education, completely and forever.' He lived in an age before the concept of 'lifelong learning' had taken hold. Nevertheless this deliberate closing of his mind at an age when he had so much to learn about the world and his place in it was discouraging.

CHAPTER FOUR

Travels

His journey abroad could be presented to the world as an educational experience. The Heir had tasted life in the army but Russia was also one of the world's great maritime powers, with a navy that had been founded personally by Peter the Great. His father wanted him to see something of the wider world, and in particular the Far East, where Russia's neighbours were the huge but shambolic empire of China and the small but powerful empire of Japan. Russia wished to establish a strong presence in the region and the Trans-Siberian Railway, at that time under construction, would facilitate this. Nicholas would undertake a voyage, it was decided, with his brother George and a few friends, fellow aristocrats and officials, aboard a warship called the *Memory of Azov*. He would go first through the Mediterranean, stopping in Athens to pick up a further passenger – Prince George of Greece. The ship would then stop in Egypt while they saw the usual monuments. They would proceed to India, Ceylon, Siam, the British Straits Settlements, Japan and China. The Tsarevich would then leave the ship at the Russian port of Vladivostok and travel back overland through Siberia.

The voyage was not a complete success. Alexander had 'micromanaged' his son's itinerary to the extent that he made detailed lists of the things that Nicholas was to be shown at each stopping place. He contacted the Russian diplomatic representatives in each case to tell them precisely how the Tsarevich was to be received. For the welcoming ceremonies on Russian soil during the return journey, he even wrote the addresses that were to be read out by provincial Governors and other officials. He thus managed to eliminate more or less all the spontaneity from the experiences they would have. He also made sure that this group of young men would not become too high-spirited by putting them under the authority of Prince Bariatinsky, an elderly general who was the Tsar's aide-de-camp. The Tsarevich himself, with a characteristic air of indifference that we have already noted, showed little outward interest in anything he saw, whether it be the Pyramids or Suez Canal or the exotic presents he received (these included several live animals, such as a panther and elephants). One of the few strong reactions he seemed to have toward anything was his weariness, in India, at seeing so many scarlet British uniforms everywhere.

The young men aboard ship were quickly bored by the monotony of days at sea, and sat listlessly gazing at the horizon as the ship ploughed its way eastward. An Anglo-Saxon passion for sports would have helped them pass the time with deck games but they knew no such tradition, and that sort of high-jinks would have met with disapproval. They were, after all, not on a pleasure cruise but engaged in an official tour aboard a naval vessel. What fun they managed to have was often accidental and clandestine. Off the coast of Egypt they suffered a major misadventure. Grand Duke George, whose health had always been delicate, suffered a fall – he may or may not have been drunk at the time – and was knocked unconscious. His father, who followed the vessel's progress daily and to whom every incident was reported, ordered George straight back to Russia to be put under the care of specialists. He therefore departed before the voyage had properly begun. He would not feature much in Nicholas's life from then on.

This was for Nicholas a very heavy loss. George had been his best friend, his only schoolmate and his constant companion all his life. They had embarked together on this adventure and suddenly, without warning, George was removed from the company and sent home. The Grand Duke would prove to be fatally ill and would spend the rest of his life – a period of nine years – living as an invalid far from his relations, who would scarcely see him again. For a family as close as the Romanovs, this must have been a considerable sadness.

From India, where this unassuming young man, good at shooting and politely interested in field sports, had been popular with his British hosts, the Imperial party sailed further east. In Siam Nicholas made a favourable impression on the Royal Family. In Japan he was well received, the first member of Russia's ruling House to visit the country. In a small town called Otsu, near the city of Osaka, he was to view a very sacred Shinto shrine, a rare honour that had never before been given to a European. He and his friends travelled by rickshaw, and they dined with the local Governor. Afterwards, as the Tsarevich was climbing into the vehicle, there was a sudden movement – the swish of a sword blade through the air. He had been attacked. A Japanese man, later identified as an off-duty policeman and assumed to suffer from mental illness, had been so offended by the notion of a foreigner trespassing on sacred ground that he sought to prevent it. He struck Nicholas once with a sabre, drawing blood from a wound just above the right ear. He tried to swing the blade again, and this second stroke might have been fatal, but was knocked aside by one of the party, Prince George of Greece, who then pinned him down. Other onlookers helped wrestle him into submission.

This incident – an international outrage committed against such a distinguished guest – put an abrupt end to the tour. The Japanese Government immediately sent a cable to Alexander, offering fulsome apologies. The Tsar accepted, but decided to bring his son home without further delay. He and the Empress had been informed by telegram of the attack on the day it happened, and had passed hours in terrible suspense as they waited to hear details of any injury 'We were at the end of our strength,' Marie told her son afterwards. He would, as planned, travel by way of Siberia for the return journey, and indeed he attended the official opening of the TSR station at Vladivostok on his way through the city, being pictured in his dress uniform pushing a wheelbarrow filled with earth. He also stopped off in the city of Tobolsk in which, in a later chapter of his life, he would spend nine months incarcerated.

The affair in Japan, though Alexander officially considered the matter closed, was to be a major grievance for the Romanovs. Nicholas – and his father – already thought of the Japanese as 'monkeys', and this word was used by Nicholas when referring to them in his diary. Notwithstanding the hospitality he had otherwise received in that country, he regarded them thereafter as savages. The white shirt he was wearing at that moment was kept as a relic. It has survived – bloodstains and all – and is in the collections of the State Hermitage Museum (it would be used for DNA-testing when his remains were identified). Every year on the anniversary of the attack, 29 April, there was a thanksgiving service attended by the family for his deliverance, though he was to suffer headaches throughout his life as a result of it.

His impressions of foreign lands may have become a blur of boredom and inconvenience, but the sights he saw on his way home left a deep impression, and prompted the most passionate outburst we have yet heard from this inscrutable young man, who told his uncle, the grand Duke Alexander Mikhailovich, that: 'I am in such raptures about what I saw that only in speaking can I convey my impressions of that rich and wonderful land.'

CHAPTER FIVE

Apprenticeship

Returned to the capital, Nicholas did not resume his nominal military career. His father felt it was time he learned at first hand something of the administration of the Empire, and had him take part in meetings of both the State Council and the Committee of Ministers – tasks which the Heir found dull and uncongenial. Alexander, like other rulers, was open to criticism that he did not give his heir more useful opportunities to experience public life. He could, for instance, have made Nicholas Governor of a province, or aide-de-camp to a general. Alexander, however, considered that even if his son benefitted from these appointments, he might show little talent for the work. He openly despaired of the Tsarevich's apparent inability to take an interest in anything, and he somehow did not think of putting him in situations where he would be forced to react, to speak in public, or to take responsibility. If the heir to an important position is visibly lacking in the necessary outlook and abilities, would it not be useful to make him practise and acquire them? We can only assume that Alexander relied upon God to do the necessary work – to provide a miracle when the moment came. However, he gave a small amount of assistance himself when he agreed with his most able Minister, Sergei Witte, that the Tsarevich could be invited to chair the Committee that directed the building of the Eastern Siberian Railway. The region had obviously taken the young man's imagination, and he had already been involved, in a ceremonial capacity, with the project. This could give him a useful insight into the running of an important enterprise. The railway would in any case be the defining Russian achievement of that generation, enabling the exploitation of the vast resources of this remote land. It was a symbol of the riches and the greatness that were to come, during Nicholas's own reign. It would be well for the next Tsar to be associated with it.

Nicholas, however, had other preoccupations. He had not forgotten Mathilde Kschessinska, and took up with her again. He was, however, keen to marry, and whatever his infatuation with her there was never any question of taking the relationship seriously. It had been a matter of genuine affection, but she must now fade out of his life as someone else took her place. She did not suffer. She would go on to a stellar career as a dancer both in Russia and abroad. She would be the companion firstly of Grand Duke Sergei Mikhailovish – by whom she had a son who was ennobled – and then of Grand Duke Andrei Vladimirovich. She would make her home in a beautiful, art nouveau mansion that remains one of the wonders of St Petersburg and, fleeing the Revolution, live until 1967 – a considerably happier fate than was visited on many in the circles in which she moved.

Meanwhile Nicholas had decided, as long ago as 1884, whom he would seek as a wife. In that year he had made the acquaintance of a young woman who had enchanted him. She was half-German, half-English, and brought up at the Court of Queen Victoria, whose favourite grandchild she was. Her name was Princess Alice (Victoria Helen Brigitte Louis Beatrice) of Hesse-Darmstadt. She was, in other words, a minor German princess of the type that for centuries had been marrying into the royal houses of Europe. 'Alix', as she was known (as well as 'Alicky' and 'Sunny'), had lost her mother as well as a younger sister at an early age, and carried with her an air of sadness that lasted all her life. She already had a connection with the Romanovs because her older sister Elizabeth had married Nicholas's uncle, the grand Duke Serge. It was at their wedding that the two young people had met. That there was a mutual regard – though no more than an adolescent crush – is proved by a window-pane at one of the smaller palaces at Peterhof. Their names – 'Nicky' and 'Alix' – are scratched on the glass. Five years after that, in 1889, Alix again visited Russia. She stayed for six weeks and, as Nicholas confided in his diary, this encounter confirmed his feelings. Auburn-haired and with beautiful grey eyes, she was very like him in nature. She had a shyness as painful as his own. Like Nicholas she came from a close-knit family but had few friends. Like him (for he proved this by his pursuit of her) she was capable, beneath an outer diffidence, of stubbornness.

Though he was certain he had found the woman he wanted, there were difficulties. For one thing, neither of his parents liked her or regarded her as suitable, and would not be likely to bless such an alliance. Nicholas broached the matter with his father, who brushed it aside. Despite his longing to marry Alix, Nicholas was still attached to the dancer Kschessinska, so his affection was not as pure as it might have seemed and his parents may have doubted his readiness to settle down. As with all parents in their position, Alexander and Marie had studied the possibilities for the marriages of their children, and they wanted Nicholas to wed a princess from the tiny Balkan state of Montenegro. This small kingdom was Russia's only ally, and it was a source of amused pride to Alexander and his subjects that their country was too mighty to need any friends. The only one they had was a small and out-of-the-way country that was of no military or economic importance. Members of its ruling family had already married into the Romanovs, and this connection could be strengthened.

As for Alix, the Tsar, as superstitious as many other Russians, objected to his son's choice of a bride from the Duchy of Hesse. Twice before, women had come from that principality to marry Russian rulers. One had been the wife of Tsar Paul. The other had been the consort of his own father, Alexander II. Both men had met tragic ends. To believe that ill-fortune was brought to the dynasty from this place may seem fanciful nonsense and yet . . . this third marriage to a Princess of Hesse was to end in greater tragedy than the dynasty had ever known.

A second important point was that Alix was a pious member of the Lutheran Church and was unwilling to change her religion. However fond she may have been of Nicholas, this was no mere formality. Her faith was essential to her character and identity and she was deeply reluctant to change it. This was a major sticking-point and might have proved an insurmountable obstacle. It certainly delayed any commitment on her part.

The betrothal might never have taken place had not the Tsar's health, in the autumn of 1894, begun a serious decline. Alexander was forty-nine but, suffering from a sudden and excruciating kidney disease, he lost his legendary strength with a speed that astonished those around him. He abandoned the family's customary summer holiday in Denmark, and went instead to Polish hunting lodges, in the hope that fresh air and simple surroundings would help him. He continued to decline and was told by doctors to seek a warmer climate, so he and his family set off for the Crimea. He would stay in his palace at Livadia for an initial recuperation, and then perhaps move on to Corfu.

He realised that he would not recover and that the process of preparing his heir would have to be, as it were, fast-tracked, or indeed given up altogether. In no sense was Nicholas ready to take over. There had been no time even to satisfactorily finish off his military education, let alone give him a sufficiently wide experience of the workings of government, the law or the Church. One wonders if Alexander felt any guilt. His son had not met nearly enough people. His formative years had seen so much wasted opportunity. He had had the possibility of meeting more people than any young man in Russia. Through the palace doors could have come any subject his father chose to summon – thinkers, writers, travellers, administrators, churchmen, artists, wits, theatrical producers. Nicholas could have listened to the most informed and erudite conversation available in this era of Russian cultural triumph. He could have learned about his future realm from the people who had upheld its greatness. Yet he had instead entered adulthood disadvantaged, not blessed, by his position, in that he had less knowledge of how to live as an adult than many young men of the merchant class. He did not even have qualifications for the rarefied and ceremonious life for which Fate had chosen him. He had no notion how to address an audience, receive an ambassador, confer a decoration. Thankfully, at least, his mother and his battery of uncles would remain and could give him advice.

It was in this climate of sudden urgency that both of Nicholas's parents agreed to his marriage. If he had a wife, the succession would be one step nearer to being continued. Their son was a weak man who would need emotional support. It would give him a home life that would help him to deal with the stress of his approaching destiny. In these rapidly changed circumstances, Alix finally ended her opposition to a change of religion and, after long talks with her sister Elizabeth and others, agreed to convert to Orthodoxy. It took an enormous personal struggle to reach the decision, even though two very powerful people – her grandmother Queen Victoria and Kaiser William – pushed hard for her to accept the Tsarevich. Ahead of her was a formidable task. She must not only learn the complicated language of her husband's country but study the theology of its Christian Church, learn new observances, a new calendar of saints, new ways of praying – and she would have to adopt a new name that would be more fitting for a Russian. Princess Alice would become Alexandra Feodorovna. We are, of course, accustomed to thinking of Nicholas and Alexandra as a couple, but they were not necessarily seen by others as 'made for each other'. Though they shared some traits they otherwise had little in common.

Her personal sacrifice, in terms of her religion, should not be underestimated. To those of sentimental inclination the courtship was charming and magical. *The Girl's Own Paper* described to its impressionable young audience, in a series entitled 'The Romance of an Empress', how 'she was courted by a prince who was heir to a mighty crown. "Sunny" lost her heart to the royal wooer, and he pledged himself to her – persistently courted her against wide opposition – turned a deaf ear to the counsels of emperors and queens who tried to discourage the match, and after years of battling with diplomatic intrigue and personal restraint he carried his purpose, married the German princess, who was truly the bride of his heart, and raised her from the obscurity of her own home to the rank of empress.' This is, of course, a somewhat fanciful description of events, though he certainly had had opposition to overcome and he was not without romantic instincts – he summoned, to Darmstadt all the way from Russia, the choir of the Preobrazhensky Regiment to sing for her, a gesture the like of which few suitors could hope to make. It is worth remarking that, whatever her feelings in this matter, her decision was unpopular in the principality from which she came. Instead of a sense of pride that she would become the consort of a mighty Emperor, her father's subjects believed she was being handed over to a semi-barbaric foreign state for political reasons. They respected her reluctance to change her beliefs and felt sympathy for her. A newspaper expressed a view that was common, and it is worth quoting at some length because of the perspective it offers on how contemporaries viewed this fairy-tale wedding:

> The German people cannot consider this marriage with joy nor with the charm of things of the heart alone in question. If we cast a glance upon the Tsar fighting against the throes of death; upon the 'private life' of the bridegroom; upon the renunciation of the evangelical faith of the Princess, a faith to which she has belonged to this day, sincere and convinced as to its truth – we consider that only an heroic nature can overcome all these terrors. After the German people had, until the last hour, reckoned with the rupture of this union, which cannot bring any happiness for the bride, it only remains to feel ashamed that, in this country of liberty of conscience and of conviction, one can make to political considerations the sacrifice of one's faith and one's heart. One would learn with a deep joy that the Princess had found by the side of her husband real and lasting happiness. In the meanwhile we can only indulge in wishes for her welfare, and hope for the best in presence of this dark and uncertain future.

The marriage had to be put in hand with speed, because time was running out. The Tsar, now a shadow of the man who had towered over courtiers and demonstrated his strength by bending silver coins in his fingers, was an invalid. Alix was summoned at once from Germany to meet her prospective father-in-law, who might last only a matter of days and who would not be alive for her wedding. She travelled across half of Europe with the speed of one who fears to arrive too late, but she had to come by ordinary train because in the midst of the crisis no arrangements had been made to bring her. In the event, her prospective father-in-law lingered for over a week. The atmosphere at Livadia was understandably miserable. To see her fiancé losing the man he most loved and admired was bad enough. The prospect of taking over from her hostess, in the very near future, the role of Empress of this giant, bewildering land was asking a very great deal of any young woman of twenty-two even if, unlike Alix, she had been of an outgoing nature or had had some kind and sympathetic mentor.

Because Russians knew nothing about Alexandra, a whole 'familiarisation process' had to be gone through. Pictures of her – expensive chromo-litho images, in colour to show off her hair and eyes – were printed in the hundreds of thousands and distributed throughout the country. Press articles praised her modesty, her intelligence (it was even claimed that she was a graduate in philosophy of the University of Heidelberg), her ability to play the piano, her suitability to be a mother. Since the majority of Russia's population could not read, this information was not widely influential, but that she was the sister of the devout and popular Elizabeth will have counted for something. Such was her shy and distant nature that, even years after Nicholas had ascended the throne, millions of his subjects still knew little about her. Her picture continued to be seen everywhere, but she made no speeches and appeared in public as a mute companion to her husband. From being simply 'the wife of the Tsar' she would become 'the mother of the Heir'. She was to make little impact on the Russian people until the Russo-Japanese War and then the advent of Rasputin.

When Nicholas's father came to the throne he had not yet reached middle age. His robust health suggested he would live for many years yet, if he escaped bomb or bullet. As other monarchs have done since, he courageously carried out official duties that involved appearing in public in spite of the risks, because he would not allow criminals to upset the life of the State. The Heir was in no hurry to learn to rule. There would surely be time for that once he had dealt with more immediate issues, such as starting a family and bringing them up, furthering his military career, reaching senior rank and commanding a regiment, travelling and becoming more familiar with the Empire. He might serve an apprenticeship as Governor of a province, experience war by taking part in some minor campaign, gradually take over from his father some ceremonial functions and even important duties. He could, over a decade or two, ease his way into the role of Tsar so that when the day came it would all be familiar, safe, simple.

And then suddenly he was the country's ruler. He was like a student who finds that final exams have started before he had got around to revising. He was caught completely unprepared. He would have to obfuscate, filibuster, rely on half-remembered formulae, make things up as he went along. In this case it was an unkind fate and not entirely a wanton idleness that had put Nicholas in this position, and he should not have felt unprepared – he had, after all, by his own admission finished his education some years earlier. Now, however, like so many other monarchs before and since, he would have to learn on the job.

His father's death – he died quietly in his chair on the afternoon of 20 October – was the sharpest blow to Nicholas, whose youth had so abruptly ended. Despite having already witnessed one sudden transfer of authority when his father took the place of his grandfather, he had no idea what to do or say. He wept with genuine bewilderment and self-pity, saying to Grand Duke Alexander Mikailovich, who was nearby; 'What shall I do? What will happen to Russia now? I am still not prepared to be Tsar! I can't rule the Empire! I don't even know how to talk with Ministers.' He must suddenly have regretted the opportunities he had wasted, sitting in State Council meetings, half-listening, on the assumption that he would have long years in which to become familiar with it all. Several of those who were present at Livadia and saw the young man assume power – and perhaps a great many others throughout Russia – remarked on the sense of desolation that followed the passing of Alexander. His successor was so visibly incapable that they could only view the future with foreboding. How could this stripling, on his own, rule so vast an Empire with its hundred and forty million subjects, and impress foreign powers as a Russian Tsar ought to do? To these observers it seemed clear that a golden age had ended and that the future could only be uncertain, disquieting and unfortunate.

The late Tsar had been – as would be expected from someone in his position – a devout believer in the Divine Right of Kings. With this went a belief that God would bestow the necessary gifts, at the appropriate moment, on the one He had chosen to take up the task of kingship. Though Nicholas, in other words, might seem unpromising at the moment, he might suddenly – instantly – gain wisdom and insight through some mystical power in the moment of accession. Alexander had experienced something akin to this himself on that afternoon in 1881, when those present had remarked on the sudden, decisive nature he had displayed. Miracles happened, and it was not expecting too much to look for such an occurrence now – after all, nothing less than the fate of the holiest, most godly nation on earth depended upon it. The Almighty could not possibly be indifferent, or unwilling.

Perhaps Nicholas was expecting this too. He was also a man of firm belief in God. But nothing happened. There was no miracle, just a continuing feeling of abandonment and inadequacy. A bad omen for this successor of Job to absorb and come to terms with.

At least there was one *good* omen. He had the wife he had set his heart upon. After years of hope, he was to be married. He would be able to replicate the atmosphere of warmth and love that had characterised his own childhood. Like his father, whose disapproval of marital infidelity had been legendary (he would force the resignations of generals or officials on hearing of any such moral lapses), Nicholas never even thought of straying. He and Alexandra shared a communion of souls such as very few monarchs – or commoners – experience (even another couple of legendary devotion – Victoria and Albert – had had vociferous rows!). For the new Tsar there was the comforting knowledge that, whatever challenges lay ahead, he could at least expect to have a very happy home life.

Alexander's leave-taking was suitably impressive. The funeral car was drawn by eight horses and driven by his most senior coachman. Twelve aides-de-camp held the supports of a canopy over the coffin, and twelve generals walked behind, accompanied by pages carrying lighted torches. Behind them came the new Emperor, on foot. The crowd eyed him with sympathy. They had been astonished by the suddenness with which the robust Alexander had turned into a shadow and then declined to death. They knew his son was not ready, or proficient, to take over the throne. For the moment, at least, they wished him well, but a feeling of foreboding had settled over Russia. People sensed that the new era would have none of the confidence or the certainty of the last reign, that the country was taking a step in the dark. The young ruler looked melancholy, and deeply apprehensive. He seemed to express, in his sad eyes, that he shared this sentiment. No one was aware that Nicholas would have problems to deal with during his reign that were considerably worse than anything his more able progenitor had had to address.

CHAPTER SIX

Monarchy

Alexander had left his realm to his son in a very strong position. Russia seemed within years of rivalling North America in the swiftness with which infrastructure came into being. In a ten-year period, industrial output doubled, and so did the amount of railway track. This meant new opportunities for exploiting resources – timber, furs, precious metals, coal – in the vast interior. In the year of Nicholas's coronation – 1896 – Russia held an international exhibition in Nizhny Novgorod to display both her achievements and her potential. The world was highly impressed by both, and began to accept the Tsar's domain as a coming industrial power. Russian and foreign newspapers were filled with images of mighty new railway bridges, ships being launched, great buildings taking shape in the fashionable neo-Muscovite style. Even for a huge country, the scale of things was becoming grander. This was the moment at which, from a foreigner's viewpoint, a handsome and charming man took over the country. He had none of the personal gruffness or the crudely threatening manner of his father. To outsiders he seemed to represent a more benevolent spirit, to guide an era of new wealth. The foreign press was optimistic in its predictions about his future and his realm's.

Exactly a fortnight after the funeral of the late Tsar, his son was married in St Petersburg. Alexandra was fetched to the wedding by the Dowager Empress, a journey that cannot have given much pleasure as there was already a chilly atmosphere between them. At the wedding, said Princess Bariatinsky, the bridal pair seemed sad and preoccupied. The year-long period of mourning, both private and official, had already exhausted them both and a sense of gloom lay over even this happy event. She commented that 'the foreboding of calamity and unrest that they felt then never left the Emperor Nicholas throughout his reign.' The couple moved into the Anitchkov Palace, the home of Marie and of the new Tsar's siblings, where they occupied the small rooms that had been Nicholas's bachelor quarters. They would share this building for some years.

Alexandra was not liked by her mother-in-law. There is no disguising this fact and it must have added considerably to the strain under which the young woman lived. One eyewitness recalled:'I remember the day when Nicholas Alexandrovich was married. The Tsar had just come down from his private apartments, and the Dowager Empress swept down the room toward him, without even noticing the gentlemen-in-waiting who were lining the walls. She was in a towering passion. She went up to her son like a fury, and exclaimed: "I wish that you may be brought back from your wedding as your grandfather was brought back from the Winter palace!"' This was, of course, a reference to the assassination in 1881. He went on: 'You may imagine the effect which his mother's blessing had on the Tsar! From that day to this the life of the Tsaritsa has been a perpetual torment . . . '

Marie's biographer, Coryne Hall, has demonstrated that the animosity was not all in one direction. The new Tsarina was a person of surprisingly strong will who resented the fact that, now mistress of a sixth of the world, she was obliged to behave like a guest in someone else's home: 'Although politeness was maintained – they called each other Motherdear and dearest Alix – the atmosphere soon became strained. The Tsar never questioned his mother's authority. If Alicky gave an audience she had to ask permission to use one of the State Rooms.' We are left with a clear, and, it seems, accurate, picture of Nicholas caught in the crossfire between two determined women, and trying to please both.

The Empress Marie was a woman of legendary strength of character who was aware of her popularity. Active in mind and body – she would live to be 80 – she had no desire to retire from public affairs, and she was unwilling, in any case, to fade into the shadows in favour of her son's wife, for she knew that she represented for many people a better era and a higher standard. She therefore refused to give up any of the 'good works' in which she was involved. She stood at the head of a network of charities and institutions that brought her considerable gratitude and admiration from the people. She should have made way for Alexandra, who was idealistic and willing to take on these tasks – to have provided opportunities and introductions – but she would not. She sat firmly on the plums of public office and refused to budge.

Alix's unpopularity had begun almost at the moment she took her wedding vows. She had taken over as consort so quickly from a woman so entrenched in the public regard that she could only suffer by comparison. That she became at once a stickler for form who insisted on having her hand kissed (a custom her mother-in-law had allowed to lapse) by Court dowagers caused them to take against her with all the venom of the seasoned backbiter. She was not gracious with her ladies-in-waiting (she would never permit them to sit down in her presence, a considerable ordeal for those who were older) and did not seek or appreciate the advice of those who had spent longer amid the surroundings of the Court than she had. It began to be noticeable that members of great families did not care to attend royal functions unless obliged by etiquette to do so. The Empress had little to say to them anyway, and seldom smiled. Her most glaring mistake had, without question, been to decide that ladies whose conduct was known not to be of the highest order should not be invited to Court balls. She discovered who such people were merely by listening to gossip, and then struck off their names from the guest lists. This was the same thing that had been done in Britain by her grandmother – and example – Queen Victoria, under the influence of Prince Albert, fifty years earlier.

The Russian Court, however, was not willing to tolerate this behaviour, these attempts to purify the moral atmosphere, from a young and callow foreigner. The move was quickly rescinded because it left so few interesting guests available that functions would have lost all semblance of pleasure. The Dowager Empress, who could be expected to lend a sympathetic ear to complaint, readmitted many of the guilty. The damage was done, however. Alexandra would never be liked, or forgiven, by those in Society in her new country. At the first New Year's reception she attended as consort, she cannot have been unaware of the atmosphere of icy disdain, even outright dislike, among guests who did their best to avoid conversation with her. Bows and curtsies can seldom have been more peremptory, or more insincere. Behind her back they looked with disdainful amusement at the pocket-handkerchief principality from which she came, and wondered how she had the nerve to put on distant airs with them.

One significant problem was that she had become Empress at a time of official mourning. This meant that for a period of a year there could not in any case be any Court celebrations (mourning had been suspended for the single day of the wedding). The highest echelons of Russian society were obliged to put away their finery out of respect for the late ruler. The period of time during which the young sovereign and his wife might have been getting acquainted with their Court, and especially with those members who were of their own age group, was not granted them. Another difficulty arose in Alexandra's unfortunate choice of Princess Maria Galitzine as her Mistress of the Robes. This lady controlled all access to the Empress. She was an embittered, sarcastic and unpleasant woman who had made enemies for decades at Court and who greeted visitors with such snobbish disdain that they were put off her mistress. Nicholas and Alexandra were never to recover from the loss of this opportunity. When, two years after her husband succeeded to the throne, the Empress arrived by carriage at his coronation her reception – the muted response of the crowd – was in audible contrast to the genuine enthusiasm for the Dowager Empress. Dislike was mutual. Alexandra was incensed that her new country did not recognise her good intentions or grant her the affectionate respect to which she felt entitled. Like a bad-tempered child who refuses to make up after a squabble, she distanced herself from Russia, its aristocracy and institutions, and withdrew into the world of her family. Her husband, who with his quiet nature usually fell in with her wishes, followed her, for a life of domestic solitude was after all the only existence he understood. She was to hate St Petersburg which, as she came to identify more and more with her adopted country, she reviled as being 'not one atom Russian'. Her disdain for the city would never leave her.

Even in the privacy of her home there were opportunities to make mistakes and cause offence. It was reported back to the gossips of Petersburg that, one evening when guests were present and the Empress wished to retire, she turned to Nicholas and said: 'Now come, my boy, it is time for me to go to bed.' This was spoken in English. A familiar, affectionate remark, it perhaps lost something in translation, but to Russians it was inconceivable that even the wife of the 'God on Earth' should use such language toward him. This simple incident brought damage out of all proportion to both wife and husband. To Alexandra because she was seen as insolent and disrespectful. To Nicholas because he was seen as a dominated weakling.

If she made little impression on people beyond the Court, it was only because they were not aware at that time of her private influence over the Tsar. Alexandra was more intelligent than Nicholas. She held stronger views than he did and she had a firm belief that she was right. She was capable of putting thoughts in his head and of providing him with opinions. Had she had an analytical brain, an ability to digest reports, interview ministers, coax her husband to make decisions, she would have been a blessing to his country and his people – literally a 'power behind the throne'. She could have given him the appearance of being a capable ruler, even if he were only repeating her views, and thus seen to it that there was consistent and relatively stable government. She could have been Prince Albert to his Victoria, creating a 'dual monarchy' in which husband and wife together pored over official documents and consort helped ruler to understand and to act. But such an arrangement would not have been accepted in Russia – all she could do was nag and lecture, reinforcing his inflexible instincts, deepening his conservatism. She reminded him continuously that he was appointed by God and thus not to be challenged by his ministers. Once she had produced an heir, she urged him never to forget that it was his duty to pass on the autocracy intact and that none of his powers should be given away. In the latter years of his reign, when the situation was unravelling and tsardom was heading for the abyss, her advice would become more strident and her manner more hectoring. She showed a strength and a resolve that he lacked, even in extremis, but her rallying-cry would by then be irrelevant.

Nicholas's first years were relatively untroubled. Nihilists and 'People's Will', the sinister terrorist brotherhoods that had made organised attempts at assassination during the '70s and '80s, were inactive owing to vigorous policing and very harsh punitive measures. The coronation saw no political violence or serious threat of disorder, and had a tragic accident not occurred it would have been remembered as a glittering start to the reign. This would be the last significant breathing space Russia would enjoy. Nicholas and Alexandra could travel relatively safely through the streets of the capital. Though shadowed by police and with their route planned in advance, they could even sit in an open carriage, recognised and saluted by their subjects (a big, scarlet-coated Cossack seated next to the driver might give away their presence!). This was a time in which pointless anarchist terrorism was claiming the lives of rulers and heads of state everywhere, and other dynasties were by no means spared the trouble that had stalked the Romanovs. In 1898 the Empress Elizabeth of Austria was stabbed to death, for no reason, while boarding a boat in Geneva. The King of Italy, Umberto I, was similarly stabbed while attending a sports display in 1900. In the same year the President of the United States, William McKinley, was stabbed at a trade fair in Buffalo, New York. If Russia seemed fortunate in avoiding such outrages it was soon to lose that innocence. The new century would bring back political violence with a vengeance. Russia, already a country synonymous, to outsiders, with violent extremism and with equally savage repression, was to consolidate its reputation for both in the time ahead.

The year after their wedding, 1895, saw the arrival of their daughter Olga, the first – for monarchists concerned over the succession – of the disappointments. Many people in this superstitious country viewed this as another ill omen. Yet her parents were absolutely delighted with her. Nicholas commented diplomatically that: 'I am glad our child is a girl. Had it been a boy, he would have belonged to the people; being a girl, she belongs to us.' Shortly after the child's birth, her parents were due to travel abroad, to visit two heads of state. They simply were not willing to leave her at home, and so she accompanied them. First they went to Balmoral in Scotland, where they saw Alexandra's grandmother, Queen Victoria, at a private family meeting. Then they made a public, official visit to Paris.

The tone that would be characteristic of Nicholas's reign was set early. In February 1895 he was visited at the Winter Palace by deputations from local councils, or Zemstva. One group, from Tver, asked politely in the course of their speech for the right to be granted to Russian subjects to 'express their opinions'. This was a reference to representative government, and the Tsar took it as a personal challenge that must be met at once. He lectured them on the folly of such notions, calling them – his voice rose to a near shriek – 'impossible dreams'. This phrase, reported in the press, fell like a cold shower on liberal Russians. It would reverberate for the rest of his life, becoming his most infamous single utterance. In the midst of a sunny new era in the nation's life, when new wealth was creating that essential component of any advanced society – a middle class – the new Emperor could have signalled that he was in tune with the times. Instead he had announced that his father's reactionary regime would continue unchanged.

It was Nicholas's' first and most important dilemma: as his country became prosperous and began to take its place among the industrial nations, it inherited the social problems that go with such a transformation – slums, low wages, sweated labour – and which lead to social discontent and political extremism. How could Russia enjoy the fruits of prosperity while keeping intact the nature of its very distinctive monarchy? The answer was that it could not. He was never to solve the problem, and the stance he took would ultimately cost him the throne.

CHAPTER SEVEN

Consecration

The coronation took place in Moscow, as was traditional, for it followed a ceremonial that predated the foundation of Peter's city. It was held nineteen months after his accession, but this was not unusual (his father's coronation had been two years after he succeeded). The period of official mourning lasted a year, and the preparations took months. The rites themselves were nearly a month in duration. The Tsar and Tsarina arrived near Moscow but stayed outside the city in the Petrovsky Palace, where they would pray and meditate for three days before entering the gates. Events began at seven o'clock on the morning of 14 May with the pealing of church and cathedral bells and the firing of 21-gun salutes. Nicholas wore the dark-green uniform of the Preobrazhensky Regiment, over which would be placed the gold and ermine coronation robe. Alexandra was dressed in white and she too would have a golden robe. His mother, similarly clad and wearing a crown, made a third member of the royal party.

It was not only the principal performers in this spectacle who were dressed uncomfortably. There was an escort of officers from the Chevalier Guards, the finest and most aristocratic of Russia's cavalry regiments. This unit, which attended the monarchy on state occasions just as the Household Cavalry does in Britain, contained some of the tallest men in the army. One of them was Carl Mannerheim, a Finn who was later to become Generalissimo of his country's armies. He and his comrades can be seen in the coronation procession – for it was photographed and even filmed – accompanying the canopy under which the Emperor walked. His regimental gala uniform, surely the most elegant in the world, consisted of a white tunic with scarlet collar and silver braid. He wore skin-tight breeches of elkskin that had to be soaked and put on wet over bare skin. He was required not only to march in this uniform but to stand to attention through the

entire proceedings with his weighty sword 'at the carry' (held verti-
cal). His right arm would have been parallel with the ground all this
time, and must have been in agony throughout. Not surprisingly, he
described the coronation as: 'the most exhausting ceremony I have
known', explaining that 'I was one of the four officers who, with the
highest dignitaries, lined the broad steps which led from the body of
the Cathedral to the two thrones on the dais. The air was heavy with
incense as we stood immobile, with a heavy cavalry sabre in one hand
and the helmet crowned with the Imperial Eagle in the other, from
nine in the morning until half-past one.' Prince Yussupov was also
a witness. He recalled: 'the sun was particularly bright that day, and
played on the gold and gems of the glittering costumes. Such a sight
could be seen only in Russia.'

The presiding clergyman was the Metropolitan of St Petersburg.
Firstly, Nicholas was asked to say the Creed. Then he was decked in
the cloth-of-gold robes. He was given the crown, orb and sceptre, and
then spoke the coronation prayer, followed by a series of responses
between himself and the Metropolitan, who represented the Russian
people. He next entered the sanctuary – in Russian churches this is
divided from the congregation by a huge, icon-covered screen called
an iconostasis – and took communion, out of sight of onlookers. Only
clergy are normally entitled to do this. It gave substance to his sym-
bolic role as head of the Russian Church. As dictated by tradition he
crowned himself (for as 'God on Earth' he needed no churchman to
do this for him) and also placed the crown on Alexandra. As he had
walked up the steps to the sanctuary, dragging the heavy robe with
him, the chain came undone on the big, clumsy collar of the Order
of St Andrew, which fell off. He had, in any case, been visibly wilting
under the weight of crown and robes, and had had to be revived with
water. To make matters worse, he dropped the sceptre. On top of everything else, one of the Tsarina's ladies-in-waiting pricked her finger on
the clasp of the coronation cloak, and drops of blood fell on it. All of
this represents such an accumulation of bad omens that one wonders
how the new Tsar was able to reign even for a week. Fortunately in this

instance very few people saw what had happened. Given the rarity of coronations and thus the fact that few of those present have previous experience, given the complexity of what happens and the number of people involved, it is unlikely that *any* has gone without this sort of mishap (at Queen Victoria's there were even worse disasters!). In a land of such superstition, however, these things assumed an importance they need not have had.

The congregation had to remain on their feet throughout. It was exceedingly warm and there were hundreds crammed into a building that is tiny by the standards of Western cathedrals. Some ladies fainted.

Once the Tsar had been blessed and crowned he and the Tsarina made their way, still in the heavy and cumbersome robes and crowns, to the Great Kremlin Palace for the traditional repast, 'of which,' continued Mannerheim, 'I managed to get a glimpse'. He shares this with us: 'It took place in the ancient Granovitaia Palace. In the banqueting hall they were waited on by the highest Court dignitaries, mostly fairly aged, who, with trembling hands, bore food and wine to the Emperor's table, flanked by officers of the Chevalier Guards holding drawn sabres. The serving dignitaries were compelled by etiquette to leave the room walking backwards, no easy task on the highly polished parquet floor.'

As with other tsars, an album of pictures was produced to show the event. It was as sumptuous in its production as it was in its subject matter. It was the work of several artists who were making sketches throughout. It allows us to appreciate the sheer visual splendour of the scene inside the Cathedral – the dazzle of gold from icons and paintings and robes and braided uniforms. The deep red velvet hangings, carpets and awnings that gave contrast to the brighter colours worn by participants. The candlelit mystique of the service itself, with the officiating priests and bishops providing a magnificence of their own. The pictures give no hint of the cloying scent, the stifling heat, the sheer exhaustion of standing through the interminable hours, or that those fortunate enough to be inside might envy those outside. A surprising number of the memoirs of those who saw it were to mention the feeling that this would be the final such event – that they were seeing the coronation of a Tsar for the last time.

Nicholas was invested with all the titles – a lengthy list (small wonder that the proceedings lasted so long!) of his positions. He became, in full: 'Emperor and Autocrat of all the Russias, Tsar of Moscow, Kiev, Vladimir, Novgorod, Kazan, Astrakhan, of Poland, of Siberia, of Tauric, Chersonese, of Georgia, lord of Pskov, Grand Duke of Smolensk, of Lithuania, Volhynia, Padolia and Finland, Prince of Estonia, Livonia, Courland and Semigalia, Samogotia, Bialostock, Karelia, Tver, Yougouria, Perm, Viatka, Bulgaria, and other countries; Lord and Grand Duke of Lower Novgorod, of Tchernigov, Riazan, Polotsk, Rostov, Yaroslav, Belozero, Oudoria, Obdoria, Condia, Vitebsk, Mstislav and all the region of the North, Lord and Sovereign of the Circassian Princes and the Mountain Princes, Lord of Turkestan, Heir of Norway, Duke of Schleswig Holstein, of Storman, of the Ditmars, and of Oldenburg' and so on, and so forth. However outlandish some of these names and styles may sound, they fulfilled the important function of asserting his authority over all the regions conquered, or claimed, or in which an interest had been declared, by his family and their predecessors. These resounding titles were a summing-up of centuries of history: military glory, alliances of birth and marriage, of agreements made and deals done and of far-flung peoples who had to be reminded that they owed fealty to the ruler in Moscow.

The procession from the cathedral was the part of all this that the public and the cameras could see. The swaying canopy, carried by Grand Dukes, gave a touch or oriental splendour. It captured both the opulence and the exotica of the Russian Court. The setting – inside the huge fortress with its green-roofed towers and clusters of gilded cupolas and with its sweeping view over the river (the buildings would be illuminated when darkness fell) – made this an awe-inspiring spectacle. When the bells of all the churches, monasteries and cathedrals rang, the sound filled the whole city.

The Khodinka Meadow was a nearby military exercise field. It was here that the 'Goulanie', or People's Fete, was to take place and that the populace would celebrate the coronation. There were tents for feasts and sideshows. There were coronation gifts of food and drink, and a commemorative mug. This object, a handle-less beaker of enamelled tin, was pretty by the standards of mass souvenirs. It was decorated in a strapwork design of blue and red (the national colours) and bore the imperial eagle, the date 1896 and the ciphers of Nicholas and Alexandra beneath a crown. It would become known as 'the cup of tears'.

The man responsible for order at this event was the Prefect of Police, whose task it was to make a tour of the grounds before the public was let in. For some time, impatient people had been trying to break through the barriers onto the field. As the police pushed back the overanxious, there developed a general scrum. A rumour had apparently gone through the crowd that there were not enough mugs. Another suggested that one of them, or some of them, would contain a gold coin. Some people broke through the barriers and began rushing across the field, but fell into trenches dug in different places, and were then trampled by those behind. The crush was awful, the screams of the trapped and injured were horrible. Order broke down, panic was everywhere. It was to be an hour before the field could be cleared, and then were revealed the corpses, lying everywhere, some so mutilated as to be unrecognisable.

Word was, naturally, conveyed at once to the Tsar, and much was made by his enemies of his apparent indifference on hearing the news. However it is worth mentioning two things: one was that the death toll was not known at that time – no figure could be given him, which would have provided some notion of the scale of the tragedy. Secondly, those reporting this news would naturally have wanted to play down the size of the disaster. This had happened in the middle of a series of national celebrations. Of course there was a desire to assess the damage before cancelling anything.

Within hours of the tragedy, the Tsar and Tsarina were due to attend a ball at the French Embassy. Of all the events taking place at that time, this was perhaps the most delicate. France, the country's new ally, had staged a massive celebration. Furniture and fittings had been imported from the Palace of Versailles to create a setting of unequalled splendour. To fail to attend – no matter what the circumstances – could be seen as an international insult.

The Tsar and Tsarina had to solve a dreadful dilemma. If they went to the ball, they would be seen as frivolous and uncaring. If they did not – and instead spent the time visiting the injured in hospital – they would risk offending Russia's ally. Should they make a populist gesture by being with their people, or a diplomatic one by acknowledging the generosity of their country's friends – in particular the Ambassador, the Count de Montebello, who was greatly liked in Russia? They both weighed opinion. Alexandra was advised by her sister, the immensely popular Grand Duchess Elizabeth, to attend the ball. It was the wrong choice.

They went, and reaped all the outrage from public opinion that they had feared. They derived no pleasure from being there, for onlookers commented on their melancholy and preoccupied manner. Princess Bariatinsky remembered that: 'Although the Emperor tried to smile and be courteous, we could see what an effort it cost him, and that his thoughts were not in tune with the festive occasion; he looked pale and sad, and on the Empress's face there were traces of tears.' Nicholas only took part in one dance. They left early to visit the injured in hospital, but their credibility was badly compromised and their critics and enemies had valuable ammunition to use against them.

This verdict was extremely unfair. Though they may not have known at once the extent of the death toll, the Tsar and Tsarina were well aware that this was a major disaster. As soon as possible, they began visiting the hospitals to see the wounded and to bring what comfort they could. For the Empress, whose withdrawn nature made it difficult to talk to strangers even of her own rank and in happy circumstances, this must have been an especially demanding task, yet she did it without flinching. They also attended a commemoration service for those who died. The Tsar founded an orphanage specially for children of the victims. He paid the entire cost of religious burial for each of the dead, who received a separate coffin (there was no question of anonymous mass-burial), and each victim's family was given the sum of 1,000 roubles in compensation. Critics accused the government of tying to hush up the matter but in fact a full report of it appeared in the press the day afterward and the rumour-mill (deaths were estimated at up to 5,000 – the figure was in fact, according to police records, 1,300) had no chance to exaggerate the number. To those willing to see objectively, it was obvious that Nicholas and Alexandra were deeply upset by what had occurred and that they made sincere efforts to help in whatever ways were possible. It was simply malicious propaganda to suggest otherwise. Nonetheless, opinion was hostile enough to give him little credit.

On a more positive note, the couple travelled more widely than any predecessor since Peter the Great. Alexander had only stirred from his domains to visit Denmark. Nicholas and Alexandra travelled extensively, going in 1896 to Austria, Germany and France – for Russia the most important foreign country.

CHAPTER EIGHT

Settings

Nicholas and Alexandra lived for some years in the capital, but their preference was for the kind of seclusion in which the Tsar had grown up. They could not occupy the same palace, because Gatchina was still the home of the Dowager Empress. They chose another of the residences that lay scattered throughout the surrounding countryside and from the fateful year of 1905 it became their winter home. This was yet another disappointment to those of their subjects who had hoped for a new era. Alexander's self-imposed isolation had been more than simply a family decision to live a more private life. It had been the removal of the living heart of the nation. Russians, passing the huge Winter Palace in all seasons and weathers, had glanced at this building (unlike Buckingham Palace, which is set far back behind railings, the Tsar's windows looked directly onto the street) at night, seeing lights on – perhaps in the rooms known to be occupied by the Emperor – and been aware that their monarch was sitting up late, at work for their benefit. They knew, too, that he watched from those windows the life of his capital as it flowed past on the streets and waterways. He might look out at shipping with a telescope, remark the figures of soldiers moving on the fortress ramparts opposite, spot a postman or a street porter struggling with a heavy load against the wind. It was known that once Alexander II had been horrified to see, amid the fury of a winter blizzard, an elderly general crossing Palace Square in the teeth of wind and snow. Upon enquiring, he discovered that the man could not afford to keep a carriage. The Tsar at once ordered that one of his own vehicles must always be available to take this distinguished veteran to and from his home.

At the portals of this great building there had been all the important bustle, the comings-and-goings, of a busy seat of government – officials hurrying in and out, soldiers standing sentinel, gorgeously dressed generals, councillors, court officials arriving in carriages for meetings, or beautiful women attending court balls. Russians had loved this symbol of their nation's might and importance. They had liked living cheek-by-jowl with their ruler, and they had a genuine love of the building, which they knew to be the biggest in Europe. Here the great decisions were made. Here the foreign ambassadors came to pay their respects, here great assemblies were held, proclamations read out, awards given. Here, too – for the Palace contained its own cathedral – the christenings and weddings and funerals of the ruling family had been celebrated for generations. Here was the Hermitage, an art collection surpassed only by the Louvre. Here, in other words, both the business and the pleasures of their government and rulers could be seen to be going on. This was the centre of society. The entertainments were lavish. Citizens loved to crowd into the great square and see it filled with carriages or sleighs, to see the long rows of lights blazing from the Palace, to hear the strains of music from an orchestra or a military band. These things were an important part of the communal life of the Imperial capital, a magic that any spectator could enjoy and feel pride in.

With Alexander's move to Gatchina, this largely ended. Though the balls still happened, periodically, during the winter season, there was not the same life about the place. The great building was used only for occasional meetings, or as a home for a few minor Romanov relations. The business of government went on somewhere else, the urgent hurrying messengers no longer crossed the square. The troops still stood at their posts but they were no longer guarding anything living, merely a series of empty rooms. For most of the time the Palace stood silent through the endless darkness, its windows unlit, its portals unvisited. It was a sad place for many of the pedestrians who took a short-cut through the square. The glory of Russia had departed. One commented that the Palace: 'Once so animated has taken on the appearance of a lumber room, and presents to the visitor an unkempt, forlorn, dirty, neglected sight.'

Those who hoped that the new Tsar would breathe life into the shuttered and dust-sheeted rooms were to be quickly disappointed. Nicholas, whose association with the Palace had ended abruptly at the age of twelve and who could not dissociate it from the bleeding and mutilated form of his grandfather, had the same disinclination to live there as his father had had. He did have apartments prepared, and in particular he had a personal library established – a comfortable, mock-gothic chamber, it impresses visitors today, who sometimes remark that it is the one room they have seen that they would actually like to live in. Nicholas did not live there. His home in the city was the Anitchkov Palace.

Not only did the lack of gaiety cause disappointment among the aristocracy, it probably spelled serious losses for the shops of St Petersburg – the milliners, tailors, costumiers, jewellers and all the others that served the beau monde during the winter social season. These patrician shops, set along the Nevsky Prospect and famously never open before noon because their clientele, sleeping off the excesses of the previous night, would not dream of going out until later in the day, will have suffered from considerable loss of trade. So would those others who supplied the minor wants – flower-sellers, say, or cab-drivers. Other wealthy and stylish people gave balls, of course, and there were enough rich in the capital to keep much gaiety going. Nevertheless, society revolved around the Court and when the Court did not lead society, many could be affected.

Yet wherever the Romanovs were, the rituals of monarchy went on. In the corridors and on the staircases of their homes could be glimpsed the vividly costumed functionaries who personified the splendour of the Court – there were heralds in the plumes and tabards of the seventeenth century, footmen in the wigs and livery of the eighteenth, pages and major-domos in the gold-braided uniforms of the nineteenth. There were ladies-in-waiting in the brooches that were their badge of office (they wore the monogram in diamonds of the personage whom they served), and Ethiopians still stood sentinel outside the private rooms of the Tsar. The atmosphere was 'timeless', as it tends to be in virtually all royal residences that reflect tradition and continuity. This was not an attempt to hide from the present, which entered the portals every day in the shape of officials and reports, but an ambience that reflected the long-term values and the dignity of the nation.

With the effective ending of public Court life, it is perhaps worth noting that aristocratic society became bored and sought other distractions. If the idle members of that class could not spend their time in gossip, in dress fittings and in attending balls, they would look for some other diversion. A number of them became 'politically aware' as a result, increasing the opposition to the state and making Nicholas's task of ruling harder in the long run.

While the Dowager Empress retained Gatchina, the young couple's preference would eventually settle on Tsarskoe Selo. This small town, set on a hilltop some thirteen miles south of Petersburg, was not a single residence but a vast estate filled with buildings, gardens and parkland. Its name meant originally 'High Village' but was corrupted to the similar-sounding 'Tsar's Village', or 'Royal Village', and it had been associated with the Romanovs since it was given by Peter the Great to his wife Catherine in 1708. Decades later, the favourite architect of the Empress Elizabeth, the Italian Rastrelli (who was also responsible for the Winter Palace) had cleared a huge stretch of land and created for her a structure that was intended to outshine Versailles. A thousand feet long, boasting six hundred rooms and painted a dazzling blue and white that makes it look as if it were made of porcelain, it is one of the world's most impressive buildings. It came to be known as the Catherine Palace to distinguish it from a smaller, plainer residence that was erected in 1796 a short distance away – the Alexander Palace. This latter, with its two hundred rooms, was to be the residence most associated with Nicholas and his family, and not least because after the abdication it would become their first prison. It had its own park but was plainly visible from the road. It was arranged in two wings (the Family inhabited one of them, the rest of the great building was used for other purposes) that flanked a domed central hall, thus forming three sides of a square while an elegant screen of pillars closed off the fourth. By the time they moved here permanently, in 1905, they had five children. Olga was to be followed by Tatiana (1897), Marie (1899), Anastasia (1901) and Alexis (1904).

Their apartments, which today are open to visitors, were decorated for them in Jugendstil, or art nouveau, style (known in Russia as 'Style Moderne'). The rooms are elegant and comfortable, relatively informal and liveable-in from a modern perspective, for the style has never gone out of fashion. By the standards of their time, however, they were almost shocking. We are accustomed to the notion that everything to do with the Romanovs was huge, impressive, overwhelming. We find Nicholas and Alexandra's home to be intimate and . . . bourgeois. The Tsar's study, with its billiard table and the big, staring portrait of his father, or Alexandra's 'mauve boudoir' in which she spent long hours in real or psychosomatic pain, the wall above her bed colonised by a collection of icons that reflected her growing and obsessive spirituality, both of these are out of keeping with other palaces and royal residences. The furniture for them was ordered from Maple in London's Tottenham Court Road. This firm, which had begun trading in 1842, had a long and honourable tradition of furnishing the homes of young couples of the English middle class. To find that they supplied the Imperial Family of Russia was something of a surprise. Prince Yussupov was horrified: 'In spite of its modest size, the Alexander Palace would not have lacked charm had it not been for the young Tsarina's unfortunate "improvements". She replaced most of the paintings, stucco ornaments and bas-reliefs by mahogany woodwork and cosy corners in the worst possible taste. New furniture by Maple was sent from England, and the old furniture was banished to storerooms.' While it is certainly true that putting Style Moderne furniture and decorations into neo-classical interiors is regrettable, it is these 'cosy corners', with their clutter of cushions and flowers and Fabergé frames, that visitors today will usually find most evocative and admirable. For the Empress and her husband England was a place of very happy memory. They had spent the most carefree weeks of their lives there, and it was there that much of their courting had been done. The English atmosphere they created was a gesture to romance and nostalgia, whatever others may have thought of the result.

As a retreat from the world and as the setting for a pleasant family life, it promised well. It was a town without industry, slums, or ugliness of any sort. Every vista was beautiful, the result of continuous labour by architects, builders, gardeners and landscape designers. The town beyond the park railings was filled with pretty villas for the aristocracy, for courtiers, officers and administrators. It was also a place to which such people liked to retire, and its cafés and restaurants were filled with both serving and former officials and their wives. Regular trains brought sightseers from Petersburg to its quaint little station. Its streets resounded with the tinkle of streetcar bells, the rattle of carriage wheels, the clop-and-jingle of horses as some cavalry squadron trotted by on its way to the great exercise grounds, or the sound of drums and trumpets and the tramp of marching infantry, for this was a major garrison town.

A guidebook described it as: 'the Windsor of Russia and winter residence of the Imperial Court. It has 30,000 inhabitants. There are two palaces, eight churches, many barracks, hospitals etc. The straight streets and the numerous country houses give the town a pleasing aspect.' Actually, its appearance had little in common with Windsor – which is dominated by a single great building – and it much more closely resembled Potsdam, the residence-town of the Prussian kings. Like Potsdam it was a toy landscape littered with caprice, folly, whimsical nonsense-buildings erected just for the fun of looking at them, or in reference to some private joke, or to offer a hint of some far-off country – Turkey, Greece, Egypt, China – to those whose position meant they could not travel abroad. There were more than eight hundred acres of artificial countryside. There were magnificent monuments, statues, obelisks, lookout towers. There were follies in the shape of Turkish baths and Chinese pavilions. There was a lake with a boathouse manned by sailors, who looked incongruous amid parks and trees. There was a canal spanned by an eccentric, three-legged 'Chinese Bridge'. There were rows of hothouses, filled with the smell of exotic flowers or orange trees. There were meadows, islands, groves and copses. In modern terms – though the description is absurdly vulgar – it was more a 'theme park' than a royal park, a sort of Disneyland, but one in which everything was designed and completed by the greatest architects and horticulturalists. Typical of it was the Children's Island accessible only by a boat rowed by sailors, on which generations of young Romanovs had played in the child-sized house. On still evenings might be heard the splash of oars from a lake, the shouts and squeals of children, the call of exotic aviary birds or even the trumpeting of an elephant from the menagerie (feeding this creature was one of the Tsarevich's favourite pastimes), the creak of a weathervane on some pavilion (there was and is one that is famous for this sound) and perhaps the drifting strains of orchestral music, or the clatter of polite applause, from some building where candlelight winked in the falling dusk. Naturally there had to be an enormous staff to tend this idyll. Every autumn hundreds of soldiers were drafted in to strip the trees of their leaves so that they would not fall and look untidy. This was truly the perfection of nature.

Much is made of the fact that this was a 'private world' – that this magic realm was only for the use and enjoyment of a single family, but this was absolutely not true. The Catherine Palace was one of Russia's most visited tourist sights (tickets had to be obtained, but admission was free, which is certainly not the case today!) and the park was open to the public at times of the year when the Family were not there. While it would naturally have been heavily guarded and a suspicious-looking visitor might be questioned, anyone could otherwise wander the paths, sit on the banks or admire the monuments. The only real proviso, in deference to the Tsar's security and privacy, was that 'the New Palace may not be inspected'. However it was perfectly common for visitors to see, through the railings of the park, the Imperial children out for walks with their nurses or governesses, to see them ride in a donkey cart attended by a top-hatted groom, or to glimpse them romping with their dogs. They may have lived a private existence, not only through their own inclination but for reasons of security. They may even have seemed like prisoners in this very gilded cage, but they were not out of sight of those of their subjects who cared to look.

Not surprisingly, given that this community was founded by the monarchy and inhabited by generations of Romanovs, it became a symbol of the dynasty and of the autocracy, for good or ill. Robert K. Massie, in his seminal book *Nicholas and Alexandra*, describes Tsarskoe Selo as 'an isolated, miniature world, as artificial and fantastic as a precisely ordered mechanical toy', and quotes Gleb Botkin, whose father served as Court Physician, as saying that 'To loyal monarchists, it was a sort of terrestrial paradise, the abode of the earthly gods. To the revolutionaries, it was a sinister place where bloodthirsty tyrants were hatching their terrible plots against the innocent population.'

Nicholas loved to roam the park with a shotgun, shooting at crows in the trees. In summer he bathed in the canal, in winter he liked to drive his wife in a sleigh, or go skating with his children. At all seasons he sawed logs, dug the soil or simply took invigorating walks. He lived as outdoor a life as was possible for a man whose position required him to deal so much with documents, with visitors and with ceremonies. When at home in Tsarskoe Selo or Peterhof he made time each day for some form of exercise. Like his own parents, he and Alexandra were very close to their children. Though the Tsarina, with a growing list of ailments, would shut herself away for days on end, Nicholas saw his children every day. In the tranquil domestic life that he had arranged all the time and energy that as a ruler he might have given to society – to sociable collective pastimes with friends, ministers, officials – was deliberately devoted instead to his family.

Alexandra, who did not have his passion for nature, was in any case often confined by pregnancy or ill health. Trouble with her legs made her unable to mount a horse, and the running about involved in tennis or badminton was beyond her, even as a young woman. She spent hours every day, while her husband dealt with administration, in work of her own. She learned the Russian language. She made a detailed study of Orthodox theology. She practised the piano. She did the routine work of an Empress which – wherever her mother-in-law had left opportunity – involved patronage of charities, schools, orphanages and other institutions.

If Tsarskoe Selo was beautiful, the Family's summer residence was even more so. Some of the warmer months were spent at Peterhof, which was as far to the west of the capital as the 'Tsar's Village' was to the south. This too was not a single building but a community of residences, widely differing in age, size, setting, architectural style and historical associations. The most overwhelmingly conspicuous was the palace of Petrodvorets built, from 1720 onward, for Peter the Great. Set on a ridge and – like the Catherine Palace – designed to match Versailles in splendour, this building had an advantage neither of its rivals could boast: it was set on the coast, overlooking the blue waters of the Gulf of Finland, to which it was linked by a canal. It stood opposite the great island fortress of Kronstad, which defended the approaches to Petersburg, and endlessly the traffic of the oceans went past. The white sails – and later the black smoke-trails – of the Russian Fleet could be watched from its windows, and orders could be signalled to the ships. On its landward side, the Palace windows looked down on a series of huge fountains – another touch of Versailles – that were truly the equal of their French inspiration. Here was a landscape as entirely filled with fantasy and caprice as were the parks of Tsarskoe Selo. There was the same clutter of monument, grotto, folly, lake and island.

Once again there were hordes of sightseers who made the excursion from the city. The great palaces around St Petersburg were tourist attractions as much then as they are now, though with the added interest that they were peopled not by ghosts but were actually inhabited by the Imperial Family and that members of this – or their vehicles, their officials, their soldiers – might be glimpsed.

The main palace was a long range, painted canary yellow and with a turreted rococo pavilion at each end that looked as perfect as a jewellery box. Exterior and interiors were as sumptuous and excessive as the vast wealth of the Tsar could command and such buildings were, of course, intended to convey, to reflect, such power, wealth and taste. Here especially this was the case, since Peterhof was built on land that had belonged to Sweden. It was an act of defiance, a show that Russia was here to stay.

Though naturally breathtaking, the Palace was not to the liking of all generations of Romanovs, or even of its founder. Peter had already, before construction began, built the modest manor house called Monplaisir that stood some distance away, surrounded by gardens. Here he had lived while supervising the huge project that followed, and in its smaller rooms he was perfectly happy. As with other dwellings of his, this original house had been preserved as a monument to him so that future generations could marvel at the simplicity of his life. Another comparatively understated structure was a small palace called Alexandria Cottage. This dated from the reign of Nicholas I. It was intended as an intimate family home, and was furnished in the historicist style that might be termed 'Walter Scott gothic' (the Emperor had been an immense admirer of Scott's works, and had told his own great writer, Pushkin, to produce similar novels). This neo-gothic appearance was much in evidence in Potsdam, the Prussian royal town from which Nicholas I's wife had come.

Once again any notion of a 'private world' is overstated. Visitors strolled the paths, photographed the views, laughed when their friends were caught by sudden jets of water from the hidden fountain, peered past the sentries to catch a glimpse of the Imperial children in the private reservation that surrounded their home. They might well have seen Alexis and his carefully chosen playmates in their white sailor suits, drilling with rifles under the supervision of his naval nurses, Nagorny and Derevenko. The park surrounding Alexandria Cottage is very much associated with Nicholas's children, and it is very appropriate that a statue of Alexis, once again in a sailor suit, now stands here.

CHAPTER NINE

Their First Decade

Alexandra, despite her background in a small and powerless dynasty, had quickly become accustomed to the scale and the influence of the Russian Imperial Family. She adopted from the time of her arrival, as we have seen, an aloof demand for deference, a distance between herself and even the most high-born of her ladies-in-waiting. Though her daughters would be brought up simply, they too were to be treated with deference by courtiers. Even members of the Family – her husband's cousins and their children – were kept at arm's length. This attitude extended to the general public. At the insistence of the Empress, when the Family was travelling by train all platforms in stations through which they passed were to be cleared of passengers, and the carriage blinds lowered. Again, our modern notion is that a royal family should be accessible. This would not have been considered, in the context of that time and place, acceptable. Nevertheless the aloofness demanded, in the name of privacy, by Alexandra was considered somewhat excessive.

She was not merely shy. The word used repeatedly by historians and biographers is 'timid' – the kind of person who is unable to look others in the eye, or to initiate a conversation. Such a person would not normally have thought to meddle in affairs of state, making suggestions and offering opinions on matters of government business. Yet she did so. She saw that her husband found it difficult to cope with this on his own, and she believed it was her mission to help him. Her failure to win the affection of his subjects did not cause her to redouble her efforts to do so, rather she gave up almost at once and became not only even more withdrawn but resentful. Her relations with the Dowager Empress were never to vary, or improve. Once she began having children Marie, like so many mothers-in-law throughout history, disapproved of the way they were being brought up – an attitude that rose to a virtual crescendo as the girls grew up starved of the company of other young people and denied more than a glimpse of life beyond their family.

Alexandra was as conscious as her mother-in-law of the need to defend the autocracy against any concession to popular representation. She was privy to all her husband's thoughts and was, if anything, more of a defender of tradition than he was. By an extraordinary quirk of personality this timid, frightened woman was also capable of firmness, anger and stubbornness. Where her position, or her husband's, was concerned she was a strong personality, less diffident, less afraid of standing up to advisors or ignoring political protest. She believed more fervently even than Nicholas in the idealised Russia of devout peasantry and inherent, respectful affection for the throne. Doting on her son, she would not let her husband forget his duty to pass on to Alexis the same powers he had inherited. Compromise was weakness. No matter the threat or the danger, she took it as an article of faith that God wanted the autocracy to continue for the sake of this holiest of nations and that whatever troubles and temptations came their way they had a duty to persevere.

It was not for the Romanovs to court, or win, public favour, or to worry about whether they were popular – to plead for their subjects' respect. Nicholas was not a constitutional monarch or an elected leader but God's viceregent, appointed by the Almighty and thus beyond the criticism of his subjects. If he were experiencing difficulties, this simply meant that God was testing him. If he did not flinch under this pressure, he would win Divine favour and, if it were God's will that Russia go through a time of trial, they must accept this. It was a simplistic view of their situation that took little account of actual circumstances, let alone possible solutions. The influence the Empress received from mystics was passed on to the Tsar. To what extent he regarded this as the voice of God is not clear, but he did not visibly differ from his wife's views.

Unsurprisingly, Nicholas was given to routine. A glimpse at his timetable, in the years when his children were growing up, may be useful.

Typically, he was up by seven or eight o'clock, and ready to start work at nine (his fellow Emperor, Franz Josef of Austria, who was almost four decades older, always started at five). He ate a simple breakfast and read the morning papers as well as beginning to read the reports that would flow in throughout the day, making notes as he went along. After two hours of this he was, according to his timetable, to have an hour of relaxation in order to take a walk in the park with his collies. In fact, the receiving of visitors and reports from Court officials usually ate into this, and he was left with only a remnant of the time to gain some air. Until one o'clock he received more visitors, this time Ministers or heads of administrative departments, to hear about developments in the cities and provinces, in the civil service and in embassies abroad, but while this was going on he participated in the time-honoured custom of a commander-in-chief of tasting the rations of his soldiers. He did this every day, alternately sampling the food of two local regiments, His Majesty's Own Infantry Regiment and His Majesty's Imperial Escort. In both cases a non-commissioned officer brought the locked steel dishes containing the food and stood to attention, his right arm in a rigid salute, while the Tsar ate. Whatever his verdict, it was passed on to the officer of the Day.

His own midday repast was taken in company with his family. This was probably the first time he had seen them during the day though the Tsarevich, once old enough, might already have joined him for his walk, and had perhaps been allowed to help try the rations. Like breakfast, lunch was a simple meal. The Emperor would quiz his wife and daughters about what they had been doing, perhaps asking details of their lessons or making admiring noises when shown drawings or needlework. Yet more audiences followed, until about four o'clock. The Tsar was involved in scores of organisations, schools, charities and military units and merely hearing about the progress of these could take up much of his time. If anything were left he would spend it, once again, walking with his dogs. At five o'clock he had tea with his family, perhaps reading aloud, as he liked to do. It was not, however, from novels or poetry that he read, but from highlighted passages in reports he had received. In this way he sought his wife's opinions on current developments, and she maintained a knowledge of events. This afternoon tea was an almost sacred rite, and was completely private, with no one present but the Family. When later they dined the Tsar would read again, this time from the works of Gogol or another of the nation's renowned authors.

From six o'clock until eight he resumed work, dined from eight until half past nine, then returned to his desk until midnight or perhaps later. No matter how fatigued, he would without fail make an entry in his diary of a few brisk and factual sentences. His day reportedly involved ten or twelve hours' work, about a third of which was spent alone, reading papers and signing them. Though the Family had dinner together they were not in the habit of having supper before retiring for the night.

What is surely missing from this routine is any discussion of events or issues with counsellors or other qualified people. He and Alexandra lived in a comparative solitude that, though it was not absolute, was nevertheless highly unusual. Monarchs are seldom alone because they are attended by a suite of officials. These may not be actual friends, but the function of some of them is to advise. The Romanovs of course had attendants, but they were by nature such self-contained personalities that they did not confide in these or involve them in their lives. An observer was to note that: 'The Emperor and Empress have no friends, no people with whom they can talk or discuss the events of the world. The solitude in which they live is complete, their isolation from mankind entire, and in view of this disastrous fact one can only wonder that the mistakes they make are not even more serious than is the case.'

For exercise the Tsar also shot at the crows, cycled in the park or, somewhat unusually, went out in a canoe. He was rather skilled at propelling this craft, and sometimes took his son with him on his knees. At Tsarskoe Selo he had lakes and the canal to traverse. At Peterhof he went out in the Gulf of Finland. Because he liked to do things with his hands, he shovelled snow in the appropriate weather, building it into sculptured figures or castles for his children. He dug trenches, and he also worked with wood, either chopping it for the pleasure of swinging an axe, or performing simple carpentry tasks, at which he apparently had some skill. In sports he enjoyed skittles, rifle marksmanship, tennis and swimming. He was a graceful diver.

His handwriting was clear and compact. He had a good memory and could recall details in other documents for cross-reference. He wrote quickly and liked simple language and, as we have seen, he disliked foreign words or expressions enough to avoid them himself and to cross them out when others used them. He was a great scribbler of notes, even to people in his family or in the same building; he did not like the telephone, and did not have one in his study. He saw it as his duty to have a view on everything, as seen in a note he wrote on a report about teacher training: 'The Ministry of National Education should concern itself particularly with the special preparation of schoolmistresses, taking measures at the same time to protect them from the hard moral and material conditions which place defenceless female workers in such a helpless position.'

He did not like to listen to, or read, lengthy reports, and had a short attention span. He would constantly be urging conciseness and coming-to-the-point. Ministers knew he would be as unimpressed with flowery language as he would with the use of foreign expressions. If he were to listen to a report being read he would insist that the business be conducted standing (as happens with the British Privy Council today, and for the same reason – if people are uncomfortable, they will deal with matters more quickly!). When receiving a visitor with a report to give, he did not like to initiate conversation and would expect the man to start at once without preamble. His study was a sea of papers, yet he knew the whereabouts and the purpose of each one. He had in readiness numerous piles of different-sized envelopes in which to seal these and send them, and he did that work himself. He was sparing with materials and used pencils until they were mere stubs, passing them on to the Tsarevich for drawing with.

On some days the meeting of people took up all of his time.

Sizeable delegations might arrive, of which he was obliged to greet and converse with every member. Despite his shyness, he mastered the royal trick of making perfunctory remarks or asking simple questions that facilitated a short exchange, suggesting interest and friendliness without committing to more than a few seconds of time. Though like monarchs today he was briefed on the basic details of those he was to meet, he did not tend to store up ready remarks, and his talk was spontaneous. 'I never prepare what I say,' he confided, 'but I pray to God and then speak what comes into my mind.' At Easter – a much more important date in the calendar of Orthodoxy than is Christmas – many thousands would come to greet the sovereign. According to Russia's Church, all are equal on that day, and all believers exchanges a kiss. The Tsar was obliged to deliver these with exhausting frequency. He had not only to embrace hordes of civilians but whole units of soldiers, leaning up to reach the faces of men who might well tower above him.

A contemporary writer, General Elchaninov, commented that 'The Tsar's kindness extends even to troublesome supplicants, for he refrains from hurting them by an irrevocable direct refusal, and usually refers them to the Minister or head of department concerned.' This can be read as suggesting that the Tsar was afraid of causing offence, afraid of making decisions and likely to change his mind once the person was out of the room. We know that, whatever his sense of discipline and his work habits, Nicholas was not a good administrator. In view of this, it must have made matters much worse that he did not even employ a secretary, which partially explains why his hours of work were so long. He was heard to say that: 'I do the work of three men. Let every one learn to do the work of at least two.'

When at Livadia in the Crimea he was officially on holiday, and his programme was different. He would set off on lengthy walks of ten or fifteen miles – enough to fill a whole day – and end these with a bathe in the Black Sea at some place that had been pre-arranged and at which a car would be waiting to convey him home. He might take this exercise alone (though doubtless shadowed by all manner of guards) but often he was accompanied by members of his suite. Many of these were less fit than the Tsar, and had had to practise before-hand to get into condition for such a physical ordeal. On more than one occasion – and this became so well known that newspapers all over the world carried the story – Nicholas, who daily sampled his soldiers' food, decided to make trial of their uniform and equipment too. Dressed as a private of a rifle regiment, he wore a high-collared blouse, a soft cap and marching boots, and carried the usual pack and ammunition pouches as well as a rifle and the characteristic, three-sided Russian bayonet. He set off through the Crimean countryside. At the brisk pace he normally used he might walk for hours, and once was somewhat amused to be challenged by a sentry who had failed to recognise him. The Regiment itself was delighted at having him thus identify with it, and Nicholas was issued with a private soldier's pay-book, in which he conscientiously filled in his details. Under the heading: 'Date of termination of service' he wrote: 'When I am in my grave.' The German Kaiser, who was much given to that sort of gesture, was reportedly furious, on hearing of this, that he had not thought of such a thing first.

Commissioned into the army as a young man, Nicholas had been promoted to the rank of Colonel in order to act as an aide-de-camp to his father. With Alexander's sudden death, there had been no time for the Tsarevich to advance any further. It was not considered appropriate for a Tsar to promote himself, and in any case Nicholas had a deep sentimental attachment to the shoulder-boards awarded him by his father. He was to wear these all his life, their crowned cipher 'A III' looking incongruous when all those around him wore his own 'H II' (H is, of course, the Russian N). It was ironic that he as command-er-in-chief of Russia's forces should be outranked by all his generals, but this title survived when all his others were lost at the Revolution.

CHAPTER TEN

'Man of Peace'

Whatever his faults, Nicholas had a genuine desire to avoid wars, and thus developed a reputation as a peace-loving ruler. This was interpreted as a sign of precocious wisdom and goodness and was much admired throughout Europe, where Russia's might was as feared as always. He had, in fact, had the opportunity to begin his reign with a war that might have brought him cheap victory and a reputation of a different sort, as a conqueror. The situation involved the Ottoman Empire, Russia's traditional enemy. It had always been the desire of tsars and their governments to control the Bosporus – the narrow channel leading through Constantinople to link the Mediterranean with the Black Sea. By doing so Russia could close the region to foreign ships and keep other powers away from her southern coasts. Nicholas's advisors suggested to him that with the Ottoman Empire at that moment involved in domestic unrest, Russia could make a sudden move and seize the straits. Nicholas refused to take up the challenge. The Crimean War had been only forty years previously, and had united four other powers (Turkey, France, Britain and Sardinia) against Russia. The issue of access to the Black Sea was serious enough to provoke another European conflict and he did not want to take on rival empires at a time when he was still finding his feet as a ruler.

He was soon to go further. In August 1898 the diplomatic representatives who attended what should have been a routine weekly briefing at the Foreign Office in St Petersburg were surprised to be given a written statement announcing that the Tsar sought to convene an international conference on disarmament and the prevention of conflict. This came to be known as the Tsar's Rescript.

It may have come from the Tsar himself, or from his cannier, more experienced Foreign Minister, Count Mouraviev, or from someone else within his government. It may have been motivated by a genuine desire for peace, by fear of neighbouring Germany's potential aggression, or – perhaps most importantly – by the need to buy for Russia a spell of calm that would enable the country to carry on with her economic development, finish the Trans-Siberian Railway and catch up with older industrial nations. It was a strange proposal in that such initiatives normally came in the midst of an existing conflict rather than a period of quiet. On the other hand, Europe was preparing for war. Though there was no sign at the moment of a cause or a crisis, the great powers were building up their fleets and armies to meet a potential threat. This arms race was to continue into the following century and to increase in speed and scale – especially between Britain and Germany – right up to the moment that war actually broke out. Russia too was caught up in this and, at a time when she needed her financial resources to develop internally, was having to spend a hefty proportion of her budget on armaments. By making efforts to restrict the use of weaponry and the likelihood of war, Nicholas was doubtless hoping to save his exchequer some billions of roubles.

Yet whatever the motive and whoever the originator, it was an inspired idea, worthy of a great leader. Such initiatives are nowadays taken for granted, because we know after two world wars and the advent of the atomic bomb that there is no survival without them. In Nicholas's time this lesson had not been learned and was not obvious. European wars were destructive and deadly, but they tended to be short – lasting rarely more than a year and often months or even weeks. The Tsar's proposal caused initial cynicism and even amusement among the chanceries of Europe, coming as it did from a man who was not known for idealism, or deep thinking, or decisive action. An American diplomat, Andrew White, probably expressed the view of many when he wrote that his: 'indifference to everything about him evident in all his actions, his lack of force even in the simplest efforts for the improvement of his people and, above all, his yielding to the worst elements in his treatment of the Baltic provinces and Finland did not encourage me to believe that he would lead a movement against the enormous power of the military party in his vast empire.'

However no one could argue that international peace was not a worthy aim and, slowly at first, it picked up momentum as the nations came to support it. The Hague, capital of the small, strategically situated and inoffensive Netherlands, was chosen by Nicholas as the site for the conference, because any more major capital city would have caused resentment among the rival delegations. It convened in May 1899 and lasted until July. It was not directly a success, and neither was its successor conference in 1907, but the idea caught on. Recruited from the lawyers, politicians and policy-makers of the world, the tribunal would be structured so that its impartiality could be guaranteed. It would not only rule in disagreements but would introduce regulations to outlaw the use of inhumane weapons (such as the explosive 'dum-dum' bullet). It was an inspired notion. Though it would not prevent the clash that was coming, it was the spiritual ancestor of the League of Nations, the United Nations and the whole apparatus of peacekeeping that would follow after 1945. There was set up an international court of arbitration, and from 1913 this had a permanent home. Andrew Carnegie (1835–1912), the American millionaire and philanthropist, donated the funds to create a vast, purpose-built complex of courthouse, tribunal rooms, library and study centre, which was opened in 1913. It has been a place of major importance ever since, and in one of its chambers – the Small Court Room – hangs a portrait of Nicholas II.

Does he deserve the credit for instigating what has become a vital element in international relations? Yes. Even if it were not his idea, he used the influence of his position and the prestige of his country – as monarchs often do in furthering some good cause – to bring about not only the initial meeting but the follow-up. He gave birth to the concept but he also saw it safely through childhood. It has been his single lasting achievement, and on its own this would be enough for one man's lifetime. A contemporary British publication paid the compliment of placing him on a level with the 'Tsar Liberator': 'It is fitting for the grandson of the Emperor who removed the bond of serf-dom from his people to endeavour to free mankind from the tyranny of war, which has, from the beginning of history, ground the world beneath its brutal heel.'

But let us briefly examine White's charges against him. He may have been indifferent to some things, but in reality it can be seen that he could and did feel deeply – passionately – about many things (his family, his country, his people, his honour), it was simply that his was an undemonstrative and self-contained personality and there was no one, except the Empress, in whom he would completely confide, for even his diaries do not completely reflect his thoughts. As for the notion that he bullied the provinces of his Empire and ignored the aspirations of the Finns and Balts – how could he possibly have done otherwise? If he had made concessions or even granted independence to one of his territories, all the others would have demanded the same and the Empire would quickly have unravelled – as it did in the 1990s when the Soviet Union ended. He was already perceived as weak. Had he given freedom to the Poles and Finns and Balts, who had never reconciled to tsarist rule, he would have horrified the Russian majority of his subjects who would have seen him as destroying their nation. In the post-1918 world the concept of 'self determination' – that even the smallest countries could choose their allegiances and forms of government – would be seen as a sacred right. Before the outbreak of the war, what mattered was that the great powers were as big and formidable as possible, so that others would not seek to attack them. Whatever the methods of his government or his police (and faced with fanatical insurrection or terrorism in which gentleness would have been seen as weakness, might was necessary), Nicholas was keeping intact the legacy of his ancestors for the benefit of his subjects and his heirs. No one could have expected him to do anything else.

CHAPTER ELEVEN

Protection

In an article entitled 'Guardians of the Tsar, Soldiers who Protect the Man of Peace' *Harmsworth's Magazine* listed the units and organisations – six altogether – that watched over Nicholas at his summer home in Peterhof. Firstly, there was the Convoy – his closest bodyguard and one that, as its peripatetic name implies, travelled with him wherever he went. It was composed of six hundred Cossacks, recruited from the Caucasus region and dressed in a splendid uniform of long blue silver-trimmed coats. Next there was the Corps of Gendarmes (an elite military police equivalent to the still-existing French Gendarmerie and Italian Carabinieri). There were regiments of the Imperial Guards, both cavalry and infantry. There was a Naval Guard that patrolled the sea with a torpedo boat and prevented any vessels from coming too close inshore; there was a Palace Police Force, and finally there was the regular, local police. All were armed with sabres and revolvers, and the Convoy carried rifles or carbines as well. The park at Peterhof, as at all Imperial residences, was ceaselessly patrolled by mounted soldiers, while sentries stood guard around the buildings. Inside, the Cossacks of the Convoy walked the corridors outside the Family's bedrooms in stockinged feet. Their passing and re-passing was remembered by Nicholas's sister Olga as one of the sounds of her childhood.

In 1905, at the height of Russia's ills, *Punch* published a mocking cartoon by the artist Edward Tennyson Reed. The lengthy caption read: 'A Nice Quiet Picnic in Finland – External View.' It went on: 'It is stated in the Press that the Tsar has several times landed from his yacht during the last few days and picnicked on the shores of Finland. Our Artist would have given anything to be present, but *this* is the nearest he could get to it. (Puzzle – to pic-Nicholas out. He is in a bomb-proof shelter inside the timber defences).' The drawing shows a cordon of fierce-looking Cossacks with sabres. Behind them is a wall of sandbags, which shelter a host of tightly packed infantrymen bristling with bayonets, and a field gun. Then there is a heavy wooden stockade. It is ironic that the security arrangements for the heads of state in many other countries today have had to catch up with those of the Tsars a century ago. Reed, were he alive in our time, could not afford to be quite so glib.

The calm that had settled over Russia in the '90s was to end suddenly with the new century. In 1900, the year after *Harmsworth's* had listed the Tsar's various guardians, political assassinations began again. Nicholas Bogolepov, who as Minister of Public Education might not have seemed an obvious terrorist target, was shot and killed by a student. A year later the Minister of Internal Affairs, Sipiagin, was murdered in the entrance to the State Council Building as he arrived to attend a meeting. It was clear that in spite of a host of spies and agents the revolutionary underground was still active and still had members committed enough to carry out these acts. Once more, as in past decades, the sound of an explosion might rip through the streets at any time of the day or night. Citizens would stop, cross themselves, and wonder who had lost their life this time.

The Imperial Family were, of course, the most important target and, no matter the protection available to the Tsar, danger continued to be constant and unexpected. Each year in January took place one of the great set-piece events of the Imperial Court – the Blessing of the Waters. This was a religious ceremony, carried out by the Metropolitan (Archbishop), who dipped a cross into the waters of the Neva as an act of benediction. Because at that time of year these waters were frozen solid, a hole was cut in the ice outside the Winter Palace, and a pavilion erected. Only the men of the Court attended (the ladies watched through the palace windows) but to do so must hardly have seemed a privilege, for it was forbidden to wear a hat, and in the low temperature to stand uncovered for the necessary hours would have been fatal. Some participants therefore wore wigs. Beyond the circle of those most immediately involved, hundreds of troops were ranged along the quays with their regimental colours on display – the link between the Army and the Orthodox Church was always extremely close – and many thousands of spectators crowded the riverbanks. Though the service itself was both invisible and inaudible to these, the spectacle of the military formations, the colour of the church vestments and the distant sight of the 'Little Father' would have justified a long wait in the cold. There was, in addition, a 101-gun salute from the Fortress.

The guns began their long and monotonous booming, the sound of the detonations echoing up and down the still river, the smoke rings drifting upward through the winter air. Yet in the midst of this a strange thing happened: after one shot, there was the sound of breaking glass, and debris fell from the Palace roof. Policemen and courtiers looked upward in alarm. The Tsar crossed himself, but gave no further sign of anxiety. The loud discharges continued, but without further damage. The salvo ended and the procession returned indoors.

It was discovered afterward that someone had infiltrated the battery and had replaced one of the blank charges with grapeshot – a vicious form of missile made up of steel balls that scatter when the shell bursts, sending death or injury over a wide area. The single round had burst harmlessly on the fabric of the Winter Palace and no one had been harmed, but this was yet another reminder that the Family could not feel safe even when surrounded by the entire resources of army and police protection.

As seen, Nicholas was more at home with his officers than with any other group of his subjects. Among soldiers, patriotism, respect and discipline could presumably be taken for granted, and therefore he could be at ease. They lived in an atmosphere of tradition and formality with which he was familiar, and their regiments had been involved with the history of his family for as long as they had existed, creating a mutual affection. He had been schooled in the profession of arms and had fitted in well with the young aristocratic officers who belonged to the smart regiments stationed in the capital. Superficial, unprofound conversation about horses and actresses, uniforms and weaponry suited his personality, so it was unsurprising that among his greatest pleasures was the making of informal visits to the officers' messes of nearby regiments, to pretend for a short time that he was just another member and did not have the weight of the country's governance upon his shoulders. In personality and in capabilities he was 'a Guards colonel of good family' – a fairly average officer.

CHAPTER TWELVE

Society

<hr>

Such officers enjoyed very considerable prestige, for Russia was structured, regulated and organised to a degree that surprised most visitors. Russians were disciplined, deferential and militaristic. This characteristic was very important, for it reflected the nature of a country very different to that of most who came as tourists. Russia had a vicious winter climate, it had been prey to invasion and spoliation, and it had vast territories that must be defended. It was therefore acknowledged that the state, which protected its citizens, was entitled, in return, to their complete loyalty. The state represented God and thus the tsar was both their temporal ruler and the reflection of their spiritual one. There could be no arguing with such a figure, upon whom depended the life of the nation and, literally, their own lives if they were not to perish from cold, starvation or the swords of Russia's enemies. Every man's energies had to be concentrated on building up the state. All service flowed upward to the throne, all reward flowed downward from it. As the Russian author Tibor Szamuely has written: 'A political system arose that was based on the unquestioning obedience and unlimited submission of the subjects, of the principle of the obligations owed by each and every subject to the State . . . The state, in the name of the common welfare, took into its full control all the energies and resources of society. Autocracy and serfdom were the price the Russian people had to pay for national survival.'

The costume of the state therefore carried great prestige, even though so many thousands wore it, and the fact that the Tsar himself dressed in the same – or a similar – uniform whenever his subjects saw him (Nicholas II never appeared in public in civilian dress in Russia. Nicholas I is said never to have worn civilian clothing *at all* after the age of ten) increased their sense of taking part in a great cause. Russia had a colossal bureaucracy and for hundreds of thousands of men, even though they might hold a fairly insignificant position in a distant province, this meant that they were entitled to share in the national glory by wearing uniform, helmets, caps, swords, brass buttons, medals, rank stripes, spurs or badges of office. Such people were often mocked in the plays and novels of the time – the self-important minor official, pompous and bungling, was a stock character in Russian literature – but they, and their ethos, were the glue that held society together. They carried the authority, and the will, of the Tsar into all corners of the Empire

And a society so organised and so disciplined was, in theory at least, easy to govern. Everything was hierarchical, everyone seemed to be either giving or taking orders. Schools, colleges, factories, choirs, sports clubs – all seemed to be set up and run along military lines, and filled with people in uniform or covered in badges and medals. Russians did not – as they still do not – waste time on politeness. Their language – especially if they are an official – is brusque, peremptory, demanding ('Passport!'). The public – pedestrians in the street, passengers on a train, even customers in a shop – may be treated like recruits on a parade ground. Russians themselves even admire this abrupt manner, believing it saves time and enables business to be done more quickly. This is, and has always been, the way of their people. It is all they know.

Russians might grumble about their government – especially as represented by its officialdom or its stern police – they did not, ever, hate the country itself. Russian peasants in any case had a sense of personal attachment to their land that would be very difficult for others to comprehend – a spiritual communion with the soil they tilled and which gave them life. They loved the vast scale of the country. They almost worshipped its natural beauty of forest and steppe and river. The more educated classes revered its music and literature and theatre. They also felt immense pride in its power, and perhaps more than anything else – its holiness. Russians grew up to see themselves as different. Their country had been especially blessed by God in the Orthodox Church. As its name suggested ('Orthodox' means 'true') this was the purest form of Christianity and the one most pleasing to the Almighty. He had given Russia the privileged destiny of being the standard-bearer for the Faith. Not for nothing was Moscow known as 'the third Rome'. The city was one of the world's greatest pilgrimage destinations. It bristled with cathedrals, monasteries, convents and shrines. It was the centre of a form of Christianity that was practised not only in Russia itself but also in Greece, Serbia and Bulgaria. The form of government that God had declared for this land – direct rule by a single individual chosen and guided by Him – was thus the best system of governance on earth.

The West was seen as a place of weakness, softness, compromised principles and dangerous ideas. Contact with the West was a source of pollution (the Decembrists – young officers who returned to Russia from the Napoleonic Wars – had been found to be infected with democratic notions. Tragically, in 1945, Stalin took a similar view of Russians returning from the fighting in Germany). Russians saw themselves as having to be purer, tougher, more determined because of their harsh physical conditions as well as this special sense of destiny. They felt a smug satisfaction at the misfortunes of other states. (In 1848 when Europe was shaken by revolutions, Russia not only stood firm against change but sent troops into neighbouring Hungary to crush the unrest there. They also looked on with glee when Britain became mired in the South African War, and some went as volunteers to serve with the Boers.) Saw their own problems as a test of their resolve. Like members of some other nations that consider themselves 'lucky countries' (the United States, Switzerland, Australia) they were grateful to belong and imagined that others must envy them.

Though Russians would grumble without ceasing about any aspect of their lives – taxes, the military call-up, the incompetence of officials – complaint was a right that only they possessed, and they would be fiercely protective if any foreigners offered a criticism. Pushkin had written that: 'I, no doubt, despise my homeland from head to toe, but I feel annoyed when a foreigner shares this feeling with me.' Their country could not be other than great. This was a law of nature. If it failed to match such expectations, its people felt betrayed. They would tolerate a despotic leader, and endure terrible domestic oppression or privation, so long as the Motherland was feared and respected abroad (this is why, to this day, some Russians feel nostalgic about the rule of Stalin). If their leader blundered and cost them this status, however, they could not forgive. As with their country, so with their system of government. To traditionalists no other European state had an autocracy like theirs – a monarchy as pure, as mighty and awe-inspiring. Other kings and even emperors were not to be compared with Russia's – it was not even worth remembering their names. Though liberals did not of course share this view, and hoped one day to see sufficient change to enjoy the freedoms enjoyed by the democracies, they too tended to be patriotic, for such an outlook was bred into Russians.

CHAPTER THIRTEEN

Soldiery

They had been specially selected for their physiques and they
soared above me like creatures from Gulliver's Travels.

Grand Duchess Olga, Nicholas's sister,
recalling the palace guards of her childhood.

Within the Army itself, there was a great multitude of different regiments and corps. There were, of course, units of infantry and cavalry whose task was to guard the sovereign. There were twelve regiments of foot guards. They were recruited from all over the Empire and not only had connections with specific provinces (the Kexholm Guards were recruited from Finland) but were required to be of standard physical types. It remains the practice in many ceremonial units throughout the world that men must be of the same height so as to give a harmonious appearance (in the Russian Presidential Guard today all men must be exactly 184 cm tall). In the Imperial Guard they also had to have the same colouring. A regiment, for instance, would recruit entirely men with brown hair and brown eyes or blond hair and blue eyes. Most unusual of all were the Pavlovsky Guards. This regiment, as its name suggests, had been founded in memory of Tsar Paul (by his son, the first Alexander, who felt remorse for his part in his father's murder). Since Paul had been remarkable for a snub nose, recruits for the Regiment were selected for having this feature, which is not especially common among the physical types of Russian men. All royal guards have to pay considerable heed to physical appearance, and this was simply one more instance of enforced uniformity.

Such attention to detail – and treating of military formations as royal playthings – was a tradition that went all the way back to Peter the Great. Tsar Paul had been legendary for his obsession with the minutiae of drill and dress. Nicholas I had followed in much the same manner – he had clamps put on the soldiers' knees to stop them bending their legs when they marched. His notion of military perfection was that a man should march in goose-step with a glass of water on top of his flat-topped shako and not spill any. Though he may have achieved the clockwork perfection he sought on the parade ground, his men were less impressive when tested in actual combat in the Crimean War.

Though such extremes were no longer to be seen in the reign of his namesake, military show was still important as a symbol of the State. Each year a great batch of those called up for military service was assembled in the capital and men were selected for the different regiments. An English author, G. Dobson, described this ritual: 'The conscripts of St Petersburg city and province are sorted out every November in the large military riding-schools, and after having had their backs chalked like cattle, to indicate the regiments to which they have been allotted, they are marched triumphantly through the streets to their respective barracks, headed by lively military music.' For the elite regiments, this gathering took place in the ballroom of the Winter Palace. The Tsar would arrive, followed by a large cohort of military personnel. He would walk along the ranks, stopping in front of each man. In these cases it was he himself who wielded the chalk, writing the regiment on the man's chest. Members of that unit would then take the recruit away. The guardians of the tsar were thus, literally, hand-picked. This regular event aroused enough international interest to be featured on the cover of the *Illustrated London News*.

Apart from the conspicuous soldiers of the Guards who could be seen in the characteristic black-and-white striped sentry-boxes that stood outside palaces, there were more specialist units. His Majesty's Railway Regiment had, as its name suggests, the task of protecting the Royal Train, but was also responsible for the security of the track on all railway routes along which it travelled, and all stations through which it passed. When at sea the Imperial Family was protected by the

Naval Equipage of the Guard, once again an elite body drafted from what the Russians call Naval Infantry, or marines. These men not only took responsibility for the security of any vessel on which the Tsar and his family were travelling but also its moorings and the surrounding harbour. When at sea, the Equipage would crew the torpedo boats that accompanied the Imperial Yacht. No other vessel was allowed within hailing-distance and any that came too close would be challenged – and then fired upon – as a matter of course.

With such a huge army, there were barracks everywhere. In the capital, where the garrison numbered thirty thousand, there seemed to be one in every street, and thus the constant sound of band music, drum signals, marching and shouted orders from behind high walls. There were also the 'manèges', or indoor riding schools, of the cavalry. Each mounted unit had its own – a long, low-roofed building in neo-classical style – and they vied with each other in grandeur. The splendid squadrons could be seen coming and going from these – long columns on black or bay or chestnut horses, with their colourful tunics and waving hackles and lances strapped to their arms.

There were specialist military schools of many sorts – for administrators, signallers, staff officers and so on. Even Tsarskoe Selo, the quaint and quiet 'Windsor of Russia' boasted two highly technical training establishments, for artillerists and engineers. The most prestigious of all – for cavalry consider themselves by far the finest branch of an army – was the Nicholas Cavalry School in Petersburg, which was known to its past and present inmates simply as 'the glorious school'. In their red-topped black hats, black tunics and blue trousers (the uniform had been designed by Alexander III) these cadets cut a considerable dash. The Corps de Pages, a military school for the sons of the nobility, was housed in a former palace. The boys, in their black-and-gold tunics, white-plumed helmets and tall black boots were a ubiquitous presence at royal events.

In the case of all these institutions, the links with the Imperial Family were extremely close. They had been founded, developed, governed by generations of Romanovs. Their own histories paralleled that of the dynasty. It is no exaggeration to say that much of the Imperial Family's time was devoted to them, for the members were constantly visiting, attending meetings of trustees or an endless succession of graduations, prize-givings, concerts and other performances. Despite the number of military schools in the vicinity of Petersburg the Tsar attended, every year, the passing-out parades of as many as he could, to kiss each graduate and congratulate him on his commission. By these means, monarchies create a bond between themselves and their officer corps. The regiments of the army often had a member of the family as its Honorary Colonel, and with a family as large as the Romanovs there were enough of them even for such a huge army. Nicholas had had this relationship with his half a dozen units since his birth, and his son would have the same. His mother was Patron of the Chevalier Guards, his wife held a similar position with another regiment, and three of his four daughters lived long enough to be given cavalry regiments too.

In addition to career soldiers there were conscripts, chosen by ballot from across the Empire. There were uniformed police of various types in the cities, and there were civil servants in uniform. Everywhere there were military academies, cadet schools, technical schools, administrative schools, charity schools, church schools. All were controlled by the State and responsible to the Tsar, and the majority of those who attended them wore uniforms. Male university students wore military peaked caps and greatcoats that looked like those of soldiers – but then so did boys of five or six at elementary schools. There were also whole sub-species of petty officials – postmen, messengers, museum attendants, civil service clerks and porters – clad in helmets, hats, epaulettes, sword-knots, chevrons, badges and medals (the latter seemed as common as confetti. Medals were given not only for great events but for the anniversaries of great events too). An elderly bearded man, dressed as gorgeously as a field marshal and covered in medals, might prove simply to be the doorman at a hotel. As with all people of that type, he would be a veteran whose position was a reward for service; teenage boys who attended the Imperial Law

College wore a uniform that included cocked hats, and made them look like miniature admirals or ambassadors.

On the 'birthday' of a regiment, it would often parade before the Tsar, at Tsarskoe Selo or on the great square before the Winter Palace. Following the ceremony the officers would lunch with the Imperial Family. Each of them would be greeted by Nicholas or Alexandra and have some moments' conversation with them. If they were awaiting, or had recently had, the birth of a child, it was likely that the Tsar would accept the position of godfather. This role was more widespread and ubiquitous in Orthodox Christianity than in the West, and there was a long tradition in the Romanov family of taking on such an honorary position. Catherine the Great, and the Empress Elizabeth, had both become godmother to numerous children of their palace guards. This paternalism went even further. Nicholas was constantly hearing stories of men disabled or poverty-stricken as a result of misfortunes when in his service. He was susceptible to these victims of circumstance, and was constantly doing things to help them. He would on the spur of the moment grant a pension to a soldier's widow, or arrange to find employment for a former member of a regiment, or even grant an instant promotion (regardless of whether the man actually deserved it or had the seniority to qualify him). These stories were numerous and they added to the legend of the benevolent Tsar who took a personal interest in the welfare of even his humblest subjects. Whether they made for an efficient army or best use of financial resources might have been another matter. As usual, however, Nicholas was blessed with a talent for the small gesture, the thoughtful action, the detail. He had greater ability to bring happiness to an individual than to deal with the wider issues affecting his Empire or his army.

CHAPTER FOURTEEN

Court and Camp

Perhaps the most potent symbol of Russia's military might was the annual camp of the Guards regiments at Krasnoe Selo ('Red Village') outside Petersburg where the Tsar, who visited each year, could live for a week every summer a life of pageantry and pretended hardship among the tents and cabins in this dusty and wind-blown landscape. There was no need for discomfort, for there was a miniature palace for the use of the Romanovs, built in the form of a Swiss chalet. Each year in May or early June the regiments would arrive, as they had since the Guards began to make their annual visits in 1819, with their bands and gala uniforms, and would turn the small cantonment and its surrounding landscape into the most fashionable place in Russia. There were barracks, but many men lived under canvas and numerous officers were billeted on local families. There were simple houses for others, and a little wooden garrison church in Russian style with a bell tower.

Not only did the Tsar stay there, his wife and children came too. So did the officers' families, and members of the Diplomatic Corps, and any number of civilian hangers-on. The conviviality of this place was considerable on a summer's evening. After the soldiers' training had finished for the day, at seven o'clock, there would be concerts by regimental bands, dinners al fresco or in marquees, and performances in the unimpressive little garrison theatre in which Pavlova, Nijinsky and Kschessinska all danced. For this short season, Krasnoe Selo took on something of the atmosphere of one of the great European watering places: Wiesbaden, Vichy or Carlsbad. An Italian visitor, Luigi Villari, described the scene: 'The troops encamped are the Guards regiments, including the Emperor's bodyguard of Cossacks in their picturesque but somewhat theatrical uniforms. At the cavalry school at Krasnoe Selo there are officers from all parts of the Empire, wild-looking Circassians in strange costumes and small-eyed Mongols from Eastern Siberia hobnobbing with smart young Guardsmen, Sheremetieffs, Yusupoffs, Dolgorukis, Galitzyns, the fine fleur of the Russian aristocracy.'

Villari went on to describe the common Russian soldiers he encountered: 'His life is a hard one; his term of service is five years, which is longer than that of soldiers in any other Continental army. His food is bad, although the poverty of the peasants in their homes is so great that by contrast it is ample in quantity; the treatment he receives at the hands of his officers is often brutal in the extreme. But he manages to keep up a certain sad cheerfulness, and beguiles the tedium of long, weary marches by singing those beautiful but terribly plaintive songs of the Russian people. To hear soldiers singing these weird and touching melodies makes one realise the sadness and sorrow of Russian life.'

The main business was, of course, to practise warfare, but it was also to impress both natives and visitors with the visual splendour of the Russian Army. This was easy, under the circumstances, to contrive. An artificial hill called the Tsar's Mound, thirty feet high, looked out over the vast exercise plain, which could be filled from end to end with infantry, cavalry and artillery. One can imagine these formations, standing or sitting their horses in straight, silent rows, with sunlight glinting on sword-points, bayonets, helmets and horse-furniture. With the yell of orders and the tap of drums they would move off in stiff formations, wheeling, advancing, retiring, pausing to fire volleys with the precision of clockwork toys. Parading by their commander-in-chief, these huge columns took a very long time to pass, the boots and hooves and caisson-wheels raising an enormous cloud while the Tsar and his generals stood motionless at the salute. A performance that seldom failed to impress visitors was the climax of each review: the cavalry would form up in the distance and break into a gallop, the horses running faster and faster, the riders – usually wild-looking Cossacks – giving blood-curdling yells. This formation plunged straight at the saluting mound and seemed intent on mowing down anything in its path but suddenly, in a single instant and with perfect discipline, the entire force skidded to a halt, sitting motionless on their panting, slavering mounts. The men gave three cheers for the Tsar. The sound was deafening, and passionate. This was the essence of Russia in a single vignette – massive, powerful, unchallengeable, and fiercely patriotic. The onlookers, not a little awestruck, applauded with enthusiasm.

The loyalty of these men seemed unshakeable, but it would prove in many cases deceptive. As the political situation deteriorated in the early years of the century, the Army was extensively infiltrated by revolutionary propaganda. Men living by the hundreds in barracks were likely to hear and discuss events and ideas. Agitators made a point of infiltrating these communities and speaking to gatherings. Though a majority could not read, pamphlets were passed around and read aloud. Officers often either did not notice this activity or did little to stop it. The result was that, even before the Japanese and German wars, the Army was infected with the revolutionary bacillus. The elite regiments were not immune, since they were the units permanently stationed in the capital. Merely having been chosen by the Emperor and having spent years standing on guard outside his home did not automatically make for personal devotion. Between the soldiery and the officers in such regiments there was no sense of joint purpose, no common ground and no sympathy. They might as well have come from different nations. There was little prospect, therefore, that officers would influence their men for good.

CHAPTER FIFTEEN

War & Revolution (i)

The Tsar himself is bringing about the destruction of autocracy more expeditiously than any hostile organisation could
do. I do not believe that the most desperate anarchists or terrorists could harm his government as he himself is harming it
by his blindness and folly. The Revolutionary party has simply
to bide its time and look on, whilst Tsardom compasses its
own downfall.

Carl Joubert, 1905.

Even without the experience of the sword attack on him, Nicholas did
not care for the Japanese, and neither did those who commanded his
armies. When the mutual interests of the two countries drifted into
hostility and involved military confrontation, there was a feeling that
this jumped-up Asiatic power should not be challenging the might of
a self-evidently greater empire, and that a lesson must be taught.

The situation was this: China was a weak country – recently made
even weaker through defeat by the Japanese – whose territory was seen
as 'up for grabs'. No European colonial power would yet annexe parts
of the Celestial Empire outright and only three countries had foot-
holds on the coast with their entrepôts: Britain (Hong Kong), Portugal
(Macau) and Germany (Tsingtao), though spheres of influence, the
established first step toward formal colonisation, were already appearing. It was predicted that there would be a 'scramble for China' to
match the 'scramble for Africa' of the 1890s. Japan – an emerging
power and a small, crowded country which wanted both living space
and prestige – had already begun this. Having annexed Korea as a
colony, Japan had moved into the Chinese province of Manchuria.
Russia did not want to see such expansion, and put pressure on China
to resist. It worked. Japan was faced down and withdrew from the

province. Russia was then rewarded with responsibility for building and running a new railway in the region – controlling the transport system and therefore the province's infrastructure. The East China Railway in fact linked two Russian territories, Siberia and the port city of Vladivostok. The Russian position was then strengthened. China was obliged in 1898 to lease to the Tsar's government the important naval base of Port Arthur for twenty-five years, and to allow a spur-line to connect it with the East China Railway.

There was some discussion in Russian government circles as to whether Manchuria should be occupied overtly by the Army and treated as a colony, or simply dominated economically and turned into a de facto Russian territory, which would save the cost of a garrison. Fate decided the issue, because this seizing by outsiders of their nation's assets created such anger among Chinese that in 1900 there was a bloody uprising (the 'Boxer Rebellion') against all foreigners. It was crushed, and China obliged to give even greater concessions. In Russia's case, this meant that the whole province of Manchuria could be occupied. The Russians, who had encouraged China to reassert sovereignty in the area, now appeared to be taking that sovereignty themselves. They no longer saw themselves as guests but as masters. There was a tiresome detail in that they had agreed not to stay – they were supposed to cede the province in stages back to China – but they felt there was no hurry and made no apparent effort to do so.

Japan believed that her unwelcome new neighbour might have designs on her own colony of Korea, and made several diplomatic requests for Russian withdrawal. All, including the most urgent one, delivered at the end of 1903, were ignored. Japan gave a deadline for reply, which was 7 January, 1904. It actually received one, with insultingly deliberate slowness, the following month. Nicholas was convinced that he could browbeat this smaller nation and get his way without the need for conflict. He liked the notion of himself as a man of peace, and trusted to fate that he would not lose such a reputation, stating that: 'All will be well; Japan will calm down. There is no danger of war. I began my reign in peace; I shall continue and end it in peace.' Four days later, while he was attending the opera, a telegram arrived at the Winter Palace to tell him that the Japanese had attacked his Pacific Fleet in Port Arthur. So much for his instincts. He had not only caused unnecessary offence in delaying his reply to the Japanese request, escalating a crisis that was already serious enough. In failing to withdraw he was breaking his word in front of the whole world.

In that era of great power confrontations, diplomatic gestures could be interpreted with considerable accuracy as warlike or conciliatory. Japan had been in no doubt about the nature of her rival's languid delay. She therefore took matters to the next stage without further attempt at diplomacy. On the night of 9 February her forces attacked the Russian Fleet at its moorings outside Port Arthur. It was a precursor of what would happen at Pearl Harbor thirty-seven years later.

One more-or-less overt ally the Russians discovered was Germany. Kaiser William II, Nicholas's cousin, had been Emperor since succeeding his father and grandfather in 1888. A bombastic, posturing man who delighted the nationalists and embarrassed the liberals among his subjects, he had an opinion on every matter and was famous for saying undiplomatic things that were widely repeated. He was known to have ambitions in the Far East, where his country had an interest, and he saw what he considered a considerable danger to European civilisation in the rise of Japan and the possible future awakening of China (an internationally distributed cartoon which he inspired, entitled 'The Yellow Peril' summed this up). The United Kingdom, the other major power ruled by a cousin, took the opposite side. King George's government had allied with Japan.

There was no role for Nicholas in this conflict other than that of distant figurehead. He would have liked to visit headquarters, meet the men in the front line, share some of their discomfort. He might perhaps even have taken over command himself, but the war was taking place at the farther end of the Empire and there was not the opportunity either for morale-boosting or for active participation. What he could, and did, do was to review the troops and the ships' companies before they set off, to make encouraging speeches, to pray for them. A famous photograph shows him on horseback, holding up an icon while surrounded by kneeling soldiers. This was taken at Peterhof in 1905. It shows members of the 148th Caspian Regiment of Foot, dressed in campaign uniforms, crossing themselves as the sovereign shows them a small icon depicting Christ the Saviour. Let it be said that the Tsar was punctilious and entirely sincere in his observation of these occasions. He tirelessly visited units, went aboard vessels, met and spoke to officers and men, and thanked them for their service. The other members of the Family did this too. The Empress, the Dowager Empress and the Grand Duchesses all attended these occasions. When men came back, wounded or otherwise, the Tsar often insisted on conferring in person the decorations they received. He and Alexandra hosted a reception at the Winter Palace for survivors of the attack on the Pacific Fleet. Once again, this shy couple made the effort to greet subjects and put them as much at ease as possible, talking to them with sympathy, seeing that they had enough to eat, sending them home with regards to their families.

One difficulty that was not sufficiently appreciated until the conflict was well under way was that supplying the armies with either men or materiel from the other end of such a vast country was very difficult. The Trans-Siberian Railway was the only direct way of reaching Manchuria. It was a single-track line, so that priority had to be allocated whenever two trains were using it – and it was not yet finished. On their way to the Front, trains had to cross the huge expanse of Lake Baikal. In winter when the surface was frozen, ice was thick enough to lay tracks and run trains across. During the rest of the year it was necessary to go by steamer. This meant long delays in getting munitions to the Front and casualties home.

General Kuropatkin, the Russian commander, did not favour direct attack on the Japanese. They were extremely well equipped and supplied because their territories were nearby. He decided it was a better strategy to draw them away from the coasts into the interior, split their forces into smaller groups and then finish these off individually. Such a notion of luring an opponent ever more deeply into one's territory had an important precedent in 1812, and would be used again in 1941. It might have worked here, too, had not public opinion been too impatient for such an approach. Russians wanted a quick and extremely glorious end to the war. There must be major battles, then a dictated peace settlement and then unrestricted Russian expansion in the Far East. Kuropatkin should get on with it.

There were major battles; the trouble was that it was not the Russians who won them. The fate of Port Arthur electrified the nation. The garrison there was besieged, but was holding on. Russians applauded the bravery of the soldiers, lit candles for them in churches, waited impatiently on street corners for newspaper special editions. The fight of these surrounded men became a national epic, an event in which every patriotic Russian took pride.

And then suddenly it was over. They could not, after all, hold on, and surrendered on 21 December. The fort was in Japanese hands and all the heroism, the endurance, the public support and emotional investment, proved to have been for nothing. Nicholas was in despair, yet his diary entry sounded as laconic as his thoughts usually did: 'It was God's will then!' Once people saw that the conflict could not be won quickly or easily, and then realised that it would not be won *at all*, a cynicism and indifference and an open grumbling replaced the earlier optimism. The Tsar and the Army both lost considerable public respect. Both had let down the country. Not only was the war not going Russia's way, it was bleeding the country white. Russia had to go cap-in-hand to her ally, France, to raise a loan, and fell into debt to the equivalent of £40,000,000. She would then, as the campaign dragged on, have to raise a further £25,000,000 from other European banks.

The fall of Port Arthur, like Khodinka, was a distinct milestone on the road to 1917 – a moment when the Russian people lost faith in their ruler and his government. Another instance was the clash between the two armies at Mukden in February. The scale was truly majestic – this was the biggest land battle since the Napoleonic Wars and involved over six hundred thousand men. The Japanese attacked a Russian force that was deployed defensively in front of the city. The Russians fought well but their opponents were able to chop their army into three and then drive it back in complete rout, capturing much of its artillery and equipment. The Russians suffered almost ninety thousand casualties and lost control not only of Mukden itself but of the eastern end of the Trans-Siberian Railway. Though they remained in the region, they did not have the resources – or indeed the will – to take on the Japanese again, and avoided contact until peace was signed.

Then, three months later, came Tsushima, an even more decisive naval defeat which made it impossible to continue the war. With the Pacific Fleet damaged and now too weak to take on the enemy there was a sudden, desperate search for other vessels. There were two other such fleets. One was in the Baltic, defending Russia from potential enemies to the west. The other was in the Black Sea. It was the Baltic Fleet – the one furthest from the conflict – that was to be sent. Though the other was considerably nearer, and included several important battleships, such as the *Prince Potemkin*, it sat idle in port. Why was this? For the important reason that some years earlier, in 1870, Russia, still smarting from defeat in the Crimean War, had been forced into a treaty by Britain in which she promised that the Black Sea Fleet would never leave the Black Sea. If it were to do so now there was a risk that Britain, Japan's ally, would have grounds for joining the war. This would mean outright disaster since Britain, with the world's largest navy, could attack Russia in both the Black Sea and the Baltic with relative impunity while all Russia's major warships were away. Petersburg was on the Gulf of Finland. It would not be fanciful to suggest that the Royal Navy could sail up this stretch of water and shell the city. A war in the farthest reaches of Russia's east was problematic, but a simultaneous one on her own doorstep would have been worse.

Not everyone took this view, especially in military circles. Captain N. L. Klado, a reform-minded Russian naval officer, wrote a book about the conflict while it was still going on. His survey was brutally realistic and gave his readers little grounds for optimism. He suggested that the Black Sea Fleet risk the ire of the British and put to sea. 'If the English Government wholly refused to come to an understanding it would be because it really wanted war, and in this event it would be wiser to give them one at once, and have the whole thing out with them.' His thoughts were formulated before the disaster of Tsushima. Once the Baltic Fleet had been destroyed there could be no question of taking on any other enemy.

The war was not popular at home. The fighting was far away and the causes either not understood or a matter of indifference. It was taken for granted by a huge nation that it would defeat a small one and that Russia's army, schooled in half a dozen conflicts during the past century and boasting recent experience against an Asiatic rabble in the Boxer Rebellion, would make short work of the unknown and untested forces of a country that had yet to catch up with European standards. This was Russia's first full-scale war (as opposed to campaigns) since the successful conflict against Turkey in 1877, and the country thus had not only recent success but a certain international heroism – Russian troops had liberated what became Romania and Bulgaria – to look back upon. As for the respective fleets, the Russians had a tradition of excellence going all the way back to Peter the Great. The warships of the Pacific Fleet had names that evoked the magnificent, all-conquering past greatness of their nation: *Prince Suvorov, Borodino, Dmitri Donskoi, Emperor Nicholas I*. Who, in contrast, had ever heard of the Japanese Navy? The Fleet left port in October 1904 to travel the width of the globe. Its journey would take months.

And it began with a terrible mistake. The ships' captains, the crews and gun-crews were in a state of high tension even as they emerged from the Baltic. There were vague intelligence reports (and a great many rumours) that the Japanese fleet was waiting for them beyond the Skagerak. It was said that the enemy had placed minefields in the North Sea, and that squadrons of Japanese torpedo boats were waiting to get in among them and cause havoc – the same type of craft that had raided Port Arthur. The torpedo boat was a recent invention. Small and fast, it was difficult to spot, and so manoeuvrable that giant naval guns could not be brought to bear on it quickly enough to fire. It was also very difficult to hit, and was, therefore, a threat especially to be feared. Lookouts were constantly sweeping the horizon for any sign of trouble, and ships would open fire at anything suspicious, for there was not time to go through the procedures of hailing and identifying. The fleet therefore fired on several merchant vessels and even on its own courier boats.

During the night of 21–22 October, as the ships churned southward through the North Sea, they were aware of small vessels in the vicinity. The Russian decks were already cleared for action and crews stood ready in the gun-turrets. Sighting bobbing shapes, they opened fire. No shots were fired in return, no white streak in the water suggested a torpedo on its way. Only with daylight did the situation become clear: the torpedo boats had been trawlers from the English port of Hull, for this was a fishing ground called the Dogger Bank. One vessel was sunk, several more were damaged and three lives were lost. In the confusion the Russian ships had also fired at each other. Only the fact that their gunnery was of a low standard had prevented greater loss of life. Did anyone seriously think, demanded an outraged British public, that the Japanese would send small naval vessels all the way from Asia to lie in wait on the Dogger Bank? Would they not wait until the Russian Fleet had reached their own part of the world before starting hostilities? There would eventually be an international court of enquiry into this event, with Russia having to pay hefty compensation. The Tsar was lucky that it had not led to war.

The immediate consequence was that the Royal Navy was put on a war footing. British vessels sailed into position around the Russian fleet and escorted it southward until it was through the Channel. Britain, which controlled the Mediterranean and the Suez Canal, refused to allow the ships to use their planned route, and they thus had to sail right down the coast of Africa, round the Cape of Good Hope and across the Indian Ocean, making a total distance of eighteen thousand miles. They had been making for Port Arthur, but this was lost while they were at sea and their new destination was to be the Russian port of Vladivostok.

The Fleet eventually arrived in East Asia in the middle of May. Though it may have looked an impressive sight when in harbour at Kronstad or Reval, it was smaller than the force it was about to meet. The ships were old, and so fouled by weed on the voyage that they were dangerously slow. To make this epic and much-longer-than-expected journey, the Russians had had to purchase coal – often of low quality – wherever they could, and this too affected speed and efficiency. Morale on board was extremely low. The Russian squadron had thirty warships and a total of 228 guns. The Japanese awaited them with 121 ships and 910 guns, but numbers were not the only thing in which they were superior. They had a more modern fleet. Their guns were of larger calibre, their ships could move faster, manoeuvre more adeptly, and had thicker armour. And they had the infamous torpedo boats. Most vitally, perhaps, their wireless equipment was far superior. It would enable them to track their enemy with ease. The Russians did not know it as, on the night of 14 May, they entered the Strait of Tsushima between Japan and Korea, but no circumstances could have enabled them to win.

The Japanese had guessed the route the ships would follow, and were waiting. They could not see their enemy in darkness and thick fog, but they followed progress so clearly through Russian wireless that they knew exactly where the vessels were. The next day the fog continued, but the fleets sighted each other in early afternoon. The battle commenced just before three o'clock.

It lasted the rest of the day, and all night. Though the Russians began well, the Japanese broke through the Russian line, firing broadsides at their enemy's bows and sterns. This manoeuvre – 'crossing the t' – was a Nelsonian device, and indeed Tsushima was to be described as the most important naval battle since Trafalgar. Russian ships were scattered and surrounded, like animals brought to bay. Ships were sinking, pounded by faster, more accurate Japanese gunnery, taking hundreds of hits. Coal stocks caught fire, ammunition blew up. The carnage was terrible.

The fight formally ended just between nine and ten o'clock the next day, when the remnants of the Russian fleet surrendered. They made three attempts to do so – by coded flag (which the Japanese did not understand), by white flag (which they did not trust) and finally by hoisting the Japanese flag. Some vessels managed to flee, and even reached their destination. Others were scuttled by their crews.

Tsushima was among the greatest disasters in Russian history. They lost 4,380 men killed and more than 5,000 taken prisoner. Japanese casualties were 117. Russia lost five battleships, Japan three torpedo boats. There could be no disguising the extent of the humiliation. With this defeat, the war was over and Russia's cause was lost, for the Japanese could now do as they liked in the region. In the Russian Orthodox cathedral in London there is a curious relic. It is a big icon, painted on metal, of St Nicholas the Miracle-Worker. It is dented in several places from the impact of Japanese bullets, for it stood on the deck of the warship *Petropavlovsk* during the battle. Not even this saint could work a miracle great enough to prevent defeat.

On land things went little better. In the retreat of Russian troops from Mukden, across a bare and freezing landscape, the troops were starving and perishing from exposure. In their panic they disregarded their officers, broke ranks and mutinied. This was a foretaste of what would happen in 1917 to another Russian army in an equally hopeless situation. When the country came to estimate the damage done by this conflict, the biggest blow had been to its pride. It had not only been bested by an arriviste power that it had not deigned to take seriously, it had – and this was far worse – seen its own proud army throw away its discipline and honour and collapse into listlessness, anarchy and mutiny.

The national trauma ended when peace was arranged through a disinterested party – President Theodore Roosevelt of the United States – who invited representatives of both sides to a conference and chaired the negotiations. Peace was quickly agreed, and was signed in

August 1905 at Concord, New Hampshire (for his part in this, Roosevelt received the Nobel Peace Prize, becoming the first American to earn this honour). Japan was given not only a lease on Port Arthur but the area of South Sakhalin and the Kuril Islands – a barely habitable but strategically important chain of islands off the east coast of Russia. Decades later, in 1945, when the Soviet Union had defeated Hitler and briefly joined the war against Japan, the islands were returned to Russia – the insult of losing them had not been forgotten.

The conflict had been an eerie, uncanny dress rehearsal, on a smaller scale, for the events of half a generation later – a lesson not only for Russia but for all the other potential combatant powers that were watching the war's progress. Here were many of the characteristics of the later confrontation.

As in 1914, the war had begun suddenly and unexpectedly. It involved the much-resented calling up of hundreds of thousands of reservists. The Front was distant, and the reasons for sending men there were not understood by most of those at home. There were major problems with transport and lack of supplies. The fighting was often a stalemate, with all the miseries of trench warfare in wintry conditions and the illness bred by this. There was the increased killing power of new technology in rifles and heavy artillery. There were losses not only in dead but in prisoners taken. There was crippling incompetence and disorganisation at all levels, with rivalries between commanders and conflicting strategies and orders, and the awful frustration of courage squandered and lives needlessly thrown away. There was a mobilisation of volunteer civilians – principally women, led by the Empress – to provide material comforts in the form of clothing, food and books, and a rush to equip hospitals and to train as nurses.

There had been, when the fighting went badly, the same tendencies among the soldiery for mutiny and mass desertion, the same defiance of officers. This set a precedent that would be followed in 1917, for at that time this previous war was still fresh in the collective memory.

* * *

War had given the Empress a sense of high purpose. Like other sovereigns and great ladies in time of conflict she had involved herself in the assembling and distribution of comforts and medical supplies. She used the Winter Palace as a depot for this, founded a society to provide staff and organised the shipment of articles to the Front. Despite her personal unpopularity, young women of good family flocked to join and to take part in this work. Almost all of them will have had connections with the Army through male relatives, and they were keen to help.

Alexandra's greatest – and unique – contribution to the Russian war effort, however, came in August 1904: in the midst of a war that was already going badly, a moment of celebration. The Empress gave birth to a son. Such had been her longing for this that the previous year she had actually had a phantom pregnancy, convincing herself, her husband and the country that a child was to be born. Medical examination eventually found that she was mistaken, and that Russia had been waiting for nothing. Now there could be no doubt, and the sense of relief and euphoria throughout the Empire, from Tsarskoe Selo to the most far-flung provinces and to the military encampments in Manchuria, was overwhelming. In the kind of public relations gesture at which he was very good, the Tsar announced that all soldiers who were engaged in fighting the Japanese were appointed honorary godfathers to the boy – a statement that cost nothing to make but which may have helped to raise morale.

The boy was to be named Alexis. This had been the name of an earlier occupant of the throne, a ruler of Muscovy rather than of Russia – the son of the first Romanov, Michael. Tsar Alexis had reigned from 1645 to 1676. He had been devout to the point of sanctity – prostrating himself hundreds of times during the course of a single church service – and he was a personal hero to Nicholas II. However, the son of Peter the Great had also been named Alexis, and this tragic young man had been imprisoned and tortured, on the orders of his father, for treason. In 1718 Peter had killed his heir with his own hands. Since that time, the name had been considered unlucky and had not been bestowed on any direct heir to the throne (though it was, of course, the name of one of the Tsar's uncles). Yet again, an ill omen – as if the unfortunate Nicholas were not already pursued by too many.

The omen proved to be true. Alexis's health was to become the lifelong preoccupation – obsession – of his mother. She would give up her own health, for this would be undermined, and all of her peace of mind, in the quest to keep him from harm, to find somehow – by any means possible – a cure for him, and to keep the throne intact for him to inherit. These questions gave her virtually no time for anything else.

CHAPTER SIXTEEN

Sorrow

The ninth of January, 1905, would live forever in Russian history. It began without any hint of the tragedy to come. A Sunday, the church bells ringing all over St Petersburg. The sky a leaden blanket, the streets deep under snow, the river frozen, as always in this season. The music of a brass band – the thump of a big drum, and the tramp of a multitude of feet in the snow. A crowd that filled the street as far as the eye could see – it was to be estimated at 140,000 – was on its way to the city's natural gathering place, the huge square in front of the Winter Palace. Indeed it could only go there, for soldiers sealed off the side streets. Its members were mostly workers – peasants transformed by industrialisation into an urban proletariat. As this was not a working day, they wore their holiday clothes – the women in bright blouses and headscarves that gave a hint of the distant provinces from which they had originally come. They brought their children. They carried banners, icons and pictures of the monarch. Their mood was happy, and optimistic. They were going to see the Tsar.

They did not realise he was not there, that he did not even live in the great building ahead of them, that he was not anywhere in the city, did not wish to see them and would not have dreamt of acceding to their demands. They did not understand that, after decades of terrorism, the soldiers and police who protected him were not benevolent but suspicious, anxious, aggressive, or that any gathering of this size – prohibited anyway under Russia's laws – was likely to be construed at once as a threat to order. Even when they saw the troops standing in line abreast across the huge, snow-covered square, blocking the way and with pointed rifles, they did not think there would be confrontation. This was no angry mob, they did not look, or feel, threatening. They were even led by a priest, the well-known Father Gapon. There was no reason for any trouble . . .

The death toll was reported by police, when it was over, at ninety-six killed and three hundred and thirty injured. The police often played numbers down, while those who sought to make capital out of the event exaggerated them upward, and in this case claimed that just under five thousand had been killed or injured.

The family of each victim was to receive the sum of one thousand roubles compensation from the Tsar – the same amount that, almost a decade earlier, had been paid to those who had died in the other great tragedy of his reign at Khodinka Field.

If Russia had a loss of innocence, this was it. Despite a history that had included more tyranny, misfortune and misery than one country or one people could be expected to endure, there had remained a notion among the cynical and fatalistic Russians that the Tsar was on the side of his people, that if he fully understood their problems and their grievances he would help them. This procession of loyal, well-meaning subjects (however misguided he might consider them to be) had represented the acceptable face of reform. That they had automatically been classed as criminals and treated like an attacking army was an insult for which the Russian people never forgave Nicholas. Though he had not been present, he had of course had warning – about a week's notice, in fact – that they were coming. Though he had not personally given any order to deal with the crowd with this level of severity, he would carry the blame for this until he himself, thirteen years later, would be shot down with a similar callousness and lack of mercy.

As well as paying compensation to the families of victims, Nicholas agreed to receive a deputation of those who had been on the march. A number of men – it is thought that the Secret Police simply dressed up a group of its own members and shepherded them into the Alexander Palace – listened respectfully to a fatherly talking-to from the Autocrat, who 'freely forgave them for having escaped the bullets and swords of his soldiers, but cautioned them not to do it again'. The public was not fooled by this charade, which did nothing to lessen their anger.

As winter turned to spring, Russia continued to be a country in the depths. 'Bloody Sunday' as the events of 9 January had become known, had caused outrage around the world. This was the Russia that her enemies had always imagined – a dictatorship ruled by vicious, unthinking brutality, a place of darkness and evil, a country civilised only in its outward forms and, beneath the surface, as barbaric as the Muscovy of Ivan the Terrible. A French journal, *L'assiette du Beurre*, depicted Nicholas with his hands dripping blood. An English publication, *Ally Sloper's Half-Holiday*, perhaps caught the essence of the situation more accurately in a cartoon entitled 'The Lily-livered Czar' – it depicted Nicholas, white-faced and shaking with fear, holding in both hands a revolver that had gone off accidentally with devastating results. Another British magazine, *Punch*, showed more gravitas with an illustration entitled 'The Eleventh Hour'. Nicholas sits brooding on his throne. Scattered about at his feet are documents labelled 'Misgovernment' and 'Massacre of the Jews'. The shade of Louis XVI, standing at his shoulder, speaks in his ear: 'Side with your people, Sire, while there is yet time. I was too late!' This tyranny and these atrocities, it appeared, reflected the true face of the 'Man of Peace' who only six years earlier had been hailed throughout Europe for his love of conciliation.

To those who sought to overthrow the state the event was, needless to say, a gift. Previously the revolution had had martyrs but there were few of them, and they were fanatics – wild-eyed students, bomb-throwers, assassins who killed innocent bystanders and therefore forfeited public sympathy. They were arrested, imprisoned and hanged. Now there were hundreds and hundreds of martyrs and they had been innocent, inoffensive, ordinary people: women, children and the elderly. They could have been anyone's neighbours, or relatives. The massacre thus brought political awareness to many who had not previously thought in terms of disloyalty. The image of corpses in the snow would remain as a lasting rebuke to the autocracy. Nothing Nicholas could do or say would wipe out the stain. Previously, subversive propaganda had only been able to paint him as ineffectual. Now he was an actual monster. Not only the massacre itself but the symbolism of it – the brusque rejection of reasonably couched requests – played straight into the hands of extremists. Now it could be seen that there was no alternative to wholesale replacement of the existing order.

Nothing this bad, in terms of social breakdown and opposition to the State, had been seen in Russia since the Time of Troubles in the seventeenth century. As Count Vassili was to write: 'No reign in Russia from the time of Peter the Great has been so unfortunate as the present one. Calamities have followed its course from the very beginning.' And Joubert wrote that: 'It is useless to search Russian history to find precedents for the present crisis. It is Russia's first awakening, and the world stands by the couch with bated breath to know how she will face the light of day.' The country had been accustomed, through its long history, to resisting aggression from outside – a powerful national myth had been built on the people's heroism, struggle and sacrifice, from the days of Alexander Nevsky to the epic of 1812. Other internal rebellions – Pugachev and Rezin in the eighteenth century or the Decembrists in the nineteenth – had been localised affairs that were within the power of the state to crush (the latter group had lasted only a single afternoon!). But what could be done now, when the enemy was everywhere? Society could not function. The country was beyond control and the authorities, which had never had to deal with such widespread or intense defiance, could not maintain order. For all the different police, gendarmerie and military units at the disposal of the state, there were not enough with the training, the experience, the organisation and co-ordination or the leadership to make an effective overall response. There was also a shortage of numbers, since so many soldiers were at the Front.

There was continuous unrest in the cities. The drab winter streets were brightened by thousands of crimson banners and armbands. Everyone in the labour force appeared to be on strike. This had begun with the railwaymen and then spread to become a general action. There were far more strikes in the month of January 1905 than in the whole of the preceding decade. Multitudes idled about the corners during working hours, listening to shouting orators, chanting slogans and singing revolutionary songs in the knowledge that the police could not arrest so many. (Besides which, it could be expected that among the uniformed ranks that confronted them would be some who took their side). Transport did not run, goods were unavailable in the shops, which were shuttered and empty. Shortages made life difficult, resulting in hoarding and looting. It was unsafe to be out after dark and even in daylight prosperous-looking people went in fear of attack. By day and night there were menacing mobs abroad, filling the streets with yet more shouting and singing, with the noise of band music or of breaking glass. Shots and explosions echoed across the rooftops.

In the countryside it was worse, for at least in urban Russia there could be the blessing of anonymity. In the provinces there were not possibly enough police or troops to keep control. Peasant mobs attacked manor houses, ransacking and destroying them (in Russia many such buildings were of wood, and thus burned easily). Landowners, merchants, wealthy peasants, indeed anyone seen as out of sympathy with the vandalism – was at risk of murder. Those connected with the State – judges, policemen, administrators and officials – would have felt they were living on borrowed time. The premises from which they operated, the court houses, police stations and government offices, were conspicuous and difficult to defend. At the top of the administrative tree, the Governor of any province was seen as the most 'high-profile target', so that it came to be felt that to accept appointment to this post was tantamount to a death sentence. Even those intellectuals and members of the professional classes who had sneered at the autocracy and wished misfortune on their government must have experienced a horrible feeling of danger and vulnerability as they sat behind closed shutters and hoped to be left alone. The protection of the Imperial Family which, as shown, had already involved hundreds of individuals, now had to be intensified even more.

And this was just in time. In the summer of 1906 a gang of armed anarchists arrived at Peterhof looking for the Tsar. The authorities discovered the plot and warned the Family to stay indoors. The group were all captured but Nicholas complained afterward, in a letter to his mother, that they had been held virtual prisoners in their own home for long hours during a beautiful summer's day. He clearly felt personally the unpleasantness of having the sanctity of his home defiled by these criminals.

Police spies were assumed to be everywhere, and were hunted down with ruthless determination. Russia, given its history of terrorist extremism, had an immense army of informers, infiltrators and *agents provocateurs*. One of them, it was believed, was Father Gapon, who had led the march to the Winter Palace on Bloody Sunday. After disappearing for some time he was found in a cabin in rural Finland. He had been hanged with a makeshift noose.

A further blow to the prestige of the state came in June when the Black Sea Fleet mutinied in Odessa. As film buffs know, the battleship *Prince Potemkin* was taken over by ratings after protests about food and conditions had been rejected by officers. There was considerable concern, too, that the component lands of the Russian Empire would demand – or seize – independence. Poland had never been reconciled to Russian control. The Baltic states – Estonia, Latvia and Lithuania – would leave if they could. The loyalty of Little Russia was not to be relied upon, and Finland would seek separation at once. Georgia and the states of Central Asia could be next. Those few months of war and revolution were the worst that any Russian could remember living through. Not only the fabric of society but the very physical structure of the nation seemed about to disintegrate. It was an experience that would be shared by other peoples in other countries both in 1918 and 1945.

The Tsar was as regular in attending the funerals of his murdered officials as circumstances would allow. He saw it as his duty, since they had lost their lives in his service, to make this gesture for them. The death toll was not huge, in comparison with the general losses of the war and the revolution, but it was certainly bad enough. Vlasheslav Plehve, the Minister of the Interior who had introduced yet more repressive measures to try and restore order, was himself a victim of *dis*order, blown up in his carriage.

Naturally such extremism would provoke reaction, and there were many citizens who opposed the revolution with a matching violence and determination. Their hatred was not based on class – for the troubles of 1905 were not entirely about that issue. They were ordinary Russians of the cities, the towns and the countryside who passionately supported the national values. They wished to see no compromise with the demands of reformers and they defended the status quo by forming into mobs. They held noisy meetings, staged church services to emphasise the spiritual nature of their crusade, and roamed the streets in as menacing a manner as the banner-waving revolutionaries. They were armed and belligerent. They broke windows, and bones. The Black Hundreds, as they were known, were proletarians. Most were industrial workers, railwaymen, stevedores or peasants. Their slogan was 'Orthodoxy, Autocracy, Nationalism', which expressed the essentials of Russian-ness. Though they were a threatening presence and caused destruction and death, the authorities did little to stop them, connived with them and were widely suspected of arming and assisting them. This is understandable from one point of view: the police were overwhelmed by violence and disorder that was aimed at the State and at anyone wearing its uniform. The Black Hundreds were on the side of authority, were a show of force against anarchy and were helping uphold order where the police were at full stretch. Small wonder that when a prominent member of the organisation was brought to trial he was either acquitted by a judge or pardoned by the Tsar.

They quickly found a scapegoat for the nation's problems in the country's Jewish population. The Empire contained about four and a half million Jews, many of them in its western regions – Poland, Little Russia (Ukraine), Belorussia and the Baltic states. Thousands of them lived peaceful and integrated lives. Others were easily identified by costume, occupation or place of residence. They dressed according to the dictates of their faith and lived in close-knit communities called Shtetls. They were often wealthy – or at least comfortably off – through plying skilled trades or dealing in finance.

Their lives in Russia had, however, largely been difficult – and sometimes horrific – over recent generations. They had been persecuted with considerable savagery in the reign of Nicholas I. He, as the most consummate autocrat, had found unacceptable the notion of millions of his subjects not belonging to the Orthodox religion. His grandson, Alexander III, had held similar ideas, and had made a similarly brutish attempt to create social uniformity. The result was the most vicious series of persecutions (the Russian word for this – pogrom – has become a universal term) seen anywhere in the nineteenth century. Thousands perished with the unofficial connivance of the state. Many more thousands fled the country – as the Tsar had intended them to do – to settle throughout Europe and America. After this outburst in the 1880s – it had coincided with Alexander's accession to the throne and his knee-jerk response to his father's assassination – the issue became dormant for some years, though it never went away. Only after defeat and revolution did it once again erupt as a nationwide epidemic.

Jews were not merely a group of obvious outsiders whose loyalty was always considered suspect, they were also associated in the popular mind with revolution. This is hardly to be wondered at. Given their traditions of scholarship and learning, they were well represented in universities and among the intelligentsia, and thus likely to have ideas for the betterment of society. More important was the fact that they had nothing whatever to gain from support of the regime. They were systematically barred from much of the best of Russia. They could not belong to the aristocracy, or serve as officers in the splendid regiments of the army. They could not hold high positions at Court or in the State Council. There was, before the first revolution at least, no political life in which they could win office and distinguish themselves. Though they could gain success through talent in the arts, very few did so. They were heavily represented in the merchant class, but were openly despised in a society in which anti-Semitism was a commonplace. They were not equal, and were not treated as such. It is not surprising that they sought to replace the form of government they knew with a fairer one – their safety and their very lives could depend on it. The most obvious representative of a Jewish revolutionary was, of course, Leon Trotsky, but he was simply the most prominent among many.

The first of the new pogroms took place in 1903, even before the war and revolution, but the explosion came two years later. During the summer and autumn of 1905, while the police stood by, this hatred swept through the cities of southern and western Russia. Eight hundred perished in the city of Odessa alone, out of a total that was to reach about two and a half thousand. Apart from fatalities there were widespread looting and wholesale destruction. As usual with mob violence, women, children and the elderly were not spared.

Though many Western countries were not without anti-Semitism (France had just had the Dreyfus case) this normally did not go further than extreme rhetoric. For Jews to be massacred in the streets of their cities was seen as an affront to civilisation. The foreign press, which could use photography to convey the horror of destroyed buildings and piled corpses (this was the heyday of the illustrated paper) fanned international outrage. This was horror on a level that would not be seen again until the Nazi invasion of these same territories in the 1940s.

And the Tsar did not seek to end it. For the government, the persecution of the Jews was a welcome relief, for it deflected animosity from those who deserved the blame. Had the public sustained its anger against the monarch, his advisors and his generals, the state might not have survived. When another enemy was found – one that was everywhere, unarmed and easy to attack – public anger could fix on that. Persecuting Jews would channel the people's anger in a safe direction. If looting property and thus enriching themselves would bring greater contentment to Russian subjects, then this was a good thing. Nicholas even shared the general antipathy, telling his wife that the Jews 'had had it coming' because they had been 'getting above themselves and putting on airs'.

There was, some commentators, argued, a strategy behind the violence that broke out all over the Tsar's domains. The authorities were aware of the fact that Russians were uniting across lines of both social class and ethnic identity, given common cause by their animosity to the Tsar. This was naturally a matter of the highest danger. It was a very useful countermeasure if disunity could be attained. As a result, *agents provocateurs* were active, moving among Russia's communities and stirring hatred against their neighbours. The Empire contained such a wealth of nationalities that this was not difficult. The hatred of Poles, Balts, Finns, Ukrainians, Belorussians, Tartars and others could be whipped into a frenzy, and was. Though this seemed a meltdown into chaos, it was actually a means of diverting anger from the Government and thus saving the State. Further, attempts were made to foster hatred of other nations as a means of focusing patriotism – Britain was accused in the Russian press of having paid for agitation, of having financed the strikes in Petersburg. The blame for shortages, stoppages, disrupted transport, loss of savings and reduction to poverty could be laid at the door of a traditional enemy. By crude methods that, in the case of ethnic tensions, cost hundreds of lives and destroyed homes and property, the autocracy sought to save itself.

Even as rioters killed members of other ethnic groups throughout his domains, the Tsar issued an Ukase that was in almost surreal contrast to events. At Easter 1905 he declared that his people – all 140 million of them – would henceforth have freedom of conscience in matters of religion – they would, in other words, be able to belong to faiths other than that of Orthodoxy without suffering penalties. And these penalties had been real. To be an Old Believer or a Dissenter or a Roman Catholic meant significant losses in terms of civic rights and career opportunities. Nicholas was, to give one instance, allowing Poles to be Catholics again – even to reopen monasteries, nunneries and shrines that had been officially forbidden. Those of other branches of faith could establish schools and legally teach their doctrines.

The Ukase was hailed throughout the world as a major step toward enlightenment and a personal triumph for Nicholas. Foreign press reports were unanimously favourable. However, putting such a policy into practice was a different matter. Religious freedom could be granted one week and revoked the next on the grounds that it was proving disruptive. The meeting houses of Dissenters would be visited by police spies, and if these suspected that they were being used for any political purpose they could be closed down at once. It is worth remembering, also, that an Ukase was not an Act of Parliament. It was not 'set in stone' and was not liable to remain unchanged if circumstances were to alter. These proclamations of the Tsar's were usually as muddled and indecisive as his mind itself was. He habitually added to his often simple and straightforward text a host of clauses and codicils. These often went unreported (who, among the foreign press, would bother to translate all that small print?) but they served the function of modifying, watering down, nullifying much that was being said or promised in the main text. Not only that, but there was nothing to prevent the ruler from issuing further Ukases on the same subject, entirely different in tone or content, undoing whatever had been said earlier. Russians could put no faith in these and regarded them with the same attitude of fatalistic cynicism with which they greeted all government measures. They were well aware (as the country that had seen the creation of 'Potemkin villages') that much of what their government did was window dressing intended to deceive both them and foreign observers. A highly significant aspect of Nicholas's offer of freedom of worship was that it made no mention at all of Jews, who remained unprotected.

For us, of course, this is an unpalatable aspect of the Tsar. We – if we are inclined to be sympathetic with him on a human level – can view him as well meaning, a man trapped by circumstances and doing his best. We sympathise further because we know that his life too was to end in violence. We are so schooled to hate all prejudice and to overcompensate for any feeling of superiority toward others that we see few things as worse than 'racism'. No concept of 'equality and diversity' had been invented in Nicholas's time and it was taken for granted that some races were better than others (when the Tsar's daughter Olga was a child, she refused to shake hands with a Siamese prince, saying that he was not a prince but a monkey. We are told he 'laughed heartily' at this and that the two later became friends). Nicholas was no worse than others of his time and situation in his view. We can understand his feeling of relief at the passing of a crisis even if we regret what happened and his failure to prevent it.

CHAPTER SEVENTEEN

Borrowed Time, Duma, 1906

At the commencement of each century Russia experiences heavy trials and disasters. The great anarchy of the 'dark period' of the seventeenth century, the unfortunate commencement of the Northern War under Peter in the eighteenth, the wars with Napoleon and the foreign invasion of a hundred years ago, and finally our terrible experiences in the war with Japan of 1904–1905, and the disorders of 1905–1906, are the disasters and calamities which Russia has experienced at successive and apparently fixed intervals of time.

General Elchaninov, writing in 1913.

Joubert commented that: 'The spirit of discontent in Russia was manifesting itself in acts of violence, in desertions from the army and in an undefined air of unrest throughout all classes. The national calamities in Manchuria were uniting all shades of liberalism, socialism, and nihilism into a compact body of opposition to the existing state of things.'

The Revolution of 1905 is naturally considered a watershed. Before these events, it is popularly assumed, Russia was governed by a blinkered and inflexible system that refused to change, and which then did so only with the greatest reluctance and ill grace. In fact, the authorities were by no means uninterested in finding better ways of doing things. What ruler, after all, would actually not want a more contented population, and thus one less likely to revolt? We have seen Nicholas as the blind upholder of a system that had outlived any plausible use, but in fact he was proving flexible enough to accept several enlightened and important measures, and very significant reforms had been in progress before the revolution. He saw himself as a modern monarch with a keen personal interest in the wellbeing of his subjects – a world away from the propaganda image of selfish decadence that his enemies wished to promote.

The great advances of his reign were the work of two very able administrators: Sergei Witte (1849–1915) and Peter Stolypin (1862–1911). Both were men of genius. Stolypin, in particular, had single-handedly made Russia into an industrial nation during the reign of Nicholas's father, and created the conditions for the country to become wealthy and modern. He had done this largely by planning the rail network that was transforming the movement of goods and thus enriching Russia almost by the hour. He was a man of drive and practicality and ideas, who had brought his talent from industry to finance and then to politics. He understood how to motivate Russia's peasantry and how to get the best out of them. He particularly knew how they hungered for possession of land, and had a scheme for dividing this so as to give each family a stake in it by allocating smallholdings. Alexander had appreciated his value, especially since he had had the vision to set in motion the country's biggest ever engineering project, the Trans-Siberian Railway. As an entrepreneur and politician who seemed able to give every Russian what he wanted, Stolypin could at the turn of the century have been elected President had he lived in a republic and not an autocracy.

Following the revolution it was Stolypin who managed both the concessions to reform and the repression of lawless elements that were necessary to make the country safe again. He did this so thoroughly that a hangman's noose came to be nicknamed a 'Stolypin necktie'. His service to the State was of immense value. He was the architect of the new Russia that emerged from the ashes of 1905, yet he fell abruptly from favour because Nicholas resented having been persuaded to make concessions. Stolypin deserved the credit for saving the dynasty, yet he took the blame for the autocracy's loss of power. In 1911 he would be assassinated in Kiev while attending the opera. The Tsar was present in the theatre with two of his daughters, and though they were naturally horrified by the murder, Nicholas, with singular ungraciousness, failed to show conspicuous sorrow at the loss of this faithful servant.

The great tragedy was that, in Stolypin and Witte, Nicholas had advisors of first-rate quality who could, with his more enthusiastic support – with a few more favourable circumstances and another decade of life – have steered the country further along the road to greatness. Both died prematurely, and they were the only gifted men that Nicholas was to have at his side.

In February 1902 a committee was formed under the chairmanship of Witte, who was Minister of Finance, to formulate agrarian reform. The purpose of this was to initiate schemes by which peasants could come into ownership of small tracts of land – smallholdings, or allotments. The notion of owning even the smallest piece of land was a dream very close to the hearts of Russia's peasants.

On 25 March 1903, the Government abolished the system of mutual responsibility. This had meant that peasants who had more wealth had had to make up the shortfall in tax payments to compensate for those who could not pay. It was a widespread source of grievance and a disincentive to enterprise.

On 24 August 1904, corporal punishment was abolished throughout the Empire.

On 16 November 1906, in the manifesto issued by Nicholas, it was announced that redemption payments were to be abolished in 1907, having been reduced by 50 per cent during the previous year. In the same document it was stated that the credit of the Peasants' Land Bank was to be increased, thus making it easier for the bank's clients to receive advances, and allowing them to borrow more readily.

From October 1906 it was established by decree that peasants could henceforward enter government service, obtain permission to travel, and attend schools on the same basis – in other words without restrictions – as other social classes. The law requiring them to remain in the district where they had been registered was annulled, as was the law that gave to the head of a country district the right to punish peasants without trial. This last represented the final ending of serfdom, which had been abolished forty-five years earlier. In view of the rural violence and the targeting of landowners by armed peasantry, this represented a serious concession.

In 1906, also, a new law granted to peasants the right to leave their community but to take with them the value of their share of communal property. At the same time the unsatisfactory system of land distribution, by which a man would farm several strips of land that were separated from each other, was abolished. All the holdings of a peasant could now be consolidated, enabling him to grow more crops, use fewer resources and not have the frustration of trudging from one patch of land to another. This measure was long overdue and was of immediate benefit to millions. The Tsar, who supported it wholeheartedly, introduced it at once on his estate at Peterhof. 'The law of November 22nd, was seen by many members of the peasant class as a second liberation – as important a date in its way as 1861 when serfdom had been abolished. Instead of being told what to plant and how to farm by a group of village elders, who might simply be passing on the bad practices of past generations, individuals could choose for themselves what to do and how to use their land. There was thus far more enterprise and more sensible use of resources. There was a considerable show of gratitude to Nicholas all over his realm for this measure – a rare instance of praising rather than blaming the ruler. Within a few short years the prosperity of the peasantry increased noticeably. Crop yields soared, surpluses built up, rural Russia was becoming richer every year. The spectre of the 1890s, when serious famine had racked the land, was fading.

Education was also making strides. His reign, in which growing prosperity meant more available resources, saw a marked increase in the number of schools opened, and five new universities. Here, as always, the Tsar and members of his family were often involved in founding, funding, giving their names and their patronage. This long tradition of philanthropy was to continue right up to the last weeks and months of tsarist rule.

Nicholas appointed, as replacement for the murdered Plehve,

Prince Sviatopolk Mirsky as Minister of the Interior. This man was known for liberal views, and his advent was hailed as representing a new era in Russia. The press, more or less overnight, seemed to become unchained and to express critical opinions. There was a whiff of freedom in the air. New journals, satirical magazines, books in great numbers appeared. There was, in fact, a publishing revolution. This was not only to give the Russian people the feeling that they were now far more at liberty to express themselves but to stifle the foreign criticism that had been so much heard. Nicholas was making concessions, with the greatest possible reluctance, but he wished the world to see that his rule could be enlightened and his people could have rights within an autocracy similar to those enjoyed by citizens of constitutional monarchies and even republics. This loosening of the bonds was, in fact, an attempt to buy off moderate opinion and divide the merely liberal from the diehard revolutionaries. The lifting of censorship was one thing, but actual political reforms did not follow, and in the meantime the state became more heavy-handed. Informers remained active, police raids were more common.

Official reaction to the disturbances of 1905 was a combination of carrot and stick. While liberal window dressing concessions were to be seen in an increased flow of ideas through the loosening of censorship, no changes had been made in laws, for instance, that prohibited public assembly. The great increase in police spies meant that there was a corresponding rise in the number of arrests for crimes that were real or perceived. During August 1905 there were 26,000 of these in Moscow and an average of 17,000 in some of the provinces.

The biggest reform and one which, unlike some of these others, was a direct result of the revolution, was the establishment of a legislative assembly. The only precedent for such a thing in Russia's history, unless it was the 'Zemsky Sobor' a kind of talking shop of council members from all provinces that had met in the seventeenth century. The Tsar continued to resist, but the assassination of his uncle, the Grand Duke Sergei, on 4 February 1905 darkened the horizon still further and proved effective in gaining further concession. Nicholas and those around him would have used the army to control the domestic political situation, but after the mutinies and desertions caused by the war, they could not assume that the soldiers were reliable and thus were reluctant to use them against the populace.

At the beginning of July a draft proposal was drawn up for the creation of a state legislature – the Duma. It was then studied by a conference which assembled at Peterhof, attended by a gathering of State Councillors, Ministers, academics and members of the Imperial Family (the Grand Dukes were present). It was chaired, naturally, by the Emperor. The draft law approved by it was published on 6 August.

The nation remained restless and unsatisfied until the autumn, when a new wave of strikes began, stopping the railways and large sections of industry. The situation was saved by Sergei Witte. This very able statesman had represented Russia at the peace talks in the United States and had, through skill and charm, gained a relatively honourable set of terms there for his country. They might not have reflected the vainglorious expectations of the Russia of 1904, but they minimised the loss of territory – it could have been much worse – and thus face was saved to a greater extent than many had feared. Now that public opinion was virtually unanimous in demanding significant political reform Witte, who recognised that it was implacable and who told his master that 'the course of historical progress is unstoppable' suggested that Nicholas jump on this bandwagon too. If the Tsar could not only accept the inevitable but do so with good grace, if he could see this as an opportunity and join his people in creating a new system, he could gain immense popularity and personal prestige. If he could pretend that this had been his and the government's intention all along, he would gain the goodwill of moderates and deprive extremists of much of their grievance. So unanimous were the voices telling him that this was not only the wisest but the only course of action that he could not ignore them. He realised that he was backed against a wall and, though all his instincts revolted against it, he would have to give way for the sake of the country and the restoration of order.

He did so on 17 October 1905. Russia was to have a constitution, ninety years after this had been demanded in vain by the Decembrist rebels – and was also to be given a constituent assembly. Nicholas actually felt that many of his subjects would lose respect for him when they heard that his power had been curtailed, but he misjudged the situation. The views of millions of rural peasants mattered less than those of the thousands of workers, students, urban intellectuals and educated people who urged a constitution and who had the power to paralyse the state and bring it down if they did not get it. He wrote: 'Yes, Russia is giving itself a constitution. We were few who fought against it, but support in the struggle did not come from anywhere. Every day a greater number of people turned from us and in the end the inevitable happened.' He added that: 'Following my conscience I prefer to grant everything at once than to be obliged in the near future to make concessions on minor matters and arrive at the same point anyway.'

The Duma was to be housed in the Tauride Palace, a former royal residence, but the speech that set its existence in motion was made in the Throne Room of the Winter Palace. A photograph, looking down on the ceremony from a gallery, shows Nicholas on the steps of the throne, the immense train of his robe draped impressively to one side. It is a pose designed to convey unshakeable power and resolve, and was entirely inappropriate for the circumstances. The crowd stands respectfully at a distance, and includes a number of men in official uniform. These, we learn, were in a state of terror. The journalist Kellogg Durand recalled that:'"To us", remarked one of the ladies of honour attached to the Empress, "it is like letting the revolution into the Palace!" Members of the Court were fearful lest the Tsar would never return from the Throne Room. Many of the nobles went in fear and trembling, and only went because they had been commanded by the Emperor and for no other reason.'

He went on to say, revealingly, that 'the nervousness of the Tsar was apparent to all, the agitation of the Grand Dukes was laughable' but that 'the Empresses alone appeared in full command of every nerve and muscle. I looked upon the Tsaritsa with absolute admiration. The picture of her strong, immovable figure is engraved for ever on my memory. Had an untoward incident occurred, the two Empresses alone would have stood solid. The exquisite poise and complete possession of the Tsaritsa commanded absolute admiration. Cold and indifferent she may be toward the people of her court, but on an occasion like this she acquits herself with rare credit.' She, and the other ladies, can be seen in the same photograph, in a group to one side of the throne. We cannot see their expressions, but something of that steely resolve is evident.

The gesture did not work – it failed to satisfy the demands of liberals, reformers, progressives and indeed anybody. It promised political concessions and representative government but was so limited, so timid and so prone to veto by the Tsar – who was known to be opposed to any concession whatever – that it was virtually unworkable.

The path on which Witte had set Russia was naturally not a smooth one. Political parties had come into being. The first and second Dumas lasted only a short time because they contained too many radical members. The system laid down by the Fundamental Laws of 23 April 1906 was that of a bicameral Parliament, with the State Council as the upper chamber and the Duma as the lower one. The two were equal, but the State Council could in practice block any measure proposed by the Duma. Voting, for which all males were eligible, was organised into colleges for different types of citizen – landowners, peasants, workers. These elected members of provincial assemblies and those in turn chose the members of the Duma. The structure was biased so that rural Russia – the loyal hinterland in which Nicholas believed – had greater influence than the urban centres, and landowners had considerably more influence than those lower down the social scale.

The Duma was therefore a deeply conservative body, by coercion if not by conviction. This was not merely because the Tsar wished to keep as much power as possible by filling the chamber with those of greater loyalty to himself, it was also because he believed that Russia could not step straight into democracy at once. The country was not ready for democracy – indeed it would probably take at least a generation for anything resembling such a condition to become familiar to Russians. The other great statesman, Peter Stolypin, was to say that for the new institutions to mature would require 'twenty years of peace at home and abroad' and this would be asking a great deal in terms of both domestic and international politics. The process could not be hurried without the risk that it would end in disaster, and in the meantime the best people to steer the ship of state were those who had the most experience of governing, running estates or organisations, holding positions of responsibility – those who had a stake in the country because they owned property. The dominance of landowners made sense when seen from this perspective. The alternative – giving power and influence to orators, social theorists and the associates of bomb-throwers – was an unthinkable political experiment. These people could not be relied upon to see the best interests of the country. Nevertheless, the opportunity for the first time to participate in government meant that the Duma members were not as supine as their backgrounds might imply, and they proved surprisingly intransigent.

The system of government brought in by this Constitution was not efficient, but no one had expected that it would be. Russia had now to catch up, as best she could and in very different, and difficult circumstances, with developments that had taken centuries in other countries. One problem was that government ministers did not work together or even, really, discuss the business of the country. Each had been appointed by the Tsar rather than by their colleagues or a popular vote. The result was that they each spoke to him only. As ever, this was a very bad means of decision-making. In addition, Nicholas had refused to budge from sole control of the most vital ministries in government – the armed forces and foreign affairs. No one could challenge him on these subjects. In theory, he could declare war and plunge the country into another expensive foreign adventure if he wished, and it was not the right of any minister to advise or to disagree with his chosen course of action. Another crucial point was that the government was not responsible to the Duma but only to the Tsar. Voters had no power over the national government, which did not need to heed their wishes or reflect their attitudes.

The concessions saved the Russian state from disappearing in anarchy but they did not stop the widespread strikes and disturbances, while the provinces continued to be a lawless, murderous place for landowners and officials. Witte, initially so successful that he had seemed the saviour of Russia (he had been created a Count), was rapidly losing standing and respect. Nicholas resented the fact that he had been talked into giving up so much of his power. Now that the immediate danger had largely past, he could afford the luxury of ingratitude. Witte, fully aware that relations with the Emperor were worsening, resigned his position in April 1906. Nicholas was relieved.

General Elchianinov provides an interesting perspective on the change in Russia brought about by the Fundamental Laws of 1906, suggesting that this was actually part of some wise and considered long-term plan: 'During the fifty years which had elapsed since the freeing of the serfs, the Russian people had gradually become educated up to, and accustomed to dealing with, social and political affairs. It became possible to revive in all its original force the custom, practised by the first Tsars of the Romanov dynasty, of giving the people, through their representatives, a share in the conduct of the State and a voice in the needs of the country. Therefore the Tsar decided to summon representatives of the people to take a part in the work of the State.' This is an extraordinary spin to put on events, in suggesting that the summoning of the Duma represented a return to Nicholas's beloved seventeenth century.

On 19 August it was announced that the Duma would be of a consultative character. It was to work with the Tsar, not replace him as the only law-maker. It was self-evident that this new system would have to learn by experience, and make some mistakes, before it could function smoothly. On 30 October the Tsar issued a manifesto to the effect that 'no law shall have force without the approval of the Duma, and that the people's representatives are assured of an active participation in the control of affairs.' Though all this sounded positive on paper, the actual workings of the legislative body remained remarkably vague and not a little mysterious., especially to foreigners. *The*

Russian Year Book, published in England for the purpose of advising those who wished to do business in the Empire, confessed to being bewildered. 'Of the competency and the rights of the Duma,' its readers were told, 'it is impossible to give an exact definition.'

Nicholas was never sincere in his acceptance of the need for representative government, and as always he saw it as a sign of Divine displeasure that Russia was facing its current crises. He declared that: 'No nation can be strong and healthy that does not maintain the traditions of its past. We ourselves have sinned against this, and God is perhaps punishing us for it.'

He told the first delegates: 'I welcome in you those "best people" whom I directed my beloved subjects to choose from amongst them. Difficult and complex work awaits you.' Yet shortly afterward he was to dissolve the assembly with stronger words: 'In those provinces of the Empire where the population has not yet developed sufficient sense of citizenship the privilege of election of members to the Duma must be temporarily withheld.'

Villari, writing in 1905 when matters were still deeply uncertain, had this to say with regard to the future:

It is to be feared that Russia is in for a long period of trouble before she settles down peacefully as a Constitutional State on modern lines. It must be borne in mind that the country has been untouched by the great movements which have moulded the history of Europe during the last five centuries – the Renaissance, the Reformation and the French Revolution – and that she has to learn these three Rs of political and intellectual development before she can evolve into a new nation. In all probability many experiments, many changes, many wild adventures will be undergone before a stable form of government, suitable to the peculiar genius of the people, is evolved. The English revolution lasted from 1640 to 1689, that of France from 1789 to 1815, that of Italy from 1821 to 1870; it would not be surprising if even that of Russia also lasted many years.

CHAPTER EIGHTEEN

Spectre

Alexandra had an interest in mysticism. This was not unusual, indeed it was a widespread fashion among the European *bon ton* at the time, and the Russian upper classes were as prone to it as anyone else. Her life had been sad before she even began her reign, and she was perhaps motivated by a need for spiritual help as much as by curiosity. Her proclivities brought her in contact with a number of questionable outsiders long before the most famous of them – Rasputin – appeared on the scene in 1905, and he was not a unique presence but simply the most powerful in a succession of favourites. The first of them was a man called 'Mitka the Fool'. A character straight from an earlier era of the Russian Court, he was the kind of freak that had entertained Peter the Great or the frivolous Empress Elizabeth. He could not speak coherently, and required an interpreter – his companion, Elprifor. Another such diversion was a woman by the name of Daria Osipovna, who claimed she was possessed by the devil. There were others, and they were not all Russian. Two came from France, another from Vienna. As the desperation of the Empress to produce a son became more palpable, so she would more obviously seek spiritual, or mystical, guidance. When this crisis was followed by another – the birth of a son and then the discovery of his condition – her search for this would become more frantic. She needed to know if her son, her husband's dynasty, their country, would be well. She was worried by both the present and the future, and sought any available insight, no matter who could offer it.

Such was her reliance on mysticism and the guidance, not of the Church as such (there were, and had been, churchmen of outstanding ability in the service of the Romanovs, most notably the saintly Father John of Kronstad, spiritual advisor to Alexander) but on anyone who, by any means, could provide what she needed, that she regarded the arrival of Grigory Rasputin (1868–1916) as a godsend.

He was introduced to the Court and to the Tsarina by two Montenegrin princesses who were married to Romanovs. There could be no doubting his ability as a faith healer, which had been seen in other cases. He came from Siberia – a remote region in which, amid trackless forests and limitless horizons, God seemed closer and miracles more believable than amid the pseudo-Western glitter of the cities. In no Western royal court could such a man have gained influence, for the tradition of the uncouth and unlettered seer did not exist there. He was something characteristic of Russia and its religion, where the scruffiness of a John the Baptist figure seemed less outlandish. The word for such a man was *staretz*, or elder.

He had, as everyone who met him recalled, a hypnotic gaze, with eyes that compelled trust or at least acquiescence. He could talk persuasively, and inspired confidence. He had the manner – and something of the substance – of a spiritual guide, and he was authentic to a tradition that was deeply ingrained in the Russian mind and soul. In this devout and superstitious country there was a long tradition of such men. They were not graduates of seminaries and they were usually lacking in formal education, which merely made their spiritual gifts more impressive to the gullible. Even one of the tsars had, according to rumour, opted to become such a figure: Alexander I, who had reportedly died in 1825 in the southern city of Taganrog, was widely believed to have faked his demise to escape the responsibilities of the throne (when his tomb was opened at the Revolution it was discovered to be empty) and gone to live the life of a religious hermit in Siberia, where he died in 1852.

Rasputin's gift of healing was, of course, what made all the difference to his credibility. Through his presence, or through a few quietly spoken words, he could succeed where the prayers of others – and the best medical care available in Russia – could not. For a mother driven to distraction with concern for the next ruler of the Empire, it was natural that she should grasp at this straw. And if he was outstandingly gifted by God in the matter of her son's health, the Empress, whose dependence on him would continue to grow, would come to wonder whether he could not be endowed with similar vision when it came to affairs of state. Why would he not have the ability to predict the future of the country, to see with clarity the policies that should be followed, to know by instinct or through prayer which were the right men to appoint to important positions?

Beyond the Family, he created less of a good impression. Rasputin was reputed to have been on pilgrimages to Mount Athos and to the Holy land. He had thus gone through some experiences that gave him credibility as a spiritual figure. More questionably, he had belonged to a sect called the Klysti which had included sexual licence in its religious services, and thus his background involved a libertine element that was tied to his aura of spirituality. His personal appetites were, in any case, fairly gross, even if they would be greatly exaggerated. A heavy drinker, he had the coarse manners of the peasant he was, and he saw virtually all women as a source of pleasure. He quickly acquired celebrity after arriving in Petersburg, his sheer outrageousness making him a sensation and something of a thrill to associate with. He attracted hangers-on among impressionable women and his home was visited by even the educated and the well-born. He boasted of his conquests among them, though this was much exaggerated. For women who wanted to be part of something exciting and risqué – to feel a whiff of scandal – it became fashionable to correspond with him, seek his counsel, visit his apartment, for he was the most talked about personality in the city. It was likely that wealthy and aristocratic people could be met in his rooms, and this will have been an additional attraction to those who sought such glamour.

It was extensively rumoured that he had a whole harem of lovers from the gentry and aristocracy, though police reports when later made public showed that this had not been the case – the women with whom his relations had been of a sexual nature were from much lower down the social scale and consisted almost entirely of those whose company could have been bought by anyone. Though such licentiousness was not against the law and adultery was not unheard of at

Court, anyone guilty of open and boastful debauchery could expect to be unwelcome in the vicinity of the Imperial Family. Rasputin, for reasons we understand and his contemporaries did not, was invited into the very heart of the Family, and he was making it unclean by association. The underground press, quick to pounce on any story that was critical of the monarchy, was delighted. Immorality and religion were nicely linked, and the scandal just seemed to keep going. Respectable people, who wished the monarchy well or who at least believed in order rather than anarchy, felt betrayed and indignant.

The presence of this man in Tsarskoe Selo also added further fuel to the flames of animosity between the Dowager Empress and Alexandra. The Tsarina reacted by doing what she always did when faced with criticism – she pursued her chosen path with even greater determination. Marie could not possibly have been unaware of the power of the staretz and therefore of why he was a vital presence in the Family.

The times through which they were living were years of frightening change, instability and threat to the traditional order. In these testing circumstances, perhaps ordained by God to punish the sins of Russia, might not God also have provided the solution in the form of a spiritual comforter – a promise that all would be well if the Family remained faithful and followed his guidance? We may feel that she and her husband were unwise, but it is not at all difficult to see why they fell under the spell of this man.

If, in addition, he was reviled by the very people the Empress most distrusted – her mother-in-law, and the senior aristocracy – would this not increase her resentment and her determination to follow her faith and her instincts? Though the Dowager Empress was naturally aware of the Tsarevich's illness, she was also aware that science had not cured it. Surely, therefore, she could understand that Rasputin offered the only solution to Russia's difficulties?

Count Benkendorff, a courtier and elder statesman who knew the Romanovs well, was to say, long after it was all over: 'I am convinced that the political influence of Rasputin was nil. The appointment of ministers, which, during the latter years, proved so fatal, can be explained otherwise. He never had any influence on the course of political events.' A much more likely reason for inappropriate or controversial political and military appointments was that the Empress, with her stubborn and opinionated nature, favoured particular men. If a candidate for a position were known to be critical of Rasputin, she could perhaps see to it that he was unsuccessful.

Rasputin's reputation in St Petersburg rapidly caused scandal. The police had him under permanent surveillance and their reports, showing who he visited and what company he kept, were shown to the Tsar. The Empress ignored, or made excuses for, his shortcomings and continued to allow him access to the Court. Such was the storm of criticism that she forbade her daughters to mention to anyone the visits he made.

Russia now possessed a satirical press, and articles and images circulated widely. These quickly came to suggest a predictable level of intimacy between the staretz and the Empress, and even with the Grand Duchesses. This too is easy to understand. The man was better known for debauchery than for anything else. That he was given what amounted to complete access to the Family, and his character excused by a woman who was notorious for moral disapproval, seemed to tell its own story. That she did not react to this by dissociating herself, by banishing him or by otherwise demonstrating that she recognised public disapproval seemed, naturally, to confirm suspicions. Even had she not had the health of her son to consider, we know that Alexandra had a disdain for public opinion that did not help matters. The Tsar, who was never as enamoured of Rasputin as was his wife, nevertheless took his side. Partly, perhaps, from the kind of weary patience that a husband might adopt to some eccentric hobby of his wife's ('it's what makes her happy') but largely because Rasputin benefitted his son and therefore Alexandra's nerves. Pierre Gilliard commented that Nicholas allowed Rasputin to wield influence because the Tsar 'dared not weaken the faith that kept the Empire alive'.

* * *

The year after Alexis arrived, Alexandra found a friend. There is something extraordinary, and very sad, in this relationship. The shy and unapproachable Empress, who could not make friends among the ladies of society, chose instead the company of a minor lady-in-waiting, an unassuming girl without beauty or talent. Anna Vyrubova (née Tanayeva), the daughter of a Court official, was to be the Tsarina's closest friend and chief confidante until they were separated by the Revolution. They spent hours together each day, singing, playing the piano, embroidering. Similarly disinclined toward the type of exercise favoured by Nicholas, they sat indoors and talked instead. The Empress liked her friend's quietude, her straightforward views, her complete and unquestioning loyalty. A year or so after they met, Alexandra even arranged a husband for Anna, having made a careful study of suitable men. Unfortunately judgement of character was among Alexandra's weakest characteristics and the one she suggested, an officer called Alexander Vyrubov, was entirely unsuitable. He was coarse and brutal. The marriage, which was never consummated, lasted only a few months before Anna left him and returned to her former life. Nicholas and Alexandra, who realised that a mistake had been made, behaved as if the marriage had not been. Anna was, however, to keep her husband's name and to make it famous through the memoirs she later wrote.

CHAPTER NINETEEN

More Settings

While summer was spent at Peterhof and winter at Tsarskoe Selo, there was another residence that the Family visited every year. This was Livadia. It was in the far south, on the Black Sea coast. This too was a holiday home. The nearby town of Yalta was the resort of wealthy and aristocratic Russians escaping the harshness of the north. It had a climate equivalent to the French Riviera and a similar landscape of coastal villages, limestone cliffs, mountains and hillside villas surrounded by cypresses and umbrella pines. The Romanovs had had an unimpressive wooden palace in which, it will be remembered, Alexander III had died. This building, gloomy both in structure and associations, was replaced by an elegant new palace that was completed in 1911 and, for what time was left to them, the Family delighted in during their sojourns there. Built in Italianate style and of a white stone that looked dazzlingly bright in the clear southern sunlight and when set against the deep blue of the sea, it was constructed around an arcaded courtyard that had a well in the middle – a cloistered seclusion that gave it something of the look of a monastery, an echo of Mount Athos, of Spain or of Italy. This was the only home the Romanovs built themselves, the only one that was not inherited from previous generations and filled with memories of others. Nicholas's delight was expressed in a letter to the Dowager Empress: 'We cannot find words to describe our pleasure and joy in having such a house built as we wished.' It is sad that this place, in which for a time they were to dream of living after the abdication, should have been the residence in which they spent the least number of years. Nevertheless, as the Empress became more infirm, they allowed the beauty of the place to seduce them and began to make longer sojourns there. The Tsar was accustomed to ruling the Empire from a distance.

In the last years before the war, the Family spent their days at

Livadia going for coastal walks and picnics, visiting local monuments, or going shopping in Yalta with an informality that they loved, for nowhere else in the Tsar's domains was this possible. Of all their residences this was, understandably, the one they most preferred, associated as it was with sunshine, relaxation and relative lack of protocol. They naturally loved the climate and the scenery. The coming of the automobile had made it possible to travel the switchback mountain roads and cover territory that was previously inaccessible.

The Family had a very highly developed system of civic duty. The Empress and her children devoted time and energy to charity work, patronages and affiliations with worthy organisations. The country had a long tradition of philanthropic institutions and of organised charity, because charity was the task of the Church and the Tsar was the head of this. When at Livadia the Empress Alexandra bought and even sold 'fancy work' such as embroidery done by the women of the Family at local charity sales. Her children also manned stalls to sell produce for good causes. The Tsar, like millions of indulgent fathers, would sometimes buy his children's items and pay more than they were worth. They were well aware that their presence would bring hordes of customers and that this would help raise funds. In April each year they were in this region, where the dry climate benefitted sufferers from tuberculosis. The children, whose uncle, Grand Duke George, had after all died from this disease, were active in a local fundraising event. The twentieth of the month was 'White Flower Day,' a curiously modern precursor of our own sellers of badges and stickers and poppies. The five of them were photographed one year, carrying staffs that were festooned with paper flowers to pin on donors and with collecting boxes hung round their necks.

There was one further place in which the family lived, and this was the Imperial Yacht, the *Standart*. This was, as such vessels usually were, an ocean-going palace. Launched from a Danish shipyard in 1896, she was at 5,557 tons and with a length of 370 feet, by far the largest private ship in the world. Black with gold trim, she had two funnels and three masts. Her figurehead was a gold, double-headed eagle that was almost twenty feet long. She was used for official purposes when appropriate, such as when the Romanovs travelled to Reval (now Tallinn, Estonia) to meet King Edward VII, or for receiving a visit from Kaiser William. Apart from this, the yacht was for pleasure. It became customary for the Family to undertake a cruise each summer along the coast of Finland. This was not far from the region where they lived – Petersburg was just opposite – but the area was deeply rural, filled with fir-forested coast, coves and islands that were a joy to explore, a touch of Swallows and Amazons, an ideal place for those who loved to climb, to walk and to swim. The landscape was largely empty of habitation, and those few people met by the Romanovs might well have been unable to speak their language. There was little need for tight security and none for etiquette. The vessel itself was entirely secure and absolutely private. Wherever they looked from the deck, they would see the reassuring smoke of escort vessels.

Standart's crew were treated with unusual intimacy. The Family knew the sailors' names and patronymics, and greeted them individually when they came aboard. They took a delighted interest in the daily tasks of the sailors, and sometimes helped with them. They watched the crew parading to receive orders, washing the deck, manning the yards, and looked on as their father tasted samples of their food. They knew the birthdays of crew members and chose presents for them. They attended the raising and lowering of the flag at morning and evening. On the expeditions ashore they were accompanied by ship's officers. Lili Dehn, who married one of the officers, became a friend and confidante of Alexandra. As had been seen with Anna Vyrubova, the Tsarina was drawn to women of obscure origin and small accomplishment. She found in their company more ease and relaxation than was available at Court.

The Romanovs were accompanied by no more than one or two attendants of each sex. Otherwise the crew provided for all their needs. There was such pleasure in this privacy and informality that they longed for the spring and summer cruises. Nowhere on land could they find this same freedom. When they went to Livadia, the

Standart was required to accompany them to the Crimea, to be on hand for similarly innocent outings along the Black Sea coast. With her instantly recognisable silhouette and huge figurehead, *Standart* was the most well-known vessel in Russia. A symbol of technology as much as of autocracy, she aroused so much interest – and envy – among monarchs that the famously tactless Kaiser William told his cousin Nicholas that he would be pleased to receive her as a present.

Though the yacht had a great deal of protection against attack, even here the Family could not take safety for granted. In August 1907, while they cruised the Finnish coast, the vessel struck a rock that had not been charted and seemed likely to sink. Thankfully, the *Standart* was accompanied by the Dowager Empress's own yacht, the *Polar Star*, and they were at once transferred on board. Seven summers later, they would be on the Yacht when news came of the assassinations at Sarajevo.

Nicholas and Alexandra did not spend summers in Denmark, as he had in his youth. Now he had a connection through his wife with another European court, and it was to Hesse that they went. Like many families, their summer holidays included a visit to relations so that the children's progress could be monitored. At the castle of Wolfsbuttel lived the Empress's brother, Grand Duke Ernest of Hesse. This building, older and smaller than any palace that the children had known, became yet another fairyland. What they loved here were not the pinewoods and parks – for they had these in abundance at home – but the ease with which they could spend their days. At home every trip they made had to be registered with the police, planned and shadowed. Spontaneity was out of the question. In Germany, even more than in Yalta, they could accompany their uncle in his automobile on drives, go shopping in nearby towns unrecognised, unacknowledged, unstared-at. They could even visit tourist attractions like any ordinary family.

These were the places in which Nicholas, his wife and their children lived out their lives. Needless to say they enjoyed surroundings that were opulent and privileged. What is perhaps surprising is that the children's lives and routines should have been so comparatively plain and even frugal. The girls – for Alexis was a different matter – had an upbringing patterned after that of their mother, who had grown up in genteel poverty. They slept without pillows, made their own beds and tidied their rooms, just as upper-class English girls might have done at a particularly Spartan boarding school. They were taught to be respectful to servants and to save them trouble where possible. Their clothing, though of quality and in keeping with fashion, was never extravagant and was sometimes decidedly plain. They dressed identically – there is not a single image in which their clothes are different – and it was not unknown that a garment made for Olga would pass all the way down to Anastasia. The girls were, in any case, genuinely good-natured and aware of their fortunate position. The lives they lived were in many ways simpler than those even of girls in the minor aristocracy.

They relished the chance to meet humble compatriots, and showed a particular affection for children. Once again, had they been a contemporary royal family, living in the glare of modern media, their unpretentious lives would have made them highly popular and would have fitted the spirit of the time. Even as it was, their goodness was relatively well known. Bolshevik propaganda was to have to work very hard indeed to demonise them.

CHAPTER TWENTY

The Heir

Count Vassili, who knew that the Tsarevich suffered from illness, was as dismissive of him as he had been of his parents, saying unkindly that: 'no child has ever been so spoiled as has the little Grand Duke, and no child has ever been brought up in a worse manner. Were he destined to live, it would be terrible to contemplate the future of Russia under his guidance; as it is, one can afford to pity him, and pity his parents, for whom he represents so much.'

Alexis was, from the moment of his birth, treated as a national mascot. His first official engagement had taken place when he was no more than a month old, for he had accompanied his father to wish farewell to ships departing for the war. Even without his position, his national celebrity and his illness, a boy with four older sisters and parents who had longed for a son was going to be heavily indulged. Everyone in his family, in the Court and in the wider public viewed him as unquestionably more important than his sisters. He was appointed Colonel-in-Chief of six regiments within an hour of coming into the world, and was on display at ceremonial events by the time he could walk. His earliest outfit still exists – a black velvet suit of jacket and knee-length trousers, embroidered with gold and with imperial eagles on the collar. Otherwise he wore the sailors' square-rig uniform of the Imperial Yacht, with the vessel's cap-tally. When the Family appeared in public, he was usually the member that people most wanted to see, proving even more popular than his father. 'Show us the Heir!' was a cry commonly heard among crowds. At sight of him, old women would fall to their knees and cross themselves. He shared the quasi-mystical status of his father as 'God on earth'.

His was an awesome position for a small boy, and he sometimes displayed an arrogance derived from never having had his wishes thwarted. Critics – and he did not lack these because he was part of an institution that many wished to attack – made much of his spoiled nature and its implications for the future. Even observers with greater objectivity told stories of his demanding nature. Kellogg Durand, for instance, was told by a naval officer of an event on board the Imperial Yacht during its 1907 cruise to Finland. The three-year-old Heir had been appointed Adjutant to his father, and this meant he was in command of not only the *Standart* but its accompanying gunboats. Unable to sleep one hot August night, the boy decided he wanted to hear the ship's band perform. The duty officer was summoned and explained that the bandsmen were asleep, but Alexis would brook no objection. They had to be roused to entertain him, and they were. Durand explained that 'very largely the Tsarevich is encouraged to do everything he is inclined to do, on the theory that the instincts and impulses of an autocrat must be right'. One cannot imagine Nicholas, with his genuine concern for others, having allowed this, yet what spirited child would not have ordered a band to play for them, had they had the opportunity?

Like his father he did not enjoy studying, though with his bright curiosity, mischief and sense of humour he would have been a far greater pleasure to teach. Nor did he like it if he failed to receive the deference expected toward the Heir, and once berated a general who had failed to stand up when he entered the room. He would obey no one except his father, yet he did not always get away with bad behaviour. A well-known anecdote tells of a lunch at Livadia at which the Heir disappeared under the table. He crawled around among the feet of the guests and pulled the shoe off a lady-in-waiting. When he surfaced and waved this at his father, the Tsar ordered him at once to return it to its owner. Alexis did, but the woman gave a horrified shriek when she found he had first put a large strawberry in the toe. On this occasion he was summarily removed.

He had, of course, really wonderful toys. Not only was his father the world's richest man, but he received gifts from the rulers of other countries, from Russian organisations and from well-wishers. He had a huge teddy bear – a new type of toy that was only just coming into popularity. The King of Italy sent him a Sicilian donkey cart and the elaborate tack to decorate the animal. He had a working miniature motor car in which he drove himself and sometimes others. Similarly, he had a miniature printing press that was fully functional. He had a cinema projector that he learned to work, and a number of films that he showed to guests. He had dogs and other animals (his most famous pet – the spaniel Joy – would accompany him into exile), and he even planted and grew wheat in the park at Tsarsloe Selo, which he then harvested himself with a sickle. He had a cohort of acquaintances with whom he played. They belonged to an organisation called the 'Potyeshnie' ('Play soldiers') which his father had created on the model of the toy regiments founded for Peter the Great in his boyhood.

The purpose, as with the Boys' Brigade and Boy Scouts in Britain, was to give male children an outlet for energy, an experience of discipline and a grounding in useful skills. Like the Scouts, there were units all over the country and they met and practised on a regular basis. Confusingly the 'play soldiers' who surrounded the Tsarevich seem always to have dressed in naval uniforms. Elchaninov described the Heir's involvement with a local unit of these boys, many of whom were of modest background and who therefore represented a wider experience of life for Alexis than his father had ever had. The General tells us that the Tsarevich: 'is thoroughly proficient in the rifle exercises, skirmishing order, the elements of scouting, the rules and requirements of military discipline, and performs the exercises correctly and smartly. There is a squad of "Potyeshnie", formed from the sons of soldiers, to join in his military instruction. When in the Crimea the Tsarevich goes three times a week from Livadia to Massandra, where on a special drill-ground the gymnastic and military exercises of this squad take place, in which the Tsarevich, according to his height, occupies the first place in the second half-squad. With them, too, he sings the songs which are an institution with all "Potyeshnie".' There was another such group at Peterhof, in which he similarly practised marching and went through the manual of arms under the supervision of his sailor-guardians, Nagorny or Derevenko. Often the boys played rough-and-tumble games in which he could not join. We see him on film, standing wistfully on a wooden jetty while they dive into the water and splash to and fro, or as they fling themselves into a hammock that is then tipped up to spill them out. Alexis could only watch.

Spala was in Poland. It was a hunting lodge and it was here that the Family stayed in the autumn of 1912 so that the Tsar could spend a few weeks shooting stags. It was, however, to earn a particular infamy in the story of the Romanovs, for here occurred the most serious illness suffered by Alexis and caused the incident that, more than any other, consolidated Rasputin's influence over the Empress.

The boy had slipped and fallen while getting out of a boat, and though nothing happened for a few days, he was suddenly reduced to agony by internal bleeding. This was to be his worst attack yet. It quickly reduced his parents to a state of traumatic anxiety. Doctors, hastily summoned, could do little. His excruciating pain increased. It was necessary to issue public bulletins, and to announce that his condition was grave. Rasputin was far away and the Empress could communicate with him only by telegraph, yet this flimsy connection was enough. He sent back the joyful tidings: 'Do not despair. The little one will not die.' The bleeding stopped.

Of all the photographic treasures from the Romanov family that we have, few images are more delightful than that which shows a scene from a play. It is Molière's *Le Bourgeois gentilhomme* and it is performed by the girls. It was staged at Spala during that time, before an audience of courtiers, friends, local aristocracy and other guests. The picture shows the younger pair, Marie and Anastasia, in an exchange. Marie is dressed as a man of the time of Molière, with a three-cornered hat and sword. Anastasia, in white petticoats and a mob cap, stands with hands on hips, looking as pert and mischievous as she was known to be. It is easy to imagine how the audience will have loved this spectacle, with the girls showing off and the artless humour of their speeches in French. They had been coached by Pierre Gilliard, a Swiss who was the children's French tutor and who produced the play. No one in the audience was aware of the reality of that evening – that while his sisters capered and his parents laughed with the other spectators, the Tsarevich was in agony only feet away. Gilliard knew, for he recorded in his memoirs that:

> When the play was over I went out by the service door and found myself in the corridor opposite Alexis Nicholaievich's room, from which a moaning sound came distinctly to my ears. I suddenly noticed the Czarina running up, holding her long and awkward train in her two hands. I shrank back against the wall, and she passed me without observing my presence. There was a distracted and terror-stricken look on her face. I returned to the dining room. Footmen in livery were handing round refreshments on salvers. Everyone was laughing and exchanging jokes. The evening was at its height.
>
> A few minutes later the Czarina came back. She had resumed the mask and forced herself to smile pleasantly at the guests who crowded round her. But I had noticed that the Czar, even while engaged in conversation, had taken up a position from which he could watch the door, and I caught the despairing glance which the Czarina threw him as she came in. An hour later I returned to my room, still thoroughly upset at the scene which had suddenly brought home to me the tragedy of this double life.

Nicholas had always, as we have seen, had the ability to hide his feelings. He was self-contained to a degree that was unusual even among royalty. This enabled him to display an impressive calm in the numerous moments of crisis that he was to encounter, but it also left many onlookers with the feeling that he was insensitive, unfeeling, or so unable to grasp the significance of events that he was simply stupid. While we know that he was not a great intellectual, we also know from our reading of his letters and diaries that he was by no means a fool. Where his family was concerned he lacked nothing in terms of sensitivity and affection, and his son's illness will have been much worse for him than if he himself had been suffering. Princess Bariatinsky claimed that evidence of his misery survived amid the documents on which he worked at the time – in some instances the ink was blurred by falling tears. The façade of normality surely cannot have been convincing. Rumours abounded, and then the news had to be confirmed that the boy's illness was serious. In a number of photographs that were taken at the time we can see in both Nicholas and Alexandra a look of haunted, baleful anxiety. They cannot hide this from the camera or from us even across the gap of more than a century. How much more difficult to conceal their pain from their contemporaries. Yet both saw it as their duty to maintain a pretence of normality for the sake of their guests. It was the same feeling that had persuaded Nicholas to attend the French Ambassador's ball on the evening of the Khodinka tragedy. Duty to subjects and allies took precedence over everything else – even a trauma as great as this.

Though Nicholas was less enamoured than his wife of the staretz, he had good reason to appreciate his ministrations and he knew the comfort that Rasputin provided for the Empress. Gibbes recalled being with him one day when the Tsar received a letter. He read some sentences and then said: 'Another of those denunciations of Gregory. I get them almost every day.' He threw it away without even reading to the end.

Though the exact nature of the boy's ailment was not known for certain outside the Family, well-informed observers could make shrewd guesses, based on the known history of European royal houses. It could not be concealed that he was seriously ill, especially after the Spala crisis. Count Vassili, who was not a well-wisher, wrote: 'The health of the little Tsarevich is such that it seems more than doubtful that he will ever reach manhood. He has no brother. The succession to the Throne is one of those shadows that darken the horizon of Russia.' In other words, even had the revolution not taken place, we are reminded that the life of Russia would have contained uncertainty and upheaval.

A series of official photographs was taken of Alexis in uniform – those of his various regiments. He appears dressed in a long Cossack coat with its silver ammunition pouches and the impressive dagger attached to his belt; in the shako of an infantry regiment with its lofty hackle; in the dress of the Horse Artillery with its extraordinary helmet – of patent leather, with peaks fore-and-aft, a fur coxcomb running from ear to ear and a pointed busby bag that hangs down behind. The boy looks splendid and in at least one picture he grins happily, but much of this was artifice. He was required to sit on a horse, though he had to be lifted into the saddle and his feet placed in the stirrups for the minutes it took to make the photograph. More tragically, there is one image in which he leans nonchalantly against a pillar. He wears overalls (the tight, understrapped trousers of the cavalry) and a busby sits at a rakish tilt over his eye. One of his legs is bent as he leans *contraposto* and the impression, which must have delighted the regiment concerned, is one of precocious urbanity and swagger. In reality, Alexis was in terrible pain. He was unable to bend his leg because internal bleeding had swelled his knee-joint. He had had to be carried into position for the photographer. It is a tragic thing to look at.

Those who knew him tell us that his illness gave him a singular perspective. While he had the beautiful toys and wonderful costumes and a certain amount of licence to give orders to adults, he was tragically aware that he could never take part in many of the happiest activities of childhood and that he would always be a semi-invalid. This knowledge gave him a precocious gravity and an empathy with suffering that compensated for any fractiousness in his nature. Since he was only fourteen when he died, we cannot know how long he would have lived (present-day medical opinion agreed with Vasilli that at that time, and with the treatment available, he would have been unlikely to survive his teens) or how successful a ruler he would have been, but the indications are that he would have been much like his father, probably less isolated and self-contained, perhaps more open-minded and comfortable in the twentieth century. His English tutor, Sydney Gibbes, later gave this thumbnail sketch of him: 'A clever boy, he was not fond of books. He had a kind heart – during the last Tobolsk days (of captivity before they went to Ekaterinburg) he was the only member of the family to give presents – and he loved animals. Influenced only through his emotions, he rarely did what he was told, but obeyed his father; his mother could not be firm with him, and through her he got most of his wishes granted. Alexis bore unpleasant things silently and without grumbling.' Among his few remembered statements was that: 'When I am Tsar, there will be no poor or unhappy people. I want everyone to be happy.' Surprisingly for a boy his age whose influence on history was so slight, he has been the subject of a biography.

CHAPTER TWENTY-ONE

Revival

While the children grew up and developed personalities, Russia was recovering from her defeat by Japan. The Tsar was determined to restore power and confidence, in the armed forces and in society. As after any difficult war, the government sought to remedy whatever abuses had been identified and in the aftermath of the Japanese debacle, Russia's General Staff had much to think about.

Significant efforts were made to improve the equipment. Russia was intent on becoming, overnight, a modern military power of the first rank. Her factories laboured to turn out armaments, because the government wanted to produce its own rather than ordering expensive foreign weaponry. Units were being re-issued with more efficient, more up-to-date, more deadly weapons. The newer aspects of warfare, such as an aeronautical service, submarines, fast torpedo boats and automobiles, were taken seriously and incorporated into the order of battle. The calibre of the men was also addressed. It must no longer be the case that service was something to be dreaded and avoided, an occupation for outcasts. Morale had collapsed so dramatically during the war that it must be rebuilt swiftly and thoroughly. Soldiers' welfare, which had become a short-lived preoccupation while the conflict was going on, was now to be a permanent characteristic, to the extent that libraries were opened for this largely illiterate army, and beginnings made in providing education for them.

Many countries that demand military service of their young men see the experience as educational – a 'school of the nation' – in which participants form a captive audience to be taught the virtues of discipline, patriotism and obedience. It also brings together men from every region, so that prejudices are broken down and integration made possible. For these reasons, as much as for defence, Russia needed its reservists. It sought to raise their standard of technical ability as well as general education. These men, who had resented being sent to the East in the war, were reorganised into two classes of eligibility, so that in future emergencies the first to be sent would be the youngest – those less likely to have responsibilities or family ties. This would probably have been a popular innovation, had not the next war been on such a scale that it simply swallowed up all the men available. It was a laudable aim but in the event it was not to succeed. There would not be time before the next war in which to implement all these ambitious notions. Progress was slow, entrenched habits continued, numbers were too great and there were other urgent issues to preoccupy those in government. It would have taken an entire generation to overhaul the huge and disparate Russian military.

The Navy, one of Russia's greatest national institutions and the biggest sufferer in the war with Japan, was similarly overhauled. The new ships, some paid for with funds raised by patriotic citizens, were thundering down the slipways of Russian dockyards. Those who would serve aboard them were, like their army counterparts, given advanced technical training – in wireless, torpedoes, gunnery and so on. The Navy even had an aeronautical branch. Russia may have been seen abroad as a backward nation, but it embraced much of the most modern technology, especially for defence.

No Tsar and Tsarina had ever been so universally unpopular. Others had been hated but feared – Peter the Great or Nicholas I. Some had been despised – Peter II, Peter III, and Tsar Paul. But none had faced the same relentless dislike from across society. The aristocracy, alienated, was highly critical. The intelligentsia, resentful of censorship, lack of genuine reform or meaningful change and of the closure for security reasons of many Russian universities, was not favourable. The Army was uninspired by Nicholas's leadership and was licking its wounds after an international humiliation. Society at large continued to see Nicholas as indecisive and weak. Those who believed in political reform, or who realised that it represented the only way forward for the nation if revolution was to be avoided, had of course given up on the Tsar from the beginning. The Empire's Jewish population, so necessary to Russia's economic wellbeing, hated Nicholas for the pogroms he allowed, and liberal Russians were aware that their ruler had done nothing to negate the country's international image as despotic, cruel, inflexible and hidebound. If any major crisis were to come – and a European war had threatened to break out several times in the years before 1914 – he was not the leader the nation required. This attitude of despair with the established order was captured by Alexander Solzhenytsin in his novel *August 1914* (1974) in which a benign old man, encountered in a Moscow street, discusses politics with the story's central character, saying to him and his companion: 'I suppose you are socialists?' When they deny this he responds: 'What! You aren't? Then I hope you are at least anarchists?'

Yet these years – from the end of the revolution and the founding of the Duma to the outbreak of hostilities in 1914 – were very good for Russia. The recovery from this national nadir was proving astonishingly swift. Stolypin's land reforms had proved extremely successful, bringing contentment and prosperity to millions. Confidence was growing, the standard of living was increasing. A glance through Russian magazines of those years will show pages of advertisements for luxury goods, aimed at the growing middle class, and a huge increase in factory-made items such as shoes, hats, umbrellas, luggage. In terms of materialism, the country was rapidly catching up with the West. Many Russian and foreign observers predicted a period of prosperity and rapid development ahead. While not wishing to bore the reader with statistics, it is worth quoting some figures published in the British press in May 1912: 'During the five years 1900–1904, the exports from Russia averaged £86,920,000 and the imports £63,400,000. In the next quinquennial period, 1905–1909, the average total per annum rose to £195,060,000, the exports being £113,020,000 and imports £82,000,000. In 1910 (the last year for which figures are available) the exports from Russia amounted to £144,830,000 and imports £108,540,000. That is to say, between 1900 and 1910, the exports from Russia were doubled, while the imports increased by 73 per cent.' It is true that industrial relations had again become terrible – in April 1912 a strike over working conditions at the Lena goldfields had erupted into violence. Troops had fired on strikers and killed two hundred and seventy of them. The result was a multiple increase in the number of industrial actions that affected the country up to the outbreak of war and beyond. In the same year that the statistics were published, the number of strikes in Russia was 1,198.

CHAPTER TWENTY-TWO

Tercentenary

The early years of the century saw a succession of anniversaries and commemorations. One of these was the two hundredth anniversary of the Battle of Poltava in which Peter the Great defeated the Swedes. Another was the half-century since the emancipation of the serfs. A third was centred on the hundredth anniversary of the Napoleonic Wars. Nicholas attended the celebrations for the centenary of Borodino, and wrote to his mother that he had met a 122-year-old veteran who had been fit enough to stand upright throughout and who had described the action to him. The struggle of 1812 – the French invasion of Russia, the retreat of her armies, the humiliations of defeat and the abandonment and occupation of Moscow were balanced by the heroic resistance of the Russian people, the reconquest of the land, the brilliant leadership of Marshal Kutuzov and of Tsar Alexander, and the final revenge as Russian armies drove the enemy all the way back to Paris, which Alexander entered in triumph. This war had made Russia a full-blown European power, feared and respected abroad. It had been the most glorious chapter in the country's history, a heroic past in which Russians could take unreserved pride, a world away from the debacle of the Crimea or the outright disaster of the war with Japan. It pointed, yet again, to the inadequacy of the present autocrat when measured against his forebears. The Napoleonic anniversaries were to be followed almost immediately by the three hundredth anniversary of the dynasty in 1913. Nicholas, Alexandra and their children would be more visible than they had ever previously been.

The year 1913 was one of celebration – it would prove to be a swansong, a final summing up of the achievements of a dynasty that would have no more achievements. There were numerous events all over the Empire to remember the accession to the throne of the modest Michael Romanov at the request of his fellow boyars. In both Moscow – where he was buried – and in the newer capital founded by his descendant there were services of thanksgiving. There were historical pageants, tours of provinces, illuminated addresses from deputations. There were yet more medals to give out – there was in fact a commemorative badge, accompanied by an impressive certificate, that anyone was entitled to receive if they had sent congratulations to the Emperor. It is not especially difficult to whip up a sense of celebration among the general populace, especially in connection with a feeling of patriotism and goodwill and bounty. If rejoicing was sincere and goodwill genuine, this was not surprising. The painful experience of the Japanese War was fading. The economy continued to expand, the standard of living was getting higher and reforms were gradually easing the lot of the worst-off. This was undoubtedly a great moment for Russia and for the dynasty.

The major commemoration took place in the capital, on 21 February. At noon, after the firing of yet another salute (thirty-one rounds this time!) from the Fortress, the Family left the Winter Palace by carriage to attend a service at the Kazan Cathedral, some distance up the Nevsky Prospect. This was, for many citizens, the first real chance to see them, since they led such a reclusive existence, and the pavements were crowded on both sides of the great thoroughfare. These spectators saw approaching a procession of three vehicles. In the first, and causing the biggest flutter of excitement, were the Emperor and the Heir. They were followed by the two Empresses, and then – in decreasing order of importance – by the four Grand Duchesses.

The capital celebrated for a further two days. There was a performance at the Mariinsky Theatre of Glinka's *A Life for the Tsar*, something of a standard Imperial entertainment, since as its name suggests it portrayed loyalty to the throne as the highest virtue. A ball followed the next evening, at the Assembly of Nobles.

Thousands of loyal subjects cheered the Family in the streets, but there were *hundreds* of thousands who would not. Revolutionary ideas had not gone away since the revolution eight years earlier. They were continuing to spread through society at large and were especially rife in the army – the very organisation that was seen as the guardian of the throne.

Carried along by the general enthusiasm, and touched by the fulsome tributes that poured in from all over his territories, was Nicholas lulled into a comfortable illusion that his people were contented and that he was loved by them? This was after all the Russia in which he believed. He received delegations from distant regions, in freshly laundered folk-dress, and thanked them graciously for their good wishes. He delighted in meeting these minor officials, prosperous merchants, policemen, priests, members of village councils. They were a cast of characters straight out of the Russian novels he loved to read, an affirmation of that traditional, pious and loyal motherland which could be found beyond the cities and the smokestacks of industrial regions. Those who defied him, criticised his wife's spiritual counsellor, printed and circulated scurrilous publications or plotted his assassination were surely not the majority, and spoke for no one but a small clique of irreconcilables. The revolution was over and they had lost. His police now kept a strict eye on them. His borders were watched to prevent the return of any who were living elsewhere in exile. He was not nearly so naïve as to think this. He had access to every police report and he knew that further terrorism was possible at any time. He was also aware that Russia was embroiled in the worst outbreak of strikes since 1905. He was perfectly appraised of the hostility toward him and his family. There was no room for complacency based on the selective goodwill of his people.

The reappearance of the Family in public was perhaps something like the return of Queen Victoria after years of private mourning. It was so long since their people had seen much of them, and observers both at home and abroad were impressed by how the children had blossomed. By this time the older girls had graduated to young womanhood and were attractive and personable, seemingly lacking the shyness displayed by both of their parents. The four daughters were as always dressed in identical styles and colours. Both Russians and foreigners were shocked, when viewing film or photographs of the events, to see the eight-year-old Tsarevich being carried in the arms of an attendant as if he were an infant. What made this an even more jarring spectacle was the fact that he was dressed in military uniform and wore the pale blue sash of the Order of St Andrew, which made him look like a miniature, invalid field-marshal. It must have been a terrible humiliation for the boy – a natural show-off – who would have liked to strut. The Family, however, made a very positive impression, fuelling an international fascination. One foreign journalist, wishing to write about Alexandra, complained that his newspaper office files contained almost nothing about her. The princesses, now that they were growing up (Olga was eighteen in 1913) could be seen to be among the most beautiful in Europe.

However endowed the Grand Duchesses were with a sense of fun, they lacked the experiences common to girls of their age – shopping for clothes, attending parties, exchanging confidences with best friends. Their manners, especially Olga's, were often brusque. They lacked, in fact, an entire dimension of refinement, politeness and social confidence that should have been taken for granted. When, in February 1913, the two eldest daughters appeared at a ball in Petersburg, they knew virtually no one in the room and did not meet or talk to the members of society. The general gaucherie of Nicholas's daughters, which was the result of their mother's overprotective regime, horrified the dowagers.

As they had been growing up, there had naturally been speculation about who they might marry. There was in Europe at that time no shortage of eligible princes. The Kaiser, to name but one ruler, had six sons. Olga was the only daughter who reached an age at which she was seriously considered as a bride. Devoted to her father and as fiercely patriotic as he was, she made it clear she did not want – as was almost automatic for a princess in her position – to marry out of her country. One prospect was Grand Duke Dmitri Pavlovich, a cousin who would later take part in the murder of Rasputin. He belonged, however, to a social set whose frivolity and extravagance offended the Emperor and Empress. Olga also found him immature, and did not like him.

A further possibility was to be explored in the last summer of peace. The Family crossed the Black Sea aboard the *Standart* to visit their counterparts in Roumania. Carol, the Crown Prince, might have been paired off with Olga, and there was speculation about them. On meeting, however, they showed little mutual interest and the idea went no further. There would in any case have been no time for a marriage to be arranged before the European conflict began.

This did not mean that the girls were without feelings for young men. As their biographer, Helen Rappaport, has shown, they had not only schoolgirl crushes but serious passions for different individuals with whom they came in contact. The subjects of their infatuations were officers aboard the *Standart*, or their army counterparts in the Convoy. These were men of good family and good manners, whose sense of discipline would have prevented them from taking liberties, but they were not suitable companions for princesses who were expected to marry into royal houses. It is surprising that Alexandra, who sheltered her daughters so effectively from contact with other youths, tolerated the flirtations that went on on deck and on tennis courts. These too horrified the senior members of society, including the girls' grandmother.

Flirtations aside, there were more serious duties. As the older two girls, Olga and Tatania, grew toward adulthood they were each given the honorary command of their own regiments. As we have seen, the Dowager Empress held such a position with regard to the Chevalier Guards. Even the girls' mother had such a position, with Her Majesty's Lancer Guards Regiment (only once did she appear on horseback at a review). On an August day in 1913, at Peterhof, the senior Grand Duchesses attended with their father a review of their regiments, each of them dressed in the appropriate uniform. From the waist up these were the same – give or take some dressmakers' tucks – as that of the soldiers, and the girls then wore long black skirts in which they sat side-saddle. Olga wore the light-blue tunic of the Elisavtgradski Hussars with its frogging and gold braid, and a fur busby surmounted with a white hackle. Tatiana was in the dark blue, plastron-fronted tunic and plumed leather czapka of the Vosnesenski Lancers. The parade was followed by lunch in the Palace and photographs of regimental groups (they sat in the middle, between their father and the Commanding Officer) and of the two girls, side by side. There would just be time for Marie, too, to be given a regiment and wear its uniform before the war put an end to all such custom. The girls each now had a group of officers to befriend and men and horses to learn about, a sense of involvement with a military unit that must have been thrilling and intriguing. Sadly, almost a year to the day after that luncheon the European war broke out. Few of those with whom they had conversed amid the clink of cutlery and glasses would survive.

CHAPTER TWENTY-THREE

War & Revolution (ii)

> In this solemn hour I wish to assure you that I have done all
> in my power to avert war.
>
> Nicholas, telegram to King George V, 2 August 1914

Russia was a vital component in the European balance of power. With formidable neighbours – the empires of Germany and Austria-Hungary bordered her territory – she had to maintain a very large standing army. The Tsars had also relished their role as arbiters of peace – the fact that they could flex military muscles, hint at alliances, show displeasure, and keep the other nations cowed. Russia, as the biggest of the Slavic nations, also felt an obligation to protect the others, and this is what dragged the country into the cataclysm that was to follow.

It will be remembered that the war began because Gavrilo Princep, a Serbian extremist, murdered the Archduke Franz Ferdinand of Austria and his wife in the town of Sarajevo on 28 June 1914. This led the Austrian Government to issue a very stiff ultimatum to Serbia. Though that country made very strenuous efforts at appeasement, the Austrians were in the mood to punish, and declared war on Serbia. Russia then mobilised her forces in support of the Serbs and France, Russia's ally, was obliged to mobilise too. Germany, Austria's ally, was likewise obliged to mobilise. Within a matter of days, while many in Europe were enjoying their summer holidays, the continent had divided itself more-or-less neatly into two armed camps. Suddenly, a minor crisis which could have been settled with arbitration was about to result in open war.

Incredibly, the last days of peace were spent in a long-arranged meeting between the Tsar and Raymond Poincare, the President of France. The President arrived in Russia, with a large military and civilian entourage, and had a number of talks with Nicholas. This was a month after the assassination at Sarajevo, and although there was tension and disquiet throughout the chancelleries of Europe, the general atmosphere throughout the continent was still largely calm. As part of the official entertainments, the President was taken to Krasnoe Selo to see the regiments, and was as impressed as foreigners always were by the scale and apparent might of his ally, for over 100,000 men filled the plain and then paraded past him as he stood, bare-headed in salute, on the Tsar's Mound. That evening, the last of his visit, he took his turn as host aboard the presidential yacht *France*. The day after he left, Austria's ultimatum was received in Belgrade.

The coming of war was welcomed in Russia, judging by the general enthusiasm that greeted the news. In Palace Square a crowd assembled with flags, banners, icons and pictures of Nicholas. The family appeared on a small balcony – the Winter Palace has nothing as impressive as the big one at Buckingham Palace – and acknowledged their cheers as the people fell to their knees. They sang 'God Save the Tsar', of which a later commentator, Sacheverall Sitwell, would write: 'Apart from the Marseillaise, there is no patriotic air that is so stirring and none that, in a few bars, paints a whole country and a people.' The sound of this, sung by hundreds in the great open square, must have been moving indeed. Their ruler read a speech (a recording of this was made and survives but, distorted by time and primitive technology, it is a most uninspiring sound).

Despite her recent defeat in the Far East, Russia had a feeling of invincibility. Her people were well aware how awestruck other nations were by the sheer scale of everything: the Army was the biggest in Europe, with a manpower pool of 1.4 million men to call upon. The Navy, though an entire fleet had been sunk at Tsushima, had made rapid strides both in replacements and in technology. Since Tsushima, a nationwide fundraising campaign had been undertaken to replace the ships (the most modern vessels had been those lost) and patriotic groups and individuals had been generous. In 1914 the Baltic Fleet was made up of five battleships, ten cruisers, fifty-nine destroyers and more than twenty torpedo boats. Aviation had been studied for its military potential as closely in Russia as in the other powers, and the Tsar's navy was equipped with reconnaissance planes. The General Staff was making good use of both motorised transport and aircraft. Russia's attitude to the war was that of a powerful, muscle-bound young man contemplating a fight, who actually feels sorry for the enemies that are about to feel his strength. As in Germany, reactionary and conservative elements actually looked forward to war as a means of distracting attention from domestic problems and building patriotism. A quick and successful war, during the most benign season of the year, would surely be just the antidote the country needed to the years of revolutionary unrest.

Not everyone, of course, shared this optimism. One who saw the threat to Russia was Witte, who told Princess Bariatinsky: 'Russia will never win; she cannot defeat Germany, who has been making preparations for fifty years, and we cannot defend ourselves for a week. It is a wild stretch of imagination if you think it is possible for a moment.' Witte knew, as did all informed opinion in Russia, that the country had begun in 1912 a thoroughgoing modernisation programme for her armed forces. This was due to be completed – with extraordinary irony – in 1917. Until this was done, the country could not fight on equal terms with her neighbours and especially with Germany, the world's most dedicated military power. Small wonder that the Tsarina exclaimed, on hearing news of the outbreak: 'This is the end of everything!'

Witte was right, though he could have known nothing of the enemy's schemes, in his belief that Germany had planned for years to attack Russia. In fact, all such preparations had been in place for almost a decade. The situation was like this: Germany's undoubted opponent in a future war would be France; that country was still smarting from a crushing defeat in 1870, and was intent on recovering provinces taken from her by Germany at that time. In the reign of Alexander III, France had allied with Russia – a most unlikely marriage of necessity between a republic and an autocracy – for the simple reasons that both had something to fear from Germany and that the Tsar was Germany's eastern neighbour. Should conflict begin, the enemy would have the might of Russia behind his back. East Prussia had no natural defences. The terrain was as flat as Holland and there were no obstacles to stop an invading army. To keep Russia's million soldiers out of this province, the Germans would have to maintain a huge garrison – men and materiel that could thus not be used against France.

The General Staff in Berlin appreciated these difficulties but knew something else: that the great bulk of the Russian Army, on the outbreak of war, could not be mustered and transported quickly. It would take, the Germans estimated, six weeks at least to assemble and equip the troops and set them on their way. This allowed time for a daring coup to be attempted. According to the calculations made by a General Staff planner, General von Schlieffen, what the Kaiser's armies should do was treat both countries – France and Russia – as enemies no matter where or why a conflict broke out, and to attack both. Firstly, the entire might of Germany must be thrown against France. Short-cutting through Belgium (which was neutral, but necessity knows no rules), the armies would bypass French frontier fortresses, seize Paris and thus knock France out of the war in a single stroke. They would then turn eastward. Transported across Europe by their country's excellent railway network, the Germans could fall upon the Russians, who would still be preparing to fight. If East Prussia's flat landscape offered an easy conquest to invaders, the same could be said for the Tsar's Polish provinces to troops marching in the opposite direction. Schlieffen died in 1905, and his plan was not altered thereafter. Everything was in readiness, to be set in motion the moment circumstances made it necessary. It is a well-known cliché of modern history that the Kaiser was unable to stop the war at the last minute because, his generals told him, the railway timetables had been worked out and could not be interfered with.

With this conflict Nicholas, the 'Man of Peace' found himself, for the second time in a decade, a war leader. Circumstances had turned him into Alexander I – the Russian component in a grand alliance similar to that which had been formed against Napoleon a century earlier. He was not commander-in-chief – that post was to be held by his cousin, the Grand Duke Nicholas Nikolaivich – but he was naturally enough the national figurehead. As always he was good at the gestures: praying for victory, inspecting troops, being photographed looking impressive in a uniform. In Russia as in Germany, the start of hostilities caused an outburst of patriotism and social cohesion as domestic grievances and internal squabbles were for the moment forgotten. Monarchy, of course, benefitted from this. In a surge of patriotic feeling, even the name borne by Russia's capital for over two centuries was regarded as too alien for the times, and in July was changed to Petrograd – literally 'Peter's City'.

However this must not be overstated. There is an illuminating passage in Solzhenytsin's great novel of that time, *August 1914*, in which the officer, Vorotyntsev, muses on how to inspire his men: 'There was no point in using words like "honour" – the concept was an incomprehensible piece of aristocratic fiddle-faddle; still less would he impress them by talking about their "obligations to Russia's allies". Should he invite them to sacrifice themselves in the name of their Little Father, the Tsar? They understood that, and would probably respond to the notion of fighting for the nameless, faceless, timeless figurehead. But to Vorotyntsev there was no eternal, anonymous Tsar – only the real, present-day Tsar, whom he despised and who headed a system of which he felt ashamed; it would be sheer hypocrisy to invoke him.'

The Tsarina, similarly, did not command loyalty. The public's already long-standing animosity toward her increased because her nationality was now an outright liability. To her credit she at once showed devotion to her adopted homeland, even though the Kaiser was her brother-in-law (her sister was married to William's brother, who was head of the German Navy). The Empress arranged for rooms in the Catherine Palace to be used as a military hospital. It would largely be filled with socially exalted patients from the guards regiments, but then these were the regiments whose home depots were in the area. The Family thus readily allowed the grim reality of war to invade the enchanted world in which they lived. The three senior women became qualified as military nurses – 'Sisters of Mercy'. They all assisted in operations, seeing at first hand the effects of modern weapons and the gruesomeness of wounds. Meanwhile the youngest daughters became hospital visitors and spent many hours talking to the wounded. The Tsar's sister, Olga, also undertook nursing training, opening a hospital on the Galician Front. The Romanovs cannot be faulted on their devotion to duty and they deserve great credit for this.

To a surprising extent, they did not receive it. Though from a modern perspective this readiness to undertake difficult and even horrible war work shows them sharing the hardships of their people, they were seen by numbers of those same people as having lost considerable status by dressing in drab nurses' uniforms and undertaking these mundane tasks. They were not supposed to be 'like everyone else,' and many were horrified to see pictures of them looking so ordinary. Western monarchies, such as those of Scandinavia, expect such gestures but this is not a view shared everywhere. Russia's attitude was similar to that which prevails to this day in Japan – that the Imperial Family are beyond the reach of everyday concerns and problems.

Russian armies thrust southward from Poland into Galicia, cutting a swathe more than sixty miles deep and surrounding the city of Prsemsyl. The Austro-Hungarians who opposed them were often lacking in aggression – indeed those of them who were Slavs felt more connection to Russia than to their own empire, and saw the invaders as liberators. Russians took many thousands of the grey-uniformed troops prisoner. For a few weeks the Tsar's soldiers carried all before them. Nicholas's ally, France, was grateful. The myth of the 'Russian Steamroller' – an uncountable army that would roll westward, crushing everything in its path – was born. For the second time in a century it looked as if this great eastern Empire was destined to save Europe.

The Russians were also to invade East Prussia, for Germany must be hammered from both directions to draw off enemy troops from the drive on Paris. For several weeks in August the Tsar's armies rolled westward over a seemingly limitless landscape of forests and lakes and yellow cornfields. Under the hot sun the great columns tramped along the tree-lined roads, raising huge clouds of dust.

But the impetus could not be maintained. Russian communications – the hundreds of trains a day that needed to be able to reach the battlefront carrying men, ammunition, artillery pieces, food supplies, medical equipment – were not available or could not travel fast enough on single-track lines. There was also a maddening level of corruption, with contractors swindling the government and local officials embezzling goods. The Germans, whose efficient organisation prevented this, whose equivalent facilities were superb and whose transport system ran like clockwork, were fighting on their own territory. When the clash came, they would have the advantage.

And it happened suddenly and decisively. On the twenty-sixth of the month the two sides met near Allenstein, in a battle that the Germans would later call Tannenberg. Because 90 per cent of Russian troops were illiterate, the use of encoding for radio signals was deemed too complicated. They were sent *en clair* and the enemy listened with ease. Fresh German troops, brought by rail and ably commanded by General von Hindenburg, who knew all the Russian plans, meant that victory was virtually a foregone conclusion. The fighting lasted four days and resulted in a major Russian defeat. Losses were immense – estimated (though even rough figures will never be known) at 78,000 dead and wounded and 92,000 taken prisoner, including no fewer than thirteen generals. The Russian commander, General Samsonov, found a quiet forest clearing and shot himself. His body was not found until the following year.

Days later a second battle – the Masurian lakes – took place in the same area. The last clash had destroyed Russia's Second Army. This came very close to inflicting the same fate on the First. Casualties this time were about 100,000 and 45,000 prisoners. Only the precipitate retreat of Russian troops into their own territory prevented them from encirclement and further annihilation.

A second offensive in East Prussia, launched in February 1915, came to grief in the Battle of Augustovo, and with those defeats the notion of the unstoppable steamroller was destroyed. There were to be no more victories, merely a soul-crushing war of attrition, boredom and defeat. This was the disaster of Manchuria again, but on a much larger scale and much nearer home. This time at least the Russian Navy was not involved, so that there would mercifully be no equivalent of Tsushima. Nevertheless, this was the second calamitous war of Nicholas's reign. To the Tsar and his generals the only compensation for the drubbing that the army was taking was that the sacrifices were appreciated by their allies – Russia could be seen to be pulling her weight.

Russia's industry had expanded remarkably over recent years, but it was not geared to war production and it could not be transformed quickly or easily. This meant that shortages were seen with extraordinary speed as soon as peacetime stocks of artillery shells had been fired. There were not enough weapons to give a rifle to every soldier even when going into action, let alone for practice when training.

Witte had been right. The Empire could not, in the long or even in the short term, compete against an opponent who had planned in detail for a decade how to invade and defeat it. All Russia could hope to do was to make up in blood and courage what she lacked in other resources and to hang on. In this, tsarist Russia was not a failure but a fantastic success. Apart from inflicting several decisive defeats on Austria-Hungary, she pinned down for two and a half years a force of a million enemy troops, most of them German, thus making a crucial difference to the fighting on the Western Front.

Some assistance came from abroad. Britain was able to send supplies through the far-north ports of Archangel and Murmansk, though not always with success. A vital supply of thousands of pairs of army boots, which could have had a major effect to Russia's war effort, were lost at sea. More significantly the great British commander Lord Kitchener died when the ship carrying him to Russia, HMS *Hampshire*, was sunk off the Orkney Islands by a U-boat. The comparative isolation of Russia made its continuation of the struggle even more impressive.

As the news from the Front got worse and remained negative, the initial euphoria vanished. It was followed very quickly by weariness, cynicism, disillusionment, and a culture of blame. And in the midst of this, Nicholas decided that he would replace his cousin as commander of the armies, which he did on 25 August 1915. Alexandra did not like the Grand Duke, and neither did Rasputin. While some naturally concluded that the Siberian mystic could replace officials with a snap of his fingers, this was not true and certainly would not have been allowed amid the high seriousness of the military situation. What did happen, however, was that the Empress could persuade her husband on a course of action. He felt he should share the experience with the men who were fighting for Russia – to take a more 'hands on' role in the war. It might have been suggested that he could do this by assuming some more modest command, perhaps subordinate to his cousin, but this was not how tsardom worked. Nicholas could not, by very definition, be anything other than in supreme command. He was now to run not only the country but its most desperate war since 1812. In departing from the capital and spending his time at headquarters, he was effectively abdicating from government. Alexandra was appointed to rule in his place, but a preoccupied invalid, suspected of treason and in thrall to what many considered a madman, was not likely to inspire confidence or loyalty.

Prince Yussupov later wrote: 'It was a great blunder to deprive the Grand Duke of his command. The whole of Russia worshipped him. The army should not have been deprived of its beloved chief at a time like this.' This was undoubtedly true. Grand Duke Nicholas was a highly respected professional soldier. He was to be replaced by an amateur whose only significant experience had been briefly to command a battery of horse artillery or a company of infantry. The Grand Duke had been untainted by the influence of Rasputin – indeed his remark that if the staretz ever visited headquarters he would hang him, had brought a sympathetic smile to all Russia.

There was a feeling among the troops that at a time of the gravest crisis they were being deprived of the one commander whom they could trust. It seemed madness, and boded very ill for their morale and their loyalty.

When the Tsar took over command of the armies he moved permanently to the Front, living in Spartan quarters at 'Stavka', the General Staff Headquarters. Here he must have enjoyed something of a return to the life of his youth – he was once again an officer living in camp with others who shared his outlook and sense of humour. He did not stay up all night attending conferences and studying maps in the company of senior officers. He set out, first and foremost, to establish a routine lifestyle that would give him exercise and time out of doors to counterbalance the hours he must spend on military matters. He brought with him his photograph albums so that he could spend his leisure time sticking in pictures and captioning them. He did not, in other words, seem a very serious commander-in-chief. His presence at Stavka also had the important effect that, preoccupied now by military matters, he would lose sight of political developments and have no notion of how the war was seen at home. While he was away, government was in the hands of his wife, an alleged German spy. Since Russians believed their armies to be the bravest in the world, the reason for their repeated defeat could surely only be some betrayal, some sabotage, that was at the heart of government. Why would anyone need to look further for this than the German wife of their inept commander-in-chief?

He also brought with him the Tsarevich. He felt that the boy needed to escape the female-dominated world at Tsarskoe Selo and to experience something of the army. He believed that the Heir should take part in these defining historical events. Alexis, accompanied by his pet spaniel Joy, came to live at Headquarters, where he shared a room with his father. He wore an ordinary Russian soldier's uniform of mud-brown cloth, with tall boots and a peaked forage cap. He was initially given the rank of Private, though his father promoted him to Corporal – an action that made him extremely proud, for he felt he had earned this advance. He naturally did not go into danger, though he toured the battlefront and did something to raise morale. He in any case had a number of quasi-military things to do: he practised drilling with a toy rifle, he accompanied the Tsar on visits to units and walked beside him along lines of troops. He dined with generals and foreign attachés, whom he predictably charmed, but he was still a schoolboy and he continued the studies he had followed at home. In the evenings he played the balalaika, at which he had some talent, and spent time with his father. The weeks spent at Stavka often seemed more like a father-and-son camping trip than a major war. Pictures show the boy engaged in pranks with officers, or in a striped bathing suit, lying in the mud on the banks of the Dnieper while his father stands over him with a spade, as if about to bury him. It all looks rather a lark. We would think we were viewing someone's holiday snaps rather than a failing military campaign, and indeed the last days of a regime and a family that was heading for disaster and oblivion. Yet both Nicholas and Alexis must have benefitted from this time together. The Tsar genuinely found it helpful to have his son's company.

In the midst of dismal times, an almost comical event occurred. Nicholas was awarded a medal for bravery. One night late in 1916, he was undertaking a morale-boosting tour of a section of the Front when his car was caught in the open during an air-raid. He was actually in some danger for a matter of a few minutes before Russian aircraft counter-attacked and drove off the enemy. The Tsar was praised for his calm demeanour. This may have been no more than his customary lack of visible feeling, or he may genuinely have sought to set an example to those around him, or perhaps after a lifetime spent under suspended death sentence from bomb or bullet he had developed a genuine coolness when under duress. Whatever the reason the local commander, General Ivanov, asked him on behalf of the St George Council if he would accept nomination for the Cross of St George. Nicholas was delighted – there was no attempt to hide his feelings this time – though he modestly protested that he had been no more at risk than anyone else who had been there. The Order of St George was a much-coveted honour. Its highest form – 1st Class – was equivalent to the Victoria Cross or the Congressional Medal of Honor. It had been founded by his ancestress, Catherine the Great, but Romanovs could not simply help themselves to it and even the Tsar could not put his own name forward. He was to receive the lowest grade – 4th Class, perhaps on a par with Britain's Conspicuous Gallantry Medal – but he was intensely proud of this. Though his chest was covered in medals, this was the only one he had actually earned on his own merits. It was pinned on him by General Ivanov and he would wear it on his uniform for the rest of his life. He lamented that the Empress had not been there to witness the occasion, and she would entirely have understood, for she confided to Anna Vyrubova that the only time in her life that she had felt proud had been when she was awarded her nursing diploma. The Tsarevich was awarded the St George Medal at the same time his father received the Cross, and for the same reason; he too had been present during the air-raid.

The war dragged on. Its third wretched winter came. The population was sick of the fighting, of the grinding down of its armies and the endlessly continuing loss of men. Transport no longer ran with even semi-regularity. Inflation was spiralling upward and making many things unaffordable for the majority of the population. People were having to sell their possessions, or live on a single daily meal. While there would be even greater hardship a generation later in the German siege of Leningrad, this was the worst suffering Russia had lived through since the Napoleonic Wars. Though every section of society hated the autocracy it was, incredibly, the upper classes – the 'Court clique', the aristocracy and the gentry – that disliked Nicholas the most. Their passionate and growing hatred would leave him without a single section of society to defend him. The autocracy, which had claimed complete power and loyalty from its subjects, had then failed to do anything that would justify these things. As one commentator put it: 'The present power is incapable of overcoming the chaos, because it is itself the source of the chaos.' Under the stress of war and the resulting breakdown of normality and order, the whole of Russia – all social classes – had become 'politicised'. So many were dissatisfied with the existing government that a coup seemed inevitable, and would have been welcomed almost universally. And then, one night in December 1916, what seemed a miracle. Rasputin, the symbol of everything that was wrong in Russia, was put to death by a small conspiracy involving the Imperial Family (Grand Duke Dmitri) and the high aristocracy (Prince Felix Yussupov).

Rasputin was shrewd and well aware of his unpopularity. He was killed by men he considered friends, whom he trusted enough to spend an evening with. The setting was the cellar of Yussupov's family home – a colossal palace – on the Moika Canal. The pretext was a small supper party at which the staretz, who arrived drunk, was given food that had been treated with cyanide (almond cakes that would disguise the distinctive smell). When these failed to take effect, Yussupov, who like the other conspirators was in a state of considerable agitation, shot Rasputin in the back at point-blank range with a revolver, several times. Though he seemed to be dead, he came to life and began crawling up the steps from the cellar and out into the stable yard. Here he was beaten repeatedly over the head with the nearest blunt object that had been available – a paperweight. Once dead his body was wrapped in a blanket, put in an automobile, then driven to the Neva and dumped through a hole in the ice. When he was found, several days later, it was discovered at the post-mortem that he had still been alive when he had entered the water.

Yussupov, who would survive the Revolution and live until 1967, would ever afterward be known as 'the man who killed Rasputin', and would be admired by some for his attempt to save Russia. He himself had the immediate problem of meeting the Empress, who summoned him to Tsarskoe Selo. She asked him outright if he were responsible for, or involved in, the incident which had occurred at his home. He solemnly swore to her that he had had nothing to do with it.

At the beginning of January 1917 the Tsar returned to Tsarskoe Selo to comfort the Empress following the murder. Observers noticed that he made no comment on hearing the news. Despite the genuine grief of the Empress, he seemed light-hearted, almost visibly happy. He undoubtedly felt that a weight had been lifted from his shoulders. Though his son's future would presumably be more difficult without the man who had been able to cure his attacks, Nicholas had realised how much the presence of the staretz had damaged the monarchy. Alexandra, needless to say, was utterly distraught. Not only had she lost the guidance of one whom she considered invaluable, she also feared for the future of her family and country. Rasputin, whose pronouncements were not to be disregarded, had prophesied that if he died the dynasty would fall. In the midst of a terrible war and a deteriorating situation, it required no great imagination to envisage this. The next time her son had a serious attack and there was no one with the skill to save him or the spiritual power to pray for him, the dynasty could fall anyway. She was to have Rasputin buried beside a church that she had founded in the park at Tsarskoe Selo, but it would not be his resting place for long. One of the first acts of soldiers after the Revolution would be to dig up his corpse and burn it.

The aftermath of his death brought a last, brief moment of happiness and optimism to Russia. As the news had spread, firstly of his disappearance and then of his undoubted, confirmed death, the country took on the mood of a patriotic holiday. Church bells rang, prayers of thanks were offered – crowds even gathered to kneel and sing hymns in the streets outside the homes of Yussupov and of Grand Duke Dmitri. They also sang the national anthem 'God Save the Tsar'. People in the streets were grinning openly, shouting the news and congratulating strangers. Might it even be possible that the tide would turn in the war? With the removal of this evil presence would the Empress with her presumed German sympathies lose all power to harm Russia? The future could surely not be worse than the present. These last moments of Imperial Russia were to be blessed, at least, by a brief false dawn.

Meanwhile, Nicholas had entirely underestimated the nature of the war and its effect on his people. Because his priority was to persist in the conflict for his country's prestige and for the sake of its allies, he paid far less attention than he should have to the effect that shortages, constant defeats and the loss of millions was having. The sight of the monarch – and even his son – apparently sharing the hardships of the soldiers was not nearly enough to make up for the negative aspects of the war. While many Russians agreed with their ruler that the struggle must be prosecuted at all costs, their numbers were diminishing all the time. The peasantry, in particular, had become weary of the conflict by the second winter. If they should mutiny, Russia's cause would be lost. He would get the entire blame for what was coming. Other than among a small part of the aristocracy that had known his friendship and experienced his charm in pre-war days, he had scarcely a single friend or admirer anywhere.

CHAPTER TWENTY-FOUR

Apocalypse

The single most important element in fostering revolution was hunger. The natural hardship of a Russian winter was made infinitely worse by a lack of basic foodstuffs. Bread, potatoes, vegetables were rationed in the cities and periodically unobtainable – yet the rich could afford to eat well and restaurants were still open. Food was known to be stored in warehouses, both for future distribution and for the benefit of profiteers and corrupt officials. Nothing would drive the populace to riot more urgently than their desperate hunger. Nothing would make the troops and police who were sent to control them more likely to take their side than sympathy with that condition.

In addition to the misery and the shortages brought by the war, Russians were deprived even of the comfort of the bottle, for at the start of hostilities the Tsar had proclaimed a nationwide prohibition of alcohol. This was the first time such a measure had been taken on a national scale, pre-dating the more famous American experiment by half a decade.

The Revolution began on 23 February 1917. Demonstrations began, and became more widespread. Within three days Petrograd was in a state not of seething unrest but of deliberate defiance. By that time soldiers were refusing to obey orders and were taking the side of the rioters. With that essential change, the second great Russian revolution had begun. Attempts to draft troops in from outside the city could not succeed because there were not the means of getting them there. The whole of Petrograd seemed to be in flames. Black smoke, and the smell of burning, hung in a pall over the city. As in 1905 there were shots and explosions, the rattle of machine-guns, the crack of rifles, the flash of tracer and even the distant boom of artillery. The streets were unsafe and yet curiosity drove people outdoors, to find out where things were happening, to gather in the raw wind and listen to speeches or rumours, to see what damage had been done, to stare at the corpses of policemen – a sight so unusual, and a testimony so eloquent, to a state that had lost control.

One rumour that proved to be true was that the Cossacks of the Imperial Guard had gone over to the Revolution. For a few days the city wavered as the direction of events remained uncertain, but even the police – hated by the mob and thus with little hope of being spared in any showdown with the people – were now refusing to obey orders. It gradually became apparent, during long days of demonstrations and long nights of gunfire, that the autocracy was over. By the beginning of March it was absolutely clear to anyone in command of a district or a military unit that this was not simply a series of riots but a widespread, groundswell revolution. There could be no restoration of order because the whole country seemed to be following this path and supporters of the old government had simply melted away.

There was a serious lack of transport to bring food to the cities, and this caused the riots on 8 March – the day that would see Nicholas's arrest – that fully fanned the flames of revolt. Russia's second revolution. Troops from the garrison joined the mob, while others travelled to Petrograd to support the insurgency, and order broke down. The President of the Duma, Rodzianko, sent an urgent message to Nicholas asking that he appoint a Prime Minister who would command general confidence, but the telegram went unanswered. Nicholas instead sent his order to General Ivanov to quell the disorder, but the troops that were dispatched could not reach the city because the lines were blocked. On the fourteenth the Provisional Government was then established by the Duma's Provisional Committee. Alexander Kerensky, a lawyer, was already *de facto* the new ruler of Russia.

Even a member of the Imperial family – Grand Duke Kiril – had marched with his troops to the Tauride Palace and pledged the loyalty of all of them to the new government – an act of family betrayal for which the rest of the Romanovs would not forgive him or his descendants (he himself would flee abroad and thus survive the Revolution).

Nicholas suspended the Duma because of the violence of many of the speeches there. He also refused to grant increased power to ministers, but it was too late for these measures to make any difference. The Tsar's views were already largely irrelevant.

Alexandra wrote to him: 'You are the lord and master of Russia. Be Peter the Great, be Ivan the Terrible, Emperor Paul – crush them all! Why do they hate me? Because they know I have a strong will and that when I am convinced of the rightness of something then I do not change my mind.' This was not why she was hated, but what in any case did these stirring words matter? His soldiers were no longer able to put down disorder.

The first of the regiments that went over to the Revolution was the Pavlovsky Guards. How could this, and other legendary units, betray the dynasty to which they had for centuries shown such conspicuous devotion? The answer was that by 1917 nothing remained of these but the names. They had long ceased to wear the parade uniforms that had brightened the streets of the capital. Russian casualties over three years, estimated at nine million but probably higher, had included an entire generation of professional soldiers. The aristocratic officers were dead, as were the old soldiers and sergeants of the peacetime army, or they were in Germany, where the number of Russian prisoners of war was larger than the entire armed forces of some countries. The ranks were now filled with young wartime conscripts (and any notion that recruits must have snub noses was long-since forgotten!). These men were not imbued with any sense of loyalty or tradition. They had not known a Russian victory, only the constant discouragement of defeat. They viewed their officers, from the highest to the lowest, as incompetent. They did not believe in the possibility of winning and – influenced by propaganda that became more virulent as the months passed – they saw no point in victory anyway, if it would mean only a continuation of their country's bankrupt system of government. They were barely even trained, so they lacked in any case the skills to take on an enemy. They had not guarded the Imperial Family, and felt no connection with it. Their officers were far removed from the type of languid young noblemen with whom Nicholas had once served. Such was the desperate shortage of manpower that sergeants and corporals had been commissioned. These too did not identify with the old order but with the public beyond the barrack gates. Like them, they were motivated by resentment that Russians starved while there were warehouses filled with food that was not made available. Without the loyalty of such regiments, the Throne was helpless.

The Romanovs were not in the city. Alexandra was at Tsarskoe Selo and had not been seen for months. The Grand Duchesses were with her. The Dowager Empress, whose popularity was undiminished, had long-since left the capital and was living in Kiev. The Tsar, of course, was at the Front. When disturbances had begun he had issued, by telegram, a preposterous command: 'I order that the disorders in the capital cease at once . . . ' No one was in a position to make this happen, if indeed anyone was listening. His Majesty set out by train for Petersburg, but his government had no control over the rail network and he could no longer go where he pleased. His train did not even reach the station at Pskov before it was diverted, on orders from the Railwaymen's Union, to a little town called Dno. And therefore he sat, for the last days and hours of his reign, in an obscure siding, waiting for whatever would happen next. For the first time since he had acceded to the throne, he was not informed of events, sent reports or given access to sources of information. He did not fully realise it yet, but Russia had finished with him.

On 2 March the Duma sent a delegation headed by two deputies – Alexander Gushkov and Vasily Shulgin – to Pskov with the clear purpose of telling the Tsar that he must abdicate. The military commanders, who were aware of the volatile state of their men, were as unanimous as everyone else in demanding this as the most fundamental requirement. If they expected on the part of the monarch emotion, anger or argument they were mistaken. They found him weary and resigned. He was not looking to save his position but to get the country, if he could, through this dangerous period of instability and he would clearly do whatever they felt was necessary to defuse the crisis. He merely asked: 'Do you think matters will be in any way improved for Russia if I relinquish the throne?' When told, firmly and by all those whose opinions were represented, that he should go at once, he immediately agreed. He did not argue, or hesitate for long. He had no thought of his dynasty coming to an end, he simply agreed to pass the Crown to the next-heir-but-one, his brother. He had done his best to keep the autocracy going. He was as stoical as always, showing little emotion. A document was prepared and, at three o'clock that afternoon, he signed it. It read:

> In the days of the great struggle against the foreign enemies, who for nearly three years have tried to enslave our fatherland, the Lord God has been pleased to send down on Russia a new heavy trial. Internal popular disturbances threaten to have a disastrous effect on the future conduct of this persistent war. The destiny of Russia, the honour of our heroic army, the welfare of the people and the whole future of our dear fatherland demand that the war should be brought to a glorious conclusion whatever the cost. The cruel enemy is making his last efforts, and already the hour approaches when our glorious army together with our gallant allies will crush him. In these decisive days in the life of Russia, We thought it Our duty of conscience to facilitate for Our people the closest union possible and a consolidation of all national forces for the speedy attainment of victory. In agreement with the Imperial Duma We have thought it well to renounce the throne of the Russian Empire and to lay down the supreme power. As We do not wish to part from Our beloved son, we transmit the succession to Our beloved brother, the Grand Duke Michael Alexandrovich, and give him Our blessing to mount the Throne of the Russian Empire. We direct Our brother to conduct the affairs of state in full and inviolate union with the representatives of the people in the legislative bodies on those principles which will be established by them, and on which He will take an inviolable oath, in the name of Our dearly beloved homeland. We call on Our

faithful sons of the fatherland to fulfil their sacred duty to the fatherland, to obey the Tsar in the heavy moment of national trials, and to help Him, together with the representatives of the people, to guide the Russian Empire on the road to victory, welfare and glory.

May the Lord God help Russia!

Could he, with a flash of inspiration and the courage to defy powerful opinion at home and abroad, have announced that Russia was suing for peace? Could he have taken his country out of the conflict, giving his people the gift of peace? No. The war was unstoppable on those terms. Had he opted out, Germany would have imposed a strict and punitive set of peace terms that would have cost Russia considerable amounts of sovereign territory, such as the whole of Poland and land in the Ukraine and Belorussia. The extent of this humiliation can be seen clearly in the peace treaty that Lenin's Bolshevik government *did* make with the Central Powers in order to leave the war. The surrender of land caused outrage at home, even among those who supported the new regime, and complainants were mollified only by the Communist belief that worldwide revolution was about to break out and that all treaties – and national boundaries – would be nullified by a new world order. Nicholas would never have bargained away the lands he had inherited. He would never have accepted the humiliation of an imposed and draconian peace settlement. It would not have saved his country or his throne. He would have been as hated, and condemned, as he was to be in any case. He would probably have been deposed by some cabal of patriots, perhaps imprisoned and tried. And events might have played out in something of the manner that they were to do in reality. It is important to remember that, from the moment the European war began and Russia mobilised her forces, the fate of the Tsar, his dynasty and his Empire was sealed.

He had come a long way during the years of his reign. He had been for three years at the helm of a nation fighting for its life. He now

considered only what was best for Russia. He did not try to negoti-
ate, to improve his position or bargain for his security. He showed no
desire to save his skin, lessen his discomfort or try to make demands
for safe-conduct or access to wealth. He gave up everything, including
his own basic rights, at once to ease the pain of Russia. Though he
had no choice in the matter, let us not forget that this renunciation of
the throne was a selfless and a very noble act. He felt that by doing so
he might avoid an internal war and a prolonged period of unrest (both
were to happen anyway.) His attitude was to be mentioned – extraordinarily – in a sermon in Moscow in 1921, by Russia's senior churchman, Archbishop Tikhon: 'He could have found himself security and
a relatively peaceful life abroad after the abdication, but he did not do
that, desiring to suffer together with Russia.'

He passed the throne to Grand Duke Michael (who thus became
Tsar Michael, giving the last Romanov ruler the same name as the
first) but his brother, who had met with a delegation from the Duma,
was not willing to accept. He had stated that he would ascend the
throne only with the approval of all political parties – a piece of nonsense, for would the Bolsheviks be expected to countenance such a
thing? Not only was their support out of the question, but he was told
his personal safety could not be guaranteed. That was discouragement
enough. Though he was nominally Emperor for the single day of 3
March, he let go the reins of government that his family had held for
three hundred and four years. Nicholas could not hide his anger and
disappointment toward those in his family who had let him down,
especially his brother, who had made no more than a token attempt
to preserve the throne. With a background untainted either by contact with Rasputin – he had not even lived in Russia for some years
before 1914 – and with no direct responsibility for wartime disasters
(in fact he had won a medal for bravery), the pleasant but inconse-
quential Grand Duke might have made a credible Tsar, provided he
had accepted the notion of being a nominal or titular ruler. Neither
he nor the Provisional Government had the time or the willingness to
examine this option. The Romanovs were finished anyway.

The new government held no ill will. There was no question of punishing the Tsar's family. He himself might stand trial in due course, so that his 'record in office' could be examined, but that could wait until the country had stabilised and there was the opportunity to think of such matters. The vast wealth of the Romanovs would be needed by the new state, so there could be no question of allowing that out of the country, but the family members themselves were, in all probability, to leave. They would be a distraction, a divider of loyalties, and should be removed. It was assumed that, with their network of relatives abroad, they would find someone to give them sanctuary – after all, even the German Kaiser, at the head of Russia's enemies, was anxious about them!

Nicholas sat in his train for a few days longer before he was allowed to go home. His mother came to see him at Mogilev station, and they spent some time together in private – and no doubt very emotional – conversation. What must her feelings have been? How would even her sainted husband have coped with disaster on this scale? Did she reproach herself that she had not tried harder to have Rasputin removed from the Court? She would be among the fortunate. She would be far from the capital when the Bolsheviks gained power, and would escape with her life. She would eventually learn, with the rest of the world, the fate of her two sons and of the grandchildren she adored. Interestingly she would refuse, for the rest of her life, to believe that the Family was dead.

When she and Nicholas parted it was for the last time. They would never meet again. He was, on 8 March, placed under arrest on the orders of the country's new Provisional Government and sent back to Tsarskoe Selo under escort. As a divisive and blameworthy figure, he was best removed both from harm's way and from the public eye. It was envisaged by the new authorities that he would remain under a benign but firm house arrest until perhaps the autumn, by which time someone would have decided what to do with him. Because there would be elements that wished him harm, the Alexander Palace must be heavily guarded, and at the request of the still-functioning Minister for the Court, a contingent of 1,500 men – for the moment, loyal – was deployed.

The Tsar's train moved slowly through the winter landscape. The only comfort available to its occupant was that he would see his family again. When the long journey was finally over and he was brought to the familiar little station at Tsarskoe Selo late at night, the majority of those in his suite who had travelled with him disappeared into the darkness as soon as the passengers disembarked. These servants and Court officials wanted to distance themselves both physically and figuratively at the first opportunity from the former Emperor and his regime.

As all students of history are taught, revolutions do not happen because a force rises up and overthrows the existing order. They happen because the old order collapses and leaves a vacuum. Without question, the tsarist regime had collapsed. It had received too many heavy blows – military defeat, loss of morale, lack of leadership, shortage of food – to be able to stand. From his position at the Front Nicholas did not realise, and neither did the Empress in her seclusion at Tsarskoe Selo, that the country they knew no longer existed – that the cities with their numerical minority of the population were, by challenging the authorities in their streets, capable of taking control of the whole of Russia. They had somehow, in spite of the evidence mounting all around them, failed to see how serious matters had become. The crash was therefore going to come as a terrible shock to them.

Reuters reported on 17 March, in a dispatch that gave an outside perspective on what was happening: 'There has been a great upheaval of popular sentiment in Russia, which has resulted in the abdication of the Tsar. This movement was aimed at pro-German influences, and established the Duma as the controlling spirit of the country. It also voices the determination of the nation to see the war to a triumphal conclusion for the Allies.'

Nicholas made a final visit to Stavka, to wish his officers farewell. He was greeted with ostentatious respect, though he no longer had any official status, and his former comrades lined up to kiss his hand. All were in a state of deep emotion. The war was over for their former chief, and their own part in it was in abeyance. This was an end to conflict that no one had seen or possibly been able to anticipate when events had begun in 1914 – an outcome that promised neither victory nor defeat but the disintegration of the country and its institutions without even having been conquered by the enemy. Though the ex-Tsar's famous emotional restraint kept his own tears in check, many of the men wept visibly and some, apparently, almost fainted. Their sorrow was overwhelming, not only at parting from their ruler and witnessing the end of the dynasty but with shame at abandoning their allies, leaving the task unfinished, losing, in the eyes of their counterparts in the other nations' armies, professional honour, and seeing three years of enormous sacrifice – and the lives of so many friends – wasted. There could only be fear for what the future would bring. All that had been familiar to these officers throughout their lives and careers was disappearing. It was Armageddon. The end of the world.

The Tsar's last message to the Army was as follows:

Carry on for the sake and honour of Russia, and do not forget our Allies are struggling hard in the cause of right and justice. This is the last time I shall address you, my well-beloved troops. After the abdication I have effected in my own name and in that of my son, the supreme power has passed into the hands of the Provisional Government, formed on the initiative of the Duma of the Empire. May God help it to lead Russia along the road to glory and prosperity. May God help you, too, my gallant troops, to defend our country successfully against the inveterate enemy.

For two and a half years you have borne continuously the hardship of military service; much blood has been shed, great efforts have been made, and the time is at hand when Russia, bound to her valiant Allies by the common desire of victory, will triumph over the last efforts of the enemy. This war, like none other, must be carried on until victory, final and complete, has been won. Whoever at this time thinks of peace, whoever desires it, is a traitor to his country. I know that every honest soldier thinks the same.

So do your duty, defend valiantly our great country, obey the Provisional Government, obey your officers, and remember that any slackening of the bonds of discipline gives an advantage to the enemy. I firmly believe that an unbounded love of your great country still burns in your hearts. God bless you all, and may the great martyr St George lead you to victory.

NIKOLAI

Though the name of St George would still have carried weight among a people that remained, for the time being, devout, it is most unlikely that any words from the Tsar would have inspired general obedience. It mattered little, for this message did not reach the Russian armies. It was suppressed by the new government, and his last public utterance was lost. There would be no final words, in the manner of Napoleon, from the Emperor to his troops. In this case, the Emperor was already an irrelevance, consigned to history. Russia had far more to worry about now than its honour, and his appeal already sounded ridiculously out of touch. His determination to see the war continue was in any case contrary to the wishes of the millions at the Front, and their desire for peace would sweep away not only tsardom but its replacement, the Provisional Government. The Army was now in the hands of common soldiers who openly disobeyed orders, set up their own councils to make decisions, defied, assaulted, and murdered their officers, and deserted in their thousands.

At Tsarskoe Selo, meanwhile, there was near chaos. The children were coming down with measles and their mother was distracted with this at the very time that the tidings came of her husband's abdication, delivered by the Grand Duke Paul. It brought her to physical collapse, but by an effort of will she kept the news from her son and daughters for the time being. Beyond the sick-room and nurseries, the servants were vanishing and water and electricity were cut off. There were shots in the park one night when a hostile force approached, but the Palace guards drove them off. Alexandra, already feeling like a prisoner, burned her private papers, including all the letters she had exchanged with Queen Victoria. She was visited by General Kornilov, now Governor of Petrograd, with the news that her husband was returning and a proposal that, once the children had recovered, the Family be sent to Murmansk, the ice-free northern port, and thence to England. 'Do what you will,' she answered, 'I am at your disposal.'

Nicholas had arrived home to find the Palace in darkness and his children ill. When reunited with Alexandra, his self-restraint for the first time left him and he burst into tears. Yet he was to salvage what he could in terms of dignity and purpose. He insisted that the children carry on with their schooling, and actually took over instruction in history and geography.

The days that followed were racked with anxiety, of course. All of the household was under arrest, even if this confinement enabled them to live among their possessions and their familiar surroundings. They were subject to a range of petty humiliations, from the rudeness of guards to the restrictions on where they could walk. Although he had ceased to have any role in the war, Nicholas was still intently following its progress through the newspapers (including *The Times*) that he received, if irregularly. He would have been elated by the initial success of the summer offensive and then horrified by the retreat that followed. After that summer the news was always, always bad.

Nevertheless, he showed a remarkably positive attitude. He adjusted far better to the new conditions than Alexandra, who had always been more regal than he. She retreated further into her world of illness and worship, and this is entirely understandable, for reality was becoming unbearable. Mysticism would be a great comfort to her.

The calm that Nicholas showed – the lack of hatred, the quiet determination to make the best of circumstances that continually got worse, the complete absence of self-pity or self-justification made this last phase of his life, without question, his finest hour. His patient nature was revealed as the gift it was. It enabled him to cope, and the example he set over days and weeks and months would inspire all the others. Without it, they would have suffered perhaps far greater anguish. It was as if Fate had been preparing him all his life for this ordeal and that through him others would be blessed.

The Tsarina had exclaimed, on hearing of the defection of members of the naval Garde Equipage: 'My sailors – my own sailors – I can't believe it! They are all our personal friends!' This was true, and expressed the horrible sense of violated trust that must have been one of the hardest things to bear. The Imperial Family often recorded their interest in those who worked for them. 'They were all friends,' Grand Duchess Olga recalled, 'I don't think they eavesdropped, but they knew far more about us than we did ourselves.' Their devotion was taken for granted and respect was reciprocated. As we have seen, among the crew of the *Standart* they were especially informal. They associated this group with travel and holidays and they shared an intimacy with them within the confines of the vessel that was not possible anywhere else. They depended upon these people and in return they trusted them. In the park at Tsarskoe Selo, these sailors had guarded the lakes, rowed the boats for them, even – in the Family's winter outings – helped them to build snow mountains or lay out toboggan runs. The sudden desertion of those who had shared their amusements and whose task it was to protect their safety will have been a grievously wounding blow.

The soldiers of the revolutionary 'First Rifle Regiment' who replaced them, in the Alexander Palace and in the park outside, were a frightening vision of anarchy – a terrible, impossible-to-ignore, symbol of change. Perhaps in no country in the world had the superficialities of military life been taken to such extremes as in the Russian Empire. Officers and men, drilled to the precision of a *corps de ballet*, in uniforms of peacock splendour, had snapped to attention at the hint of any passing Royal, saluting with a flash of sabre or bayonet.

The rooms and corridors of their home had formerly been guarded by men from regiments that were steeped in the glory of Russia – Cossacks in their lamb's-wool hats and sweeping blue or scarlet coats, and Palace Grenadiers, a formation of veterans with tall bearskins and patriarchal beards, kindly and time-tested servants of the dynasty. The uniforms had been packed away and the experienced members of these fine regiments had largely, inevitably, died in the war. Years of hardship and the resulting unrest had proved the loyalty of many to be false. Now in the same palace corridors, scruffy with lack of maintenance, were lounging, sneering, untidy men with unbuttoned tunics, dangling cigarettes, making ribald or obscene comments. The ex-Tsar was at least still known by the only title he had left – 'Mister Colonel' – but was sometimes also addressed, in a sinister echo of the French Revolution, as 'Citizen Romanov'.

Far beyond the railings of the Alexander Park, the news of Russia's revolution was greeted largely with relief and approval in the wider world. So long as the new government was willing to keep Russia in the war, her allies wished her well. It seemed possible that the country would now become a liberal democracy and join the community of similar nations. The United States, which was on the verge of entering the conflict, was now readier to do so as part of 'an alliance of democracies against an alliance of empires'. The British Labour Party sent a delegation, despite the dangers of international travel in wartime, to give its approval to the new state. One communication sent to Nicholas at this time was a telegram from the American Lewis J. Selznick. He was a Jew (his name was actually Zeleznik) who had been born in Kiev in 1870, had suffered in the pogroms of Alexander and had emigrated at the age of twelve. He had become a wealthy and successful film-distributor, and his son would be the producer of *Gone With the Wind*. The message read:

NEW YORK VIA WESTERN UNION—WHEN I WAS A POOR BOY IN KIEV SOME OF YOUR POLICEMEN WERE NOT KIND TO ME AND MY PEOPLE STOP I CAME TO AMERICA AND PROSPERED STOP NOW HEAR WITH REGRET YOU ARE OUT

OF A JOB OVER THERE STOP FEEL NO ILLWILL WHAT YOUR POLICEMEN DID
SO IF YOU WILL COME NEW YORK CAN GIVE YOU FINE POSITION ACTING IN
PICTURES STOP SALARY NO OBJECT REPLY MY EXPENSE STOP REGARDS YOU
AND FAMILY—LEWIS J. SELZNICK

It is unlikely that its recipient saw the humour in this.

CHAPTER TWENTY-FIVE

Exile

When Kerensky told the Czar of the proposed transfer he explained the necessity by saying that the Provisional Government had resolved to take energetic measures against the Bolsheviks; this would result in a period of disturbance of which the Imperial family might be the first victims.

Pierre Gilliard

The months they initially spent in captivity were, to a surprising extent, an experience that Nicholas and his family could endure. They had always led a sheltered life behind the park railings at Tsarskoe Selo. Now it was equally cut-off, though for different reasons. They were together, in the company they loved most (besides the seven of them a few faithful officials and retainers had stayed). The largely self-contained unit that they had always been meant that, to a great extent, they did not miss the society of others. After years of absence and of stress and preoccupation, the Tsar was relieved of work and worry that had always been beyond his capabilities and was free to spend his days with his wife and children. Though he bitterly regretted the attitude to the war shown by the new regime, he must have known a sense of relief that the burden had been lifted from his shoulders and the responsibility passed to others. There were no longer the trappings of court life, but then these things had been disappearing in any case through the privations of war, and were missed less than they might otherwise have been. There were guards in the park, no longer deferential and no longer there to protect but to imprison, but Kerensky, the head of the Provisional Government, had decreed that no physical abuse was to be meted out to the Family and they could rely for the time being on his protection. It was therefore still possible to enjoy the simple pleasures in which Nicholas and his children had always indulged – walks in the woods and gardens, the chopping of logs and the shovelling of snow.

It was deeply ironic that these had always been Nicholas's preferred pastimes, and that in grimly different circumstances he was carrying on with them, almost as if nothing had changed. There were also new experiences such as the planting of potatoes. The Family, and their fellow prisoners, took on the task of transforming the parkland nearest the palace into a vegetable garden. This proved to be a major undertaking but also a source of interest and satisfaction. Guards sometimes became involved in their tasks, sharing the labour of digging and carrying. An officer was always on hand to observe, but would often be genial company. The Romanovs seem to have enjoyed the novelty of working at agriculture on their former estate, and for captives having something useful to do must have helped. There was always an undercurrent of fear, a dread of the unknown and a helplessness that those now in authority either hated them or would have to defer to the wishes of others who did, but where it was possible this family, dominated by spirited young people, made the most of any opportunities for enjoyment or normality. Pictures show that they kept their sense of humour to a remarkable degree. They even had their picture taken, with their guards, next to the ornamental bridge that marked the boundary beyond which they were not allowed to go. The girls, who had all had to have their hair shaved off as part of the treatment for measles, were so lacking in vanity that they had themselves photographed with bald heads.

As a captive, Nicholas – perhaps for the first time in his life – came into his own. Convinced always that it was his lot in life to suffer, he was now doing so. His self-contained nature enabled him to endure, with a surprising amount of patient resignation, the monotony and the constant and escalating humiliations. His diary entries remained largely laconic and matter-of-fact, chronicling the weather, his modest activities, his mundane conversations with his guards. He always wore military uniform, and now this took the form of a simple soldier's khaki shirt. It made him look much the same as his captors.

His deep personal faith endowed him with a sense that whatever happened was the will of God, and though this did not bring actual contentment, it certainly chimed with his natural fatalism. His wife and children seem to have shared this feeling to a large extent. Piety was one of the few things left to the Imperial Family and their observance was punctilious. The rooms in which they would be imprisoned, whether in Tsarskoe Selo or Tobolsk or Ekaterinburg, were hung with icons and furnished with makeshift altars. They were served by local priests who were allowed to visit them in their quarters. The Empress had, of course, always been intensely devout and she retreated yet further into the comforts of religion.

Whatever it was that sustained them, whether hope of rescue, change of circumstance or a growing feeling of martyrdom, it was deeply impressive. The members of the Family had had a great deal of public criticism – even to the extent of cartoons showing the Grand Duchesses intimate with Rasputin – but from those around them had had nothing but respect and deference. Now, deprived of liberty, spied upon and insulted, they showed no hatred and no obvious self-pity. They became steadily more other-worldly. Their conduct in the final weeks and months of their lives was beyond reproach – a holiness that is inspiring.

They had access to some newspapers, both domestic and foreign, and were able to follow not only the course of the war but reaction to their own deposition. Nicholas was deeply hurt by the gloating of liberal countries at his misfortune. He also despaired of the defeatism that was apparent as public opinion turned increasingly against continuation of the war. He continued to feel responsible to Russia's allies, even though he was powerless.

The Family endured the long months of winter and spring, awaiting events, as did the rest of Russia. There was no thought of escape at this stage in their confinement. They did not see this phase of Russia's misfortunes as permanent – and after all there was no precedent for what was happening – so that Nicholas might well have had some future role to play in the state and must be available when the time came. Though they were undeniably uncomfortable, they did not feel their lives were in direct peril, and of course they assumed that negotiations were and would be going on to arrange a temporary home – perhaps a brief foreign exile – until the situation became more stable.

Some things were harder to bear than others. Nicholas was understandably mortified when told that he could not be in the same room as his wife, except at meals, which were thus the only times of day at which they could speak. The Empress was overwhelmingly identified in the imagination of the Russian public with intrigue and malevolent influence over her husband. Even though he no longer held any power or position the country was still in the war, and she suffered the equivalent of being interned as an enemy alien, as well as the lingering stigma of her association with Rasputin. The Tsar himself was equally tainted, because he was identified with military failure, and of course the Family represented a focus for any revival of loyalty – such as an uprising by officers – that might attempt to topple the government. They were a liability, and must be kept as quiet and as invisible as possible.

Kerensky, who was Minister of Justice as well as the dominant personality in the Government, was obliged to interview the Empress about alleged pro-German activities. He was not without human sympathy for the Family. Their safety had been promised. Their guards, whatever their manners, at least protected the Romanovs from worse. Kerensky knew that though other countries had empathised with the overthrow of tsardom any mistreatment of the Imperial Family would cause an outcry. He had abolished the death penalty so that, if put on trial, Nicholas would not suffer too draconian a punishment.

Beyond the palace gates, their country had become a place of frightening uncertainty. The Provisional Government, an experiment that had the daunting task of setting up a new state while in the midst of war, was not going to prove strong enough to survive. Though tsarism with its incompetence and lack of direction had gone, the country's most urgent problems – the conflict, with its huge losses of sons and brothers; the price of food, the shortage of goods in the shops – had not been solved. In the spring, Kerensky became both Prime Minister and War Minister. He thus took on himself the same double burden that Nicholas had carried, that of running the country and the war. There was to be a major offensive in the summer of 1917, but the public was sick of the fighting and did not believe in victory. Any government that continued the war would risk losing popularity as soon as an alternative policy was possible.

The Bolshevik party, which intended to provide that alternative, was low on funds and lacking in support and organisation. Its leader, Vladimir Lenin, was charismatic and determined, but he was stuck in exile on the other side of Europe, and travel was impossible. The Bolsheviks had spectacularly missed history's opportunity.

Or perhaps not. Berlin was well aware that a government led by Lenin would end the war as soon as possible on virtually any terms, and that Germany could therefore not only make big territorial gains without having to fight for them, but would be free to concentrate resources on the Western Front, with a very realistic chance of winning there. It was a stroke of genius, from a German perspective, to retrieve Lenin from exile in Zurich and convey him in secret, in a locked and shuttered train, across German territory. Smuggled the rest of the way, he arrived in Petrograd on the night of 3 April 1917. Soviet mythology would subsequently portray his arrival as a triumph, with huge crowds listening as he addressed them from atop an armoured car.

Whatever his reception, there was to be no sudden overthrow. Weeks and months passed while he undertook the work of organising, attracting members, gaining influence in the local government, the Petrograd Soviet. Meanwhile the summer offensive went ahead, a last desperate attempt by Russia to win the war on creditable terms. The troops surged forward – then were driven back in confusion. It was yet another disaster, and it was the final straw. A massive demonstration filled the streets of Petrograd after the defeat in July. The slogan on the banners: 'Land, Peace and Bread!' summed up the only priorities people had left.

It was still not Lenin's moment. For obvious reasons he was seen as being in league with the Germans, and might well have been assassinated. He fled to Finland, disguised as a railwayman.

Nevertheless, members of his party were gradually coming to dominate the Soviet – so much so that government troops were sent to suppress this body, but made common cause instead. The party was now so strong that the Provisional Government could not maintain order without its support, and the workers of Petrograd were provided with weaponry. The city was now filled with armed and dangerous men.

And then, in October, came the coup. Suddenly one night the cruiser *Aurora* appeared in the Neva, some way downstream from the Winter Palace, in which the Provisional Government had established itself and in which its leaders were then meeting. She fired shots. This was the signal for an armed Bolshevik mob to rush across the great square and 'storm' the building. In reality there was almost no resistance. The Palace was guarded by a combination of female soldiers and cadets, and both groups surrendered without resistance. Again, this scene was later made much of by Soviet propaganda – the image of an unstoppable, surging force, seizing power and vanquishing tyranny ('storming the Winter Palace' is a metaphor for such an overthrow of authority or privilege). Ironically, more people were injured in the re-enactment for Soviet cinema than in the real event – but it meant that the Bolsheviks were now in power. Kerensky fled.

CHAPTER TWENTY-SIX

Captives

For those at Tsarskoe Selo this changed everything. The guarantees of their safety and the abolition of the death penalty that would have protected the Tsar were now void. The people with whom they had dealt – the respectful officials and ministers who were largely familiar from pre-revolutionary times and who showed a genuine concern for their wellbeing, were now gone. Instead, they would be dealing with unknowns who would have, at best, no respect for them and at worst a desire for revenge. The Provisional Government did at least do one final thing for them. It decided that they would be moved from the volatile and highly dangerous environs of Petrograd, the centre of revolution, and sent to Siberia where they would be out of reach of the mob. To enable them to leave the area unnoticed, the vehicles in which they travelled were labelled, 'Japanese Red Cross Mission'.

Kerensky explained to Nicholas that they were too close to the capital, too accessible for extremists, too likely to influence or be affected by events in Petrograd. Should more radical elements triumph in this new Russia, they could be in considerable danger from mobs that could reach the little town in no more than half an hour. Better to put them safely beyond reach, at least until matters had settled down. The place chosen for this necessary exile was the Siberian town of Tobolsk, where they would have the use of the Governor's house. On 31 July the Family left their home, taking with them some pet dogs and accompanied by a group of loyal servants including a cook and several other domestic staff. With them too were Gilliard, the Swiss tutor (his English counterpart, Gibbes, would join them in exile later), the Tsar's physician, Doctor Botkin, and Nagorny, the sailor-nurse to the Tsarevich. Extraordinarily, from the moment they departed the Palace was at once to be treated as a museum – everything left exactly as it had been, including the contents of the cupboards and with books and objects littering the tables. Nicholas travelled surprisingly light. He dressed simply and therefore needed few clothes, and he showed little attachment to possessions. The ladies took much more luggage, including a great many belongings of sentimental importance – and a surprising quantity of jewels, which were hidden in their bags or about their persons. The journey was lengthy – three weeks or so – by rail and riverboat. The monotonous low fields and mudbanks through which their vessel steamed each day were often relieved by a cluster of roofs or the cupolas of a church or monastery. Once, it was the village of Pokrovskoe from which Rasputin had come, and Alexandra must have mused on his prophecy about the end of the dynasty. When their destination was reached, they were installed in the Governor's house.

Though watched, they were not uncomfortable. They looked out onto another big house, in which some of their suite were lodged, and across a square at the domes of the local church. Despite the high wooden fence that surrounded them, they were able to take part in the life of the town. Local people, who retained a high degree of loyalty to the throne, brought provisions for them day after day. Nuns from a nearby convent kept them supplied with eggs. They were allowed to attend the church, and people crowded to see them, kneeling or crossing themselves as the Romanovs walked, under guard, to and from the house. There were opportunities to stroll, and to exercise in the usual log-sawing manner, inside the fence, and indoors there was the continuation of their traditional pastime of reading aloud. Expecting to spend long periods in captivity, they had brought books to read. Now they devoured everything they could lay hands upon, and a surprising amount of it was English. They read one or two of Dickens's novels, which have always been popular in Russia, and even *The Fifth Form at St Dominic's*, an archetypal public school yarn. They received newspapers, though irregularly, and these included *The Times*, of which Nicholas was a long-standing reader. Surprisingly, their captivity included many touches of 'normality'. They had received large and regular gifts of money from monarchist members of the public and, though these decreased and largely dried up, they had enabled them to eat well and continue to employ servants. They still had their cameras and took pictures of each other and of their surroundings. They wrote and received letters, keeping in contact with friends. Alexis even had a playmate in Kolia Derevenko, the son of the family's doctor. At mealtimes they still had daily menus, handwritten beneath a printed imperial eagle.

The four younger children continued to have lessons with the tutors. Olga, now an adult and with nothing much to do, assisted with some teaching. Their rooms were decorated with familiar images – dozens of family photographs (in the room shared by the four girls there were pictures of the *Standart*) and the kind of knick-knacks beloved of people of that time. There was still happiness, of a sort, and a good deal of laughter, among the captives. At some moments they seemed almost like holidaymakers in a hotel who were trapped indoors by bad weather and forced to provide their own diversions.

The two tutors found a solution to boredom in the performance of plays. There were some playscripts among their books, and both Gibbes and Gilliard were of a theatrical bent. They decided that productions could be rehearsed on weekdays and performed on Sunday evenings – a brilliant means of building excitement and a sense of achievement. Gibbes even created elaborate programmes. Naturally, the younger generation threw themselves into these, but even the ex-Tsar allowed himself on one occasion to take part. He played the pompous and irritable Smirnov in Chekov's comedy *The Bear*. On another occasion, Anastasia brought the house down when a draught blew up her gown and revealed her underwear. These were the innocent pleasures of a family trying to forget the crushing reality of the present and the awful uncertainty of the future. They remained, however, as pious as always, and with the opening of Lent, 1918, the productions were abandoned as inappropriate. Instead, they attended to prayers and catechisms, but found that these, too, gave pleasure and filled the long hours.

While this was going on, Gibbes penned a letter to a colleague in England, a retired governess called Miss Jackson. Knowing that letters written by the Family and their staff would be read, he made the missive as innocent and matter-of-fact as possible. He described his surroundings and even helpfully drew a plan of the house to help her visualise it. It seems to have been sent on the assumption that it would be passed on to the British Royal Family and that some sort of assistance would result. As we have seen, it was expected by many that the Romanovs' relations would be making efforts on their behalf, and the Provisional Government had been in negotiations to make their departure possible. Nicholas and Alexandra did not envisage exile as permanent. In everything they wrote, there is the belief that the present troubles are temporary – a time of soul-testing hardship that would pass. Whether they imagined returning to the places or positions they had formerly occupied (they had a daydream of retiring to Livadia), they did not think of living permanently elsewhere. As months went by and no possibility of sanctuary was forthcoming the Family must, however, have felt yet more betrayed.

And they had reason, for internationally their friends had deserted them. France was their closest ally, but the country was in the convulsions of war and the Empress's German links would have caused hostility. Denmark was another possibility but, though neutral in the conflict it shared a border with Germany and was perhaps too close for comfort. Countries further afield might have helped – Spain, a neutral power and a monarchy, put out diplomatic feelers but without result. It had been thought very likely that Britain would be their destination. Not only had the United Kingdom been Russia's ally throughout the war, there were close and well-known ties between the ruling houses. The Tsar had been a British Admiral and was Colonel of a Scots regiment. Alexandra had been Queen Victoria's favourite granddaughter. Britain had for centuries – ever since the Reformation – been a haven for refugees from the Continent (even Lenin had found shelter there). It seemed almost a routine procedure that the Romanovs would, like Louis Phillippe and Napoleon III before them, go to England and live out their lives in some little-used royal palace (Louis XVIII had been offered Holyrood) or rented country house. Most importantly, King George V had indicated that he would allow them to come.

But then he changed his mind. It is difficult to believe that a man of his integrity should have reneged on such an offer and the reason, it must be assumed, was fear. The Russian Revolutions – especially the latter – which had swept away the last remnants of the old order and placed the working class in control of the state for the first time, had aroused impassioned sympathy among the proletariat in other countries. Not only did these watch the experiment with interest but with envy, and with an eye to following Russia's example. In the midst of a soul-crushing war that showed little sign of ending, the notion that a whole army could simply leave the field, and that a whole people could overthrow its rulers, was deeply attractive. Workers everywhere wished them well. Even without some spark to light the flame of revolution, the same thing could happen elsewhere. In Britain there was a dangerous undercurrent of socialism, and industrial relations often turned nasty. It would be wise, at a time when the country was at full stretch to fight the war and maintain social cohesion, not to provoke trouble. He did not so much fear for his throne. The British do not have a tradition of violent revolution and it is difficult to imagine a constitutional monarch in our modern age being violently deposed. He did, however, fear for his kingdom. What head of state would *not* be anxious to avoid the social and political chaos, the violence and huge loss of life, that had afflicted his cousin's country?

The offer of asylum was therefore not taken further. An excuse put about was that bringing them out of Russia, naturally by sea, would be too difficult when German U-boats were at large – especially as the route from European Russia would lead through the Baltic and the Skaggerak. The blame for this was laid on the Prime Minister, David Lloyd George. A Liberal, he was the most left-wing Premier Britain had had. He would not be expected to favour the notion of rescuing autocrats from a mess of their own making, and it is assumed that he had made clear to the King that public opinion would not allow the

Tsar to find asylum in the United Kingdom. Historians have found, however, that what Lloyd George had done was to take the blame for a decision that was the King's. Russian monarchists have never forgiven the British sovereign for what they see as an act of base desertion, and King George's name is anathema to them to this day. The King, who had spent pleasant days with the Imperial Family during their visit to Cowes in 1909, felt keenly the fate that befell them. It is interesting that when a somewhat similar situation developed later in 1918 – the abrupt collapse of the Austro-Hungarian Empire and the abdication of its young ruler, Karl – he sent a personal representative to escort that Imperial Family into exile abroad, even though the Emperor had been on the opposite side in the conflict.

In Tobolsk the months crawled by. Summer came, without opportunity to enjoy the warm weather. Life had become increasingly difficult for the Family. Their clothes were more patched, their meals more monotonous, their expenses harder to meet. The second revolution had removed the respectful and usually well-disposed officials with whom they dealt, replacing them with a harsh and completely unsympathetic regime. Local commanders and soldiers might be pleasant enough, but there were always others who were surly and hostile. The men were paid irregularly and this made them resentful of any perceived luxury the captives might seem to be enjoying. Funds to keep the Romanovs had run low because they were not a major concern in the distant capital, and a loan had to be raised locally. Small humiliations multiplied. Nicholas was forbidden, as were all officers, to wear the distinctive shoulder-boards of the old army (something that had always been highly prized in Russia). His, bearing the cipher of Alexander III, were his last link with his father. The Family was no longer allowed to go regularly to church, and had to have a soldier present whenever they heard mass. The ice-mountain – a sledging-run the children had built in the compound – was demolished by their captors because they had stood on top of it to wave to a departing guard detail and thus exposed themselves to view from the street.

Could matters get any worse? Yes. On 3 March 1918 – a year to the day after Nicholas had abdicated – the Bolshevik government signed an agreement with Germany that would end the war for Russia. By the Treaty of Brest-Litovsk, named after a strategic fortress in western Russia that was now enemy headquarters, Lenin gained an immediate cessation of hostilities. With nothing to offer the Germans, he got nothing in return except the departure of their forces. They, on the other hand, got everything they wanted. Russia gave up the provinces of Estonia, Lithuania, Courland, Livonia, Poland and Finland. No such loss of territory had been known in Russian history. Lenin, who would be violently criticised at home for this betrayal, justified it on the grounds that proletarian revolution was about to sweep through the whole of Europe and would come to Germany, perhaps in a matter of months. When that occurred, the ruling regime would vanish, to be replaced by soviet government and all previous agreements would be nullified. This would not be the last time he proved spectacularly wrong in his predictions, but tragically for the inhabitants of these territories they would once again come under Russian hegemony a generation later.

The former Russian commander-in-chief was predictably horrified when news of this event reached Tobolsk. He feared that he would be made to sign it, as the man who had taken Russia into the war. Thankfully he was so far removed from new developments that no such thing was necessary.

Alexis injured himself, badly. He was playing on a sled on the wooden stairs of the house and he fell, injuring his groin. This was the same type of wound he had suffered at Spala, but worse, and there was now no Rasputin to help. He was in such pain that he longed for death. His recovery was very slow and during this lengthy convalescence the Bolsheviks decided that the Family must be moved further into Siberia. Their destination this time was to be the industrial town of Ekaterinburg. This was yet another hammer blow. The region – known as the 'Red Urals' – was infamous for its active Bolshevism. Nicholas had said that he would rather go anywhere than there. In Tobolsk there had been kind and loyal people who would help the

Family in small ways. In their new home they could expect greater hostility. It was among the most dangerous places in Russia for this set of captives. Alexis could not travel, and must follow when he was able. In fact, it was decided that Nicholas, Alexandra and Marie would go together, and the rest would follow. This time, the journey was undertaken in rough and bone-jarring peasant carts (Alexandra lay on a mattress), and involved crossing two frozen rivers and travelling some distance on foot. Only for the last phase were they put on a train and, owing to a dispute between two local authorities, transferred to another train to be taken to the town. They arrived to find a large crowd, both curious and menacing.

Their new home was waiting for them. A local merchant, Ipatiev, had been evicted at short notice some months before, and his house made ready. A two-storey building in neo-baroque style, it had been screened from the busy street outside by a heavy wooden fence, and a second one would soon be built. The Family would be confined to the top floor while their captors, armed with rifles and machine-guns, lived below. The windows were whitewashed to prevent them seeing out or being seen themselves. This was to be a much closer confinement. The guards were also more savage. Inebriated louts from the streets and factories of the town, they would take pleasure in taunting and browbeating their captives, leering at the girls, noisily singing revolutionary songs. Into this purgatory, at the end of May, came the rest of the Family – Olga, Tatiana, Anastasia and Alexis.

CHAPTER TWENTY-SEVEN

Martyrdom

And when the hour comes
To pass the last dread gate,
Breathe strength to us to pray,
Father, forgive them!
Verse from a prayer, copied out by Olga while in Tobolsk.

The days grew hotter. The occupants of what had been designated 'the House of Special Purpose' were confined inside for most of every day. Unable to see out of the windows, they were not allowed to open them either, and when Anastasia briefly peered from one she was fired at by a guard below. The food got worse. It came from a local workers' restaurant. They sat out the long mornings, afternoons, evenings, still reading, doing needlework or drawing, waiting for – what?

Was there no hope of rescue? It was a reasonable assumption that bodies of men, or even individuals might be in the vicinity, biding their time. Nicholas, with his military training, would have known that attacking such a heavily defended place would have been very costly. Should such a thing happen, their captors could easily just kill them. The situation, however, did not arise. There was to be no move to capture the building. The groups that aspired to rescue were too disparate, too disorganised, too lacking in funds or facilities, too unable to trust their members. Attempts were made at contact –the area seemed to be crawling with foreign agents, and Nicholas received cryptic smuggled messages – but there would somehow not be the right moment, or anyone with the will to seize it.

At the beginning of July, the killing started. Nicholas's brother, Michael, was imprisoned in a hotel in Perm (also in Siberia) with his English manservant, Brian Johnson. In the middle of the night of the third, both were roused from sleep without warning by men who did not seem to be local Bolsheviks, and were ordered to dress at once. Michael insisted on taking Johnson with him, and their captors appeared to want this too. Driven out of the town into nearby woods, they were both shot. The precedent had been set for murdering members of the Imperial Family. Nicholas and the other captives in Ekaterinburg had little over two weeks to live.

They were losing members of their entourage. Prince Dolgoruky had been taken from them on arrival in Ekaterinburg, and must have been killed at once. The sailor Nagorny, who had intervened when a soldier tried to steal from Alexis, was arrested and shot after a few days' imprisonment.

They did not know it, but preparations were going on all around them for their deaths. The place had been planned, but the disposal of the bodies – the provision of transport, the finding of a suitably remote location where the slow process of destruction could be carried out in secret – would have taken some days. Telegrams were flying between Ekaterinburg and Moscow (the Bolshevists' new capital). Jacob Yurovsky, a gruff, silent and sinister-looking man who was in fact a member of the CHEKA, the Soviet secret police, had arrived. He was to supervise. There were new faces among the guards, too. Nicholas was to notice, in those last few days, that the guards avoided the eyes of him and his family. He wondered why.

A prominent member of the Menshevik Party, Nikolai Chkheidze, had been asked if the Romanovs would be allowed to flee abroad. His answer was revealing: 'Never,' he replied. 'He has enormous sums of money there – five hundred million roubles in gold. He'll organise such a counter-revolution for us that nothing will be left of us. He has to be rendered harmless here.' Though the act of killing the Family – all members of it, including cousins, whom the Bolsheviks were able to capture – was a terrible crime, it is understandable if seen from the point of view of the ruthless apostles of revolution. Not only could the Tsar mobilise immense funds with which to wage war abroad against the new regime, he – or any single member of his family – would be a rallying-point for opposition and thus a continuing threat. Only by getting rid of all of them could this be neutralised, though this begs the question: why were their bodies not exposed to the public gaze to prove that they had gone?

On the night of 16–17 July, it ended. They were woken without warning and told to prepare for a journey. By now they were used to these sudden departures and will probably have dressed with practised speed. They may have assumed that White forces were near the town and that they were being taken to a nearby place of safety – nothing seemed to have been said about what to bring.

Yurovsky wrote a report once it was over. In the chilling language of bureaucracy he described what has come to be regarded as one of history's great crimes. In semi-darkness the Family, in travelling clothes, descended the steps to the basement:

The Romanovs did not suspect anything. Nich. Carried A (Alexis) in his arms, the others carried little cushions and other small items. Going into the empty room, A (Alexandra) asked 'What, are there no chairs? Can we not even sit down?' The Com. (Commandant) ordered two chairs to be brought in. Nich placed A[lexis] on one chair, and A.F. (Alexandra) sat on the other. The others the Com. ordered to stand in a row. When they had done so, the firing-squad was summoned. When they came in, the Com. told the Romanovs that, as their relatives in Europe continued to attack Soviet Russia, the Urals ispolkom had ordered that they be shot. Nicholas turned his back on the firing-squad and faced his family, then, as if collecting himself, turned to the Com. And asked 'What? What?' The Com. hastily repeated what he had said and ordered the firing-squad to get ready. The men had already been told who was to shoot whom and ordered to aim straight at the heart, in order to minimise the amount of blood and to get it over with quickly. Nicholas turned again to his family and said nothing further, the others uttered a few incoherent exclamations. All this lasting a few seconds. Then the shooting started, and continued for two or three minutes. Nicholas was killed outright by the Com. Himself. Then A.F. and the Romanovs' servants died immediately. The four daughters, Tatiana, Olga, Maria and Anastasia, Doctor Botkin, the footman Trup, the cook Tikhomirov, another cook and a maid-of-honour whose name the Com. had forgotten. A (Alexis), three of his sisters, the maid-of-honour and Botkin were still alive. It was necessary to finish them off. This surprised the Com. As they had aimed straight at the heart. The whole process, (including checking their pulses, etc.) took about twenty minutes.

Accounts describe the executioners' astonishment when bullets ricocheted off some of the women. Only afterward did the reason become clear – they had jewels sewn into their bodices that had deflected the shots. As we have just seen, not all were killed outright, despite the careful targeting. Anastasia seems to have fainted. She regained consciousness seconds after the fusillade and had to be finished off with a bayonet. The maid, Demidova, was unharmed enough by the first shots to run back and forth, trying to defend herself with the cushion that had been in her hands. Otherwise it was mercifully swift.

Arguably this sudden end, horrific as it was, was preferable to further months – or years – of captivity and degradation. Time and again over that interminable, fourteen-month wait, they must have asked themselves; 'How much longer can this go on? How can we endure?' The youngest member of the Family, during their last days in Tobolsk, told Alexandra: 'I would like to die, Mama; I'm not afraid of death, but I'm afraid of what they may do to us here.' It is unlikely that the Romanovs would have been released, and they could have lived on, prisoners in some Gulag, for decades. Alexandra and Alexis would not have survived. The girls could in theory have lived until the end of the twentieth century – and thus might have seen the demise of the Soviet state in 1991. Had the Bolsheviks put Nicholas on trial he would have been made a national scapegoat and condemned to death. There would have been the same type of tragic parting from his family that was seen with Charles I. Alexandra too might have been tried, for treason – the fact that no evidence existed would not have mattered – and could have suffered her own Calvary in the manner of Marie Antionette. How much better that this close-knit family was together and that it happened without warning. One wonders why the executioners did not simply shoot them in their beds as they slept. Perhaps Yurovsky was one of those who wanted to see the Tsar stand trial, hence his brief delivery of sentence.

As the world knows, the bodies were taken to a clearing outside the town and rendered down by a crude process of dismemberment, acid and burning. They were then buried and the site of their grave was disguised. They would remain undisturbed for more than sixty years while, from the moment they disappeared, rumour and speculation and wishful thinking would keep them alive.

Had the Family been able to flee and find sanctuary abroad, they would never have known peace. The secret police of the new state were to prove extremely adept at carrying out executions of dissidents and other enemies no matter where in the world they settled, as witness the killing of Leon Trotsky in Mexico in 1940. Though a great many Russian aristocrats, and a number of Romanovs, were to live unmolested in the West for the remainder of their lives, the immediate family might not have been so lucky. They could have been – and they would have felt – hunted for the rest of their lives.

So they would have been killed anyway, but what had made the situation more urgent was the advance of a 'Czech Legion' toward the town. Its members were former prisoners of war. Though technically subjects of the Austrian Emperor they had little loyalty to a motherland from which their own territory was about to separate. They were armed and heading westward across Siberia to reach central Europe, and they were on the side of the White Russian armies that opposed the Bolsheviks. Within days or even hours they could be in Ekaterinburg and the Romanovs' captors would be forced to retreat. It was distinctly possible that Nicholas and his family might have been gunned down in haste by their departing captors. There was certainly tension, if not yet actual panic.

White forces did come, though it was not for several days that they cleared the area of Bolsheviks and entered the town. Knowing where the Family had been held, they quickly searched the Ipatiev House for any sign of them. They found mementoes by the score – furniture, clothing, jewellery, documents – and even the Tsarevich's pet spaniel – but no Romanovs living or dead. In the basement they discovered clear evidence of some act of terrible violence. There were bloodstains on the floor and the walls were riddled with bullets, which were laboriously dug out by investigators. The conclusion reached by this enquiry, the Sokholov Investigation – that the Family had been murdered – was first of all to be announced as fact, then doubted for decades as authors tried to prove different theories, and then finally vindicated when the bodies were found. Meanwhile, the corpses of other murdered Romanovs were discovered. The Grand Duchess Elizabeth was found to have been killed the day after her sister Alexandra, along with her family. A towering spiritual figure, she was canonised. A statue of her stands today among those of twentieth-century martyrs commemorated above the West Door of Westminster Abbey.

CHAPTER TWENTY-EIGHT

Sanctity

The doubt as to their fate was to give their lives an eerie continuity. Imposters began turning up almost at once after reports of their deaths were published. Sometimes these were plausible, though there would be none that convinced the surviving members of the Family. Nevertheless for decades stories continued to appear that some, or even all, had survived. It was stated that the Communist government had kept them alive for use in bargaining (if so, why were they never used?), that the whole massacre had been a hoax to put an end to monarchist hopes (but why feed and house them if you can just kill them?), or that through neglect, incompetence, connivance or miracle they had survived and scattered across the globe. Serious authors sometimes took up the cudgels for one claimant or another. Anna Anderson, who was discovered in Berlin in 1920 and was believed to be the Grand Duchess Anastasia, remained the most tenacious claimant, and wrote a memoir about her life. She settled in America with a husband who never doubted the truth of her identity. Another version, recorded by American author Guy Richards in his book *The Hunt for the Czar* (1972), announced that all of them had survived. Though he was sincere in his belief and his book was undoubtedly exciting, the details described and the photographs shown of claimants were simply not believable. Later in the decade two BBC journalists, Anthony Summers and Tom Mangold, made a thorough investigation of evidence available up to that time. The result was their book *The File for the Tsar* (1976). Again, this seemed credible, suggesting that Anastasia and Alexis had survived. The bookshelf of any aficionado will also contain Michael Occleshaw's *The Romanov Conspiracies* (1993), *The Escape of Alexei* (1998) by Vadim Petrov et al, Shay McNeal's *The Plots to Rescue the Tsar* (2001), and Andrew Cook's *The Murder of the Romanovs* (2010). Notice that these last, all of which are fascinating and well argued, were published *after* the discovery of the bones. Such is the horror and revulsion that this crime continues to evoke that millions throughout the world have *longed* to believe it did not happen. Though the bodies have been found and positively identified, such books will continue to be written for decades to come, for the mystery is not yet fully solved. The Russian Orthodox Church is currently demanding the exhumation of the remains so that more intensive DNA tests can be carried out, for it seems there is still room for doubt. Two of the Family, Alexis and Marie, meanwhile remain unburied. There may well be further revelations, more controversies, and doubtless more conspiracy theories to come.

While these questions are debated, what of Nicholas's legacy? The most weak and inadequate Tsar for a hundred years, criticised without cease by his subjects and by the international community, under constant threat of violent death from extremists, grieved by the knowledge of his son's illness, faced with problems to which there was no apparent solution (no one else could have, or did, solve them) he carried on with patient doggedness for twenty-three years. This was more of a triumph than it perhaps seems. There can be no doubt whatever that he was the wrong man for the circumstances. He lacked the qualities that would have enabled him to find a way through. Considering this handicap we, who have the benefit of hindsight and of a century of scholarship to help us analyse, must be cautious in our condemnation.

While it cannot be pretended that Nicholas was the greatest of the Tsars, neither was he the worst. Let us briefly survey what might be considered his achievements: he did not wantonly go to war in the 1890s, though this would have been popular, as the objective would have been the seizure of the Bosporus – a long-standing national dream. He was the moving spirit behind the Hague Convention and the international arbitration court that grew from it. He presided over a time of increasing national prosperity; more Russians lived better under his rule. He coped extremely well with his son's illness, keeping up a public appearance of normality and going about his duties as usual. He pursued the war in 1914, despite his own extreme reluctance, as an obligation to his country's allies (and tried to prevent its outbreak through the court of arbitration). He kept Russia fighting until the day he stepped down from command in spite of shortages, mismanagement and continuing defeats. This was absolutely vital to the Allied war effort because of the support it gave on the Western Front, which would not have held without it. He was faithful, conscientious, possessed of a high sense of honour – a good man who was uncorrupt and incorruptible, true to his principles and personally honest. When he abdicated, he could have tried to flee the country with his family and possessions. He made absolutely no attempt to save himself or to find any accommodation with the new rulers. He stayed in Russia to face a possible trial and an unknown future. Though he would have been grateful for rescue from the Bolsheviks, he did not want to go abroad, preferring to stay in Russia in case he could be useful. He accepted the progressive humiliation that deprived him of everything but the company of his family, and ultimately took his life. He did this without rancour, and even with forgiveness. He deserves the respect of all who admire integrity and revere the courage of the helpless.

As for other people and places involved in the end of Imperial Russia? The Dowager Empress was the senior survivor. Rescued from the Crimea by a British warship at the behest of her sister, Queen Alexandra (she initially refused to leave the country) she returned to her homeland of Denmark and lived in a wing of Hvidore Palace until her death. Her remains were later transferred to the new Russia so that she could lie beside her husband. Of her two daughters the older, Xenia, settled in England and ended her days (in 1960) in a grace-and-favour cottage at Hampton Court. Olga, who had married for love, lived in Denmark with her husband until the Second World War, when she moved to Canada. She too died in 1960. Her final home was a tiny apartment above Ray's Barbershop in a working-class Toronto suburb.

Of the homes in which they had lived, most, including the Winter Palace, Gatchina and Peterhof, became museums. Some were destroyed or damaged by the Germans when they laid siege to

Leningrad, though post-war restoration was remarkably thorough. The Alexander Palace, designated a museum the moment the Family left it in 1917, remained as such until the beginning of the next war. It was occupied by the Germans and much vandalised. Later it was given to the Russian Navy, which occupied it until the tourist-boom that followed the end of the Soviet Union. It has gradually been returned to the appearance it had when Nicholas and Alexandra lived there. A bust of him has been placed in the grounds and, of course, the town itself has changed back to Tsarskoe Selo after decades as 'Pushkin', a name awarded in reference to the fact that Russia's great poet had been at school there.

Livadia, the home they loved the most, looks much as it did in their lifetime, and this too has in recent times become a place of pilgrimage. After its occupants had gone, it was to gain further fame in a later chapter of history when, in 1945, it was the setting for the Yalta Conference. Churchill, Roosevelt and Stalin were famously photographed in the arcaded courtyard where the Romanovs had once strolled and sat.

And what of the *Standart*, on which so many of their happier moments were lived out and recorded for posterity? The yacht was put in dry dock in Petrograd and remained there, presumably forgotten, until 1936. Renamed *18th March (Marti)* and then *Marta*, she was converted for the Soviet Navy and became a minelayer. She took part in the Second World War and subsequently became a training-vessel called *Oka*. Unrecognisable and painted battleship-grey, she survived until 1963 when she was broken up at Tallinn in Estonia, the very port – then called Reval – in which she had once been the meeting place between Nicholas and King Edward VII.

Afterword

Ekaterinburg, after an interlude in which it was called Sverdlovsk, is once again named after the great Catherine. The Ipatiev House has gone, demolished in 1977 by command of the local communist ruler, Boris Yeltsin. On its site a church was built between 2000 and 2003. It is a memorial not only to those who lost their lives in this place but to all who perished in those terrible years. The Church of the Blood is dedicated to 'All the Saints Radiating With Light in the Land of Russia'. The Family themselves are designated, in the language of Orthodoxy, 'Royal Sufferers and Martyrs'. The crime of their murder has resonated through Russia for a hundred years and, among those who worship, has called for a national repentance. At the church's dedication the Metropolitan said that the killings 'resulted in a fratricidal civil war and years of repression which touched almost every family. All further, and even current, trends in our Homeland are the consequences of our straying from that path which Russia followed many times, leading to power and glory. This stain lies on our conscience and darkens our society's spiritual life. It can be washed away only through universal repentance and toil of the priests and children of the Church, State and People...'

Inside, their likenesses appear several times in icons. They are pictured together, though there is also one of the two males, and one of Alexis on his own that was painted in 2004 to mark the centenary of his birth. They are stiff and stylised, as the figures in icons are, and they look so unfamiliar, dressed in Byzantine costume (all of them have a crown as well as a halo) that at first glance one has difficulty telling the women apart. In the church is an historic relic – the icon of the 'Three-handed Virgin', that was in the house with them during their captivity. Here too is the body of St Seraphim of Sarov, a holy man whose original canonisation they attended. In the crypt, an altar now stands on the spot where the Imperial Family awaited their killers on that summer night. Where once the air was filled with the crash of pistol shots and the screams of the dying, there is now a peaceful, respectful hush. Looking down from the wall is yet another icon of those who ended their lives here. Nicholas, robed and crowned and bearded, looks like some figure from an earlier Russia – from the Muscovy of the seventeenth century that he so admired. It is as if he had become his hero, the Tsar Alexis.

Like other weak monarchs who lost the battle with history, he has been given by those who survived him a posthumous sanctity as a form of compensation. Henry VI of England, pious but inept, was murdered and later canonised. Two centuries later his successor, Charles I, was beheaded by his people and later venerated by them as 'King Charles the Martyr'. Nicholas, like these others, was a man of strong personal faith whose patience in the face of a horrifying, implacable fate has won admiration. He, and his family, have now gained a similar reward. How thoroughly they deserve it.

The church does not lack visitors, summoned by a sense of history, or a feeling for the victims of tragedy. The author Charlotte Zeepvat has summed up the view of many Russians as 'part reverence, part regret, part sorrow'. Pilgrims – mostly women in headscarves – bow, make the sign of the cross, hold bunches of slender, lighted candles. We look in vain here for an epitaph written by Princess Bariatinsky, who lost so many friends in the Revolution, including the seven who are honoured here. It is surely applicable in this place, among these faithful: 'May we, who escaped their fate, be worthy to join them in heaven's good time.'

Interestingly, Nicholas continued to have an afterlife a long way from his homeland. In 1894 he had been made Colonel-in-Chief of the Scots Greys, a cavalry regiment with a very impressive history. Despite already being commander-in-chief of a huge army at home, he had a genuine love for this, and took a great deal of interest in its affairs, beyond the mere formality that such an appointment might have been. He commissioned the portrait painter Serov to depict him in its uniform, and presented the result to the Officers' Mess. He also received a visit from members of the Regiment in Russia, and several books they gave him remain in his library to this day. When he met King Edward VII at Reval he again wore the uniform, with its distinctive black bearskin. He gave to the unit a *white* bearskin – an item unique in the British Army – and this is still worn by the bass drummer in the regimental band.

For their part, they have never forgotten him. Today the Greys are amalgamated with other units and renamed the Royal Scottish Dragoon Guards, but the Serov portrait still looks down from the walls of the Mess and on nights when the officers dine formally the old Russian national anthem, 'God Save the Tsar' is played. Following his death, officers and men wore black backing behind their cap-badges, and they still do – a gesture of mourning that has been observed since 1918. At the burial of the Romanov family eighty years later, members of the Regiment participated in the procession, including a piper who played haunting laments as the remains of the Family were carried to rest in the Peter-Paul Cathedral – surely an incongruous, but stirring, sound in such a setting. The Dragoon Guards possess an icon of the Tsar, a present from Scottish expatriates living in Russia, and this image of their erstwhile Colonel-in-Chief, now a saint, travels with them on operations, to offer his prayers and his protection.

Timeline

1868   6 May. Birth of Grand Duke Nicholas Alexandrovich Romanov at Tsarskoe Selo, the future Nicholas II.

1869   21 January. Birth of Gregory Efimovich Rasputin.

1870   27 April. Birth of Grand Duke George Alexandrovich.

1871   25 May. Birth of Princess Alice of Hesse, daughter of Grand Duke Louis IV of Hesse and the Rhine, and of his wife, Princess Alice. The future Empress Alexandra of Russia.

1873   June. Visit to England of Tsarevich Alexander and family. Nicholas's first experience of travel abroad.

1874   25 March. Birth of Grand Duchess Xenia Alexandrovna, sister of Nicholas.

1878   22 November. Birth of Grand Duke Michael Alexandrovich, Nicholas's youngest brother.

1881   13 March. Assassination of the Emperor Alexander II.

1882   1 June. Birth of Grand Duchess Olga Alexandrovna, the youngest sister of Nicholas.

1883   27 May. Coronation of Alexander III and Marie Feodorovna in the Moscow Kremlin.

1884   6 May. Nicholas's sixteenth birthday and coming of age. Oath taken by him before the Imperial Court.

1887   23 June. Nicholas began military career with 1st Company ('His Majesty's Company') of the Preobrazhensky Regiment, as 2nd Lieutenant. Remained with this for less than two months.

1888   17 October. Imperial Train destroyed en route for Petersburg from the Caucasus. Cause may have been a bomb, though this never proved. Dining car roof collapsed and Alexander held it up while his family climbed to safety.

1889   18 January. Princess Alice of Hesse visited Russia with her father.

6 May. Nicholas created a member of the State Council and the Committee of Ministers.

22 June. Transferred to 1st Squadron of His Majesty's Hussar Guards Regiment.

1890   1 January. Became commander of His Majesty's Squadron and served in that position until August. Met Kaiser William II who was visiting Russia.

Relationship with the ballerina Mathilde Kschessinska.

23 October. Set off on travels through the Mediterranean and to the Far East, joining ship at Trieste. Sailed to Port Said, then to India and Japan.

1891   29 April. Nicholas attacked with a sword by a Japanese policeman during a visit to a shrine. Injured but not seriously, though he was never to forgive the Japanese for this.

Resumed military career. Transferred to Horse Guards Artillery, commanding 'His Majesty's Battery'.

1892   1 January. Promoted to Colonel and put in command of 1st Battalion, Preobrazhensky Regiment.

July. Second visit to England for marriage of the Duke of York (later King George V).

1894   2 April. Attended wedding in Coburg of Princess Alice's brother Ernst.

8 April. Became engaged to Princess Alice. In June the couple were together in England for over a month.

17 September. Tsar Alexander, suffering serious ill-health while holidaying in Poland, left for Livadia, his home in the Crimea, on doctor's orders, in the hope that the climate would help.

20 October. After a month of continuing illness, Alexander died. He was forty-nine. Nicholas became Tsar.

27 October. Alexander's body travelled from Livadia to St Petersburg by train, accompanied by the Imperial Family. Arriving 1 November, it was buried in the Peter-Paul Cathedral.

14 November. Nicholas and Alexandra Feodorovna (her new Russian name) were married in the cathedral church of the Winter Palace.

1895   17 January. In the Winter Palace, Nicholas received representatives of the Zemstvas, and made the notorious 'senseless dreams' speech that was to disappoint liberals and set the tone for the rest of his reign.

3 November. Birth of their first child, Grand Duchess Olga Nikolaievna.

1896   6 May. Nicholas's twenty-eighth birthday. Start of coronation celebrations in Moscow. Nicholas and Alexandra made their ceremonial entry into the city on 9 May. The coronation ceremony was held on the fourteenth. During that summer, he made more official visits than in any other year of his reign. These included Austria, Germany, France, Denmark and Scotland, where the Romanovs were received by Queen Victoria. Nicholas made Colonel-in-Chief of the Scots Greys regiment.

1897   The heads of state whom he had visited returned the call. Nicholas and Alexandra received the rulers of Austria, Germany and France, as well as the King of Siam.

29 May. Birth of Grand Duchess Tatiana Nikolaievna.

1898   24 August. Nicholas suggested international peace tribunal to representatives of foreign powers.

1899   18 May. The Hague Conference, outcome of his suggestion, met.

14 June. Birth of Grand Duchess Marie Nikoliaevna.

23 June. Death of Grand Duke George Alexandrovish in the Caucasus.

1901   5 June. Birth of Grand Duchess Anastasia Nikolaievna.

1904   8 February. Outbreak of Russo-Japanese War.

17 June. Governor-General of Finland, General N.I. Bobrikov, assassinated.

28 July. Minister of the Interior, V.K. von Plehve, assassinated. The beginning of a new wave of terrorism.

30 July. Siege of Port Arthur by the Japanese began.

12 August. Birth of the Tsarevich, Alexis Nicholievich.

1905   2 January. Siege of Port Arthur ended in capitulation.

9 January, 'Bloody Sunday', troops shoot down peaceful demonstrators who had marched to the Winter Palace to hand petitions to the Tsar.

5 February. Assassination of Grand Duke Sergei, uncle of the Tsar and brother-in-law of the Tsarina.

20 February. Battle of Mukden began. Russian defeat.

27 May. Battle of Tsushima. Naval disaster.

17 October. 'October Manifesto' announcing the end of purely autocratic rule and granting a constitution.

1906   27 April. The official opening of the Duma with a speech by Nicholas in the Throne Room of the Winter Palace. The beginning of a new era for Russia.

6 May. Constitution ratified.

1907   18 May. Second Hague Conference opened.

1908   May and August. Nicholas visited Reval (now Tallinn, Estonia) twice aboard the Imperial Yacht for meetings with heads of state – King Edward VII and the President of France.

1909   27 June. Two hundredth anniversary of the battle of Poltava, a decisive victory by Peter the Great over the Swedes. The first of a series of military anniversaries that made the Romanovs more visible in public after years of seclusion.

1911   5 October. Assassination of the Prime Minister, Peter Stolypin, during a performance at the opera house in Kiev. The Tsar, Olga and Tatiana were present.

1912   17 April. Strikers in the Lena goldfields shot by troops. This incident was seen as a milestone on the road to revolution.

1913   21 February. Tercentenary of the Romanov dynasty. A service was held at the Kazan Cathedral in St Petersburg attended by the Family. During the month of May, they made official visits to historic cities and regions.

7 May. Nicholas visited Berlin for the wedding of the Kaiser's daughter Victoria-Luise. This was the last gathering of European royalty before the outbreak of war, and the last time that the Tsar would see his cousins the Kaiser and King George V.

1914   May–June. Romanovs made a state visit to Roumania, and received visits from the King of Saxony and the President of France.

31 July. Russian forces mobilised in defence of Serbia, a fellow Slavic nation.

31 July. St Petersburg renamed Petrograd to remove any German association.

1 August. Germany declared war against Russia in response to the Russian mobilisation against Austria.

26–30 August. Battle of Tannenberg. Major Russian defeat.

7–14 September. Battle of the Masurian Lakes. Second huge Russian defeat.

1915   22 March. Russians captured Przemysl after six-month siege. A rare success.

1916   24 August. Nicholas took over as Commander-in-Chief of Russia's armies, thus becoming associated with incompetence and defeat.

29/30 December. Assassination of Rasputin by Prince Yussupov and Grand Duke Dmitri.

1917   22 February. Nicholas went to army headquarters at Mogilev.

23 February. Beginning of strikes in Petrograd

27 February. Nicholas returned from headquarters in view of the serious domestic situation.

1 March. The Tsar's train unable to reach the capital, diverted by revolutionaries to Pskov.

2 March. Nicholas persuaded by unanimous advice of those around him to abdicate. Passed the throne to his brother, the Grand Duke Michael.

3 March. Michael refused to accept, believing that he could not save the situation. Russia was without a tsar for the first time in 313 years.

4 March. Nicholas had returned to headquarters at Mogilev where the Dowager Empress visited him.

8 March. The ex-Empress Alexandra arrested on the orders of the Provisional Government. Nicholas wrote a final address to the Army, which was suppressed by the country's new rulers. He too was arrested and escorted to Tsarskoe Selo, arriving the following day.

17 April. Lenin returned to Petrograd from Swiss exile.

31 July–6 August. After months of house arrest in the Alexander Palace, the Imperial Family was removed for safety to Tobolsk in Siberia, and placed in the Governor's house there.

1918   13 April (26 April by new style calendar). Three members of the family – Nicholas, Alexandra and Marie – left Tobolsk for Ekaterinburg, arriving on 17 April.

7 May (20 May new style). The rest of the Family joined them in Ekaterinburg, an industrial town in the Urals known for the extremism of local Bolsheviks. They were accommodated in the house of a merchant, Ipatiev.

1/2 June (12/13 June new style). Grand Duke Michael and his English manservant shot at Perm by Bolsheviks.

5 July (18 July new style). The family and their remaining servants were awoken and ordered to dress for a journey. Assembled in the building's basement, they were then shot.

5 July (18 July new style). Grand Duchess Elizabeth and members of her family murdered at Alapayevsk in Siberia.

1919   11 April. Dowager Empress Marie and other members of the Family evacuated from the Crimea by the Royal Navy.

1928   13 October. Death of the Dowager Empress.

1960   20 April. Death of Grand Duchess Xenia, sister of Nicholas II.

24 November. Death of Grand Duchess Olga, the Tsar's other sister.

1977   September. Demolition of the Ipatiev House.

1978   1 May. Family's grave found, but the discovery not revealed.

1987   1 November. The Imperial family, including Grand Duchess
       Elizabeth, canonised by the Russian Orthodox Church in exile.

1991   25 December. End of the Union of Soviet Socialist Republics.

1998   17 July. Ceremonial reburial of the Imperial Family and those
       who died with them in the Peter-Paul Cathedral, St. Petersburg.

2000   20 August. Canonisation of the Family by the Russian
       Orthodox Church in Russia, which had remained more scep-
       tical of the authenticity of the bones than its counterpart
       abroad.

2006   23 September. Remains of Dowager Empress Marie returned
       to Russia for burial beside the Family in the Peter-Paul
       Cathedral.

2007   23 August. The bones of the two missing family members,
       proved to be Alexis and Marie, discovered.

Acknowledgements

I would like to thank a number of people for their help with this project.

In Moscow, my delightful and greatly cherished friends Ekaterina Rodina and Ekaterina Morozova – whose comments on the Russian outlook were most useful – and Christina Mitina. In St Petersburg, I thank Olesia, her colleagues and pupils at one of Russia's greatest schools, 281.

At Little, Brown I am grateful to Duncan Proudfoot for commissioning the book, to Rebecca Hilsdon and Amanda Keats for supervising it and, most particularly, to Una McGovern for editing it with wisdom, efficiency – and a great deal more patience than I deserved. Any mistakes that remain in the text are my fault, not hers.

Lastly, and as always, I thank my wife Sarah, who also needed a good deal of patience.

Index